Everyman, I will go with thee,
and be thy guide

THE EVERYMAN
LIBRARY

*The Everyman Library was founded by J. M. Dent
in 1906. He chose the name Everyman because he wanted
to make available the best books ever written in every
field to the greatest number of people at the cheapest possible
price. He began with Boswell's 'Life of Johnson';
his one-thousandth title was Aristotle's 'Metaphysics',
by which time sales exceeded forty million.*

*Today Everyman paperbacks remain true to
J. M. Dent's aims and high standards, with a wide range
of titles at affordable prices in editions which address
the needs of today's readers. Each new text is reset to give
a clear, elegant page and to incorporate the latest thinking
and scholarship. Each book carries the pilgrim logo,
the character in 'Everyman', a medieval morality play,
a proud link between Everyman
past and present.*

Aischylos

SUPPLIANTS
AND OTHER DRAMAS

PERSIANS, SEVEN AGAINST THEBES,
SUPPLIANTS, FRAGMENTS
with PROMETHEUS BOUND
traditionally ascribed to Aischylos

Edited and translated by
MICHAEL EWANS
University of Newcastle, NSW

EVERYMAN
J. M. DENT · LONDON
CHARLES E. TUTTLE
VERMONT

Consultant Editor for this volume
RICHARD STONEMAN

Introduction and other critical apparatus © J. M. Dent 1996

J. M. Dent
Orion Publishing Group
Orion House, 5 Upper St Martin's Lane,
London WC2H 9EA
and
Charles E. Tuttle Co. Inc.
28 South Main Street,
Rutland, Vermont 05701, USA

Typeset in Sabon by CentraCet Ltd, Cambridge
Printed in Great Britain by
The Guernsey Press Co. Ltd, Guernsey, C. I.

This book if bound as a paperback is subject to the
condition that it may not be issued on loan or otherwise
except in its original binding.

British Library Cataloguing-in-Publication Data
is available upon request.

ISBN 0 460 87755 0

CONTENTS

for Caro

NOTE ON THE AUTHOR AND EDITOR

AISCHYLOS, son of Euphorion from the deme Eleusis in Attika, was born in 525/4 BC. The ancient biographical testimony is largely speculative, and material was invented to compensate for the lack of reliable information at the much later dates when it was compiled. The historical record for the period in which Aischylos lived is also relatively slight, compared to the wealth of surviving sources for the last thirty years of the fifth century. As a result little is known for certain about his life beyond the facts and dates recorded in the Chronology. We do know that Aischylos was of noble ('Eupatrid') birth, that he fought against the Persians at Marathon, and paid two visits to Syracuse in Sicily; he died in 456 during his second visit, at the age of 69. He probably became an initiate in the Eleusinian Mystery cult.

He created at least eighty tragedies, and won at least thirteen prizes during his lifetime in the tragedy contests at Athens. Only six dramas composed by Aischylos survive complete, together with *Prometheus Bound* (ascribed to Aischylos, but probably created later in the century by another poet). Numerous fragments – most of them very short citations – are extant from the lost works.

After his death the Athenians conferred a unique honour on Aischylos: the Archon (the elected official in charge of the Festival of Dionysos) was required to grant the necessary funding for a choros to anyone seeking to produce his dramas. Aischylos was therefore the first Athenian dramatist to have his work revived.

MICHAEL EWANS read Classics at Oxford and wrote his Cambridge PhD thesis on Aischylos, supervised by George Steiner. He was appointed in 1973 to a Lectureship in Classics at the University of Newcastle, NSW, and began teaching Drama when the discipline was introduced at Newcastle in 1974. He became Associate Professor of Drama in 1982, was Head of the Depart-

ment of Drama from 1982 to 1985, and is now Associate
Professor of Drama and Music. His publications include scholarly articles and programme notes on Greek tragedy and opera,
his other main research field, and four books: *Janáček's Tragic
Operas* (1977), *Wagner and Aeschylus* (1982), *Georg Büchner's
'Woyzeck'* (1989), and the Everyman Classics edition of *Aeschylus: 'Oresteia'*. He has directed and supervised numerous pro-
ductions at the University, both of Greek tragedy and of
twentieth-century drama, especially expressionist plays. He is a
consultant to the Australian Opera, and played a major role in
developing the Drama syllabus for secondary schools in New
South Wales. He is currently preparing a complete Sophokles in
two volumes for the Everyman Classics.

CHRONOLOGY OF AISCHYLOS' LIFE

Year	Age	Life
525/4		Aischylos born at Eleusis
499	26	Competes for first time at Festival of Dionysos
490	35	Fights at Marathon; his brother Kunegeiros is killed
484	41	Wins his first prize in the competition for tragedy
480	45	Fights at Salamis
479	46	Possibly fights at Plataia

CHRONOLOGY OF HIS TIMES

Year	Artistic & Historical Events
528/7	Hippias succeeds Peisistratos as tyrant of Athens
c. 514	First Persian attempt to invade Greece thwarted by the Skythians
514	Hippias' brother Hipparchos murdered by Harmodios and Aristogeiton
510	Hippias expelled from Athens by the Alkmeonidai
508	Constitutional reforms of Kleisthenes at Athens
508–6	Defeat of attempts by Sparta and Boiotia to intervene in Athens' internal affairs
501	Performances of tragedy first incorporated into Festival of Dionysos
499	Ionia revolts from Persia, led by Miletos; Athenian troops sent to assist
498	*Pythia 10*; first known poem by Pindar, the great composer of choral lyric poems from Boiotia
494	Persians defeat Ionians at Lade; fall of Miletos and collapse of revolt
493	Phrynichos produces *The Sack of Miletos* and is fined
490	First Persian invasion of Greece, repelled by Athenian victory at Marathon
480	Second Persian invasion under Xerxes Unsuccessful defence of Thermopylai by Spartan King Leonidas Sack of Athens by Persians Decisive Greek victory at Salamis Withdrawal of Xerxes
479	Final defeat of Xerxes' lieutenant Mardonios by combined Greek army at Plataia
478	Withdrawal of Sparta and allies from combined Greek league Athenians form Delian League
476	Phrynichos wins competition with *Phoinikian Women* Pindar visits Sicily, and composes *Olympian 1* celebrating Hieron's victory in the horse race

Year	Age	Life
472	53	Wins competition with a tetralogy which includes his first surviving drama, *Persians*
470	c. 55	In Syracuse. Restages *Persians* and produces *Women of Aitna* to celebrate the foundation of the new city of Aitna by Hieron
468	57	Defeated by Sophokles' first entry in tragedy competition
467	58	Wins competition with Theban tetralogy: *Laios*, *Oidipous*, the surviving *Seven against Thebes*, and the satyr-drama *Sphinx*
463	62	Wins competition with Danaid tetralogy, which includes surviving first drama, *Suppliants*
458	67	Wins competition for thirteenth and last time with the *Oresteia*
456/5	69/70	Dies at Gela in Sicily

Year	Artistic & Historical Events
470	Themistokles ostracized Pindar, *Pythian* 1. His masterpiece, written for Hieron (though Pindar, unlike Aischylos, did not revisit Sicily) to celebrate both his victory in the chariot race at Delphi and the foundation of the new city of Aitna
469	Victory of League fleet over Persians at Eurymedon ends Persian threat to the Aigeian
466–5	Themistokles condemned; flees to Persia
465–3	Athens crushes attempted revolt by Thasos from the Delian League
462	Ephialtes and Perikles curtail powers of the Areopagos
462–1	Pindar, *Pythians* 4 & 5. Two of his greatest compositions, written for Arkesilas, king of Kyrene
461	Ephialtes assassinated; Kimon ostracized Alliance between Athens and Argos
460–45	War between Athens and Sparta, the 'First Peloponnesian War'
c. 456	Pindar, *Isthmian* 7, critical of Athens' expansionist foreign policy
455	Euripides competes for the first time

INTRODUCTION

Persians, *Seven against Thebes* and (perhaps especially) *Suppliants* have often been underestimated. Many readers, critics and theatre performers regard them as remote from our understanding; scholars have frequently distorted or downplayed their actual qualities in pursuit of their own theories about the nature of early tragedy and the evolution of the genre; and all too often they have been compared (sometimes unconsciously) with such acknowledged summits of Greek theatrical achievement as Sophokles' *Antigone* and *Oidipous the King*, or measured against criteria more appropriate for modern naturalistic plays.

Tragoidia[1] was a complex synthesis between previously distinct poetic forms, developed at Athens at the end of the sixth century. Athens was at that time Greece's most innovative democracy, and tragedy rapidly became the central and most important of Athenian intellectual and creative activities. When Aischylos created *Persians*, the earliest surviving drama, there had been competitions for tragedy for 29 years; he was aged 53, and had been competing at the Festival of Dionysos since he was 26. It is therefore improbable that features of these dramas which some modern critics and readers have found primitive or inept would have seemed so to his fellow-performers or his first audiences. We need to learn to understand these three great dramas from within, on their own terms.[2]

The Origins of Tragedy

All Greek poetry was written to be performed;[3] but tragedy was different from earlier genres in three significant ways. It blended

---

[1] All italicized Greek words are defined in the Glossary.
[2] This book also contains fragments of lost dramas of Aischylos, and work by others which was subsequently ascribed to him.
[3] This is demonstrated in exhaustive detail by Herington 1985, 3–78.

solo performance with choral performance; the performers impersonated characters throughout the drama;[4] and they were all male, masked, and costumed for their roles.

We know for certain that:

(1) By 501 BC,[5] competitions for masked verse *tragoidia* formed part of the Great, or City, Festival of Dionysos at Athens in March of each year.

(2) By 472 BC, each competitor provided three tragic dramas and one *satyr-drama*. The normal resources for tragic dramas at that date would appear from *Persians* to have been two solo actors and a *choros* of twelve.[6]

(3) The spoken dialogue was by then primarily in the verse metre of iambic trimeters, with some use of the trochaic tetrameter.[7] The metres chosen for the sung lyrics were adopted from a number of different previous types of non-dramatic choral and solo verse, and were marked out from the dialogue, which was written in Attic Greek, by using the Doric dialect elements which were traditional in the artistic language of lyric verse.

Beyond these points almost any statement about early tragedy is speculative and hazardous.[8] Much of the evidence[9] is late and of doubtful validity; and the subject has proved a rich battleground. Some early twentieth-century scholars, influenced by the newly emerging science of anthropology, and by an intellectual trend towards primitivism, emphasized relationships between tragedy and ritual.[10] A vigorous counter-attack was launched in 1965 by Else,[11] who regarded tragedy as a rational

---

[4] Performers of epic poetry narrated in their own person, and only acted out the voices and gestures of individual characters when the story required these characters to speak.

[5] Not 534; against the traditional backdating cf. Connor 1989.

[6] A third actor was added at some time between *Suppliants* (463) and the *Oresteia* (458). However, the *choros* still remains central in the *Oresteia*.

[7] See Notes on *Persians* Scene 1. These were the two metres principally used by Solon, Athens' lawgiver and early sixth-century poet. Aristotle discusses the early metres of tragedy at *Poetics* 49a 21ff.

[8] Cf. Winnington-Ingram 1985, 258–63.

[9] Including all of the purported fragments of Thespis.

[10] Cf. esp. Murray in Harrison, 1912. Further examples cited by Else 1965, 28–9 and Garvie 1969, 91.

[11] Else 1965, cf. Herington 1985. Both authors stress the fact that much of the subject-matter was drawn from the epic ('Homeric') cycle.

and deliberate creation by two Athenians; first Thespis, who created the new, representative medium of drama by uniting two previously separate styles of poetry, iambic trimeter verse and choral lyric, and then Aischylos, who by adding a second actor 'created tragedy'.[12]

The relationship between tragedy and ritual cannot be dismissed so cavalierly. Tragedy was performed not at the Panathenaic Festival, the forum chosen in the sixth century by the tyrant Peisistratos for competitions between Homeric bards, but at a festival of the god Dionysos; it was performed there together with *dithyramb* and *satyr-drama*; its subject-matter has clear links with cult;[13] and its lyrics show signs of influence from *dithyramb* and from Dorian parts of Greece.

We should therefore not dismiss Aristotle, who had access to good information about early tragedy, when he states that tragedy had its first beginnings in improvisation, originating with the leaders of the *dithyramb*; also that it developed its characteristic solemnity 'late, since it began with slight plots and comic diction, because it developed from being like *satyr-drama*'.[14] The following summaries go as far as is reasonably possible on the evidence: 'In the second half of the sixth century the Athenian public cult of Dionysos seems to have been open to influences from earlier innovations in the northern Peloponnese. It seems that in Sikyon the tyrant Kleisthenes had incorporated hero-lamentations, described as "tragikoi choroi" by Herodotos (5.67), into a public festival of Dionysos; and a few miles away, in Corinth, Arion had turned the traditional, processional *dithyramb* into a stationary performance of a text.[15] In a similar but more far-reaching development at Athens

[12] Ibid. 2. Aischylos probably did introduce the second solo actor (Aristotle, *Poetics* 49a 15–18); but there is no reason why true tragic drama could not have been present in Thespis' lost one-actor dramas as well (*pace* e.g. Else ibid. 5 and 78ff., and Garvie 1969, 115); there are dramatic subtlety and power in the many scenes in Aischylos where only one actor interacts with the *choros*.

[13] Seaford 1994, 275–7 against Else 1965, 63. Though Phrynichos and Aischylos wrote several dramas about Dionysos, there are tragedies connected with the cults of many different gods and heroes, and this may explain the proverb that tragedy has 'nothing to do with Dionysos'. This feeling would itself explain the presence in the fifth-century festival of *satyr-drama*, which has a great deal to do with Dionysos; see below, introduction to the Fragments.

[14] *Poetics* 49a 9ff. and 19–21.

[15] *Suda* s.v. 'Arion': Hdt. 1.23.

the *dithyramb* abandoned its Dionysiac content and style, and assumed the characteristics of tragedy. And so Greek tradition associates the birth of tragedy not only with Epigenes of Sikyon and with Arion, but also with the Athenian Thespis .... Arion's *dithyramb* at Corinth was probably performed by satyrs. At Athens too satyrs accompanied Dionysos in the kind of festal procession likely to have been accompanied by a *dithyramb*. But whether the *thiasos* of Attic satyrs actually contributed to the development of tragedy, it is impossible to say.'[16] 'The context of performance came to be shifted from the procession to the altar .... The dithyrambic (and tragic) performances at the centre [of the city] become important enough to have their own sacrificial procession and evening *kômos*. And so the excursion from and return to the city, which was the original heart of the festival, celebrating the original arrival of the god, became eventually a mere preliminary.'[17]

Its development from Dionysiac ritual and cult explains the single most distinctive feature of tragedy: that the participants are masked, and impersonate other people exclusively, throughout the performance.[18] If Thespis was a travelling player, providing a secular entertainment,[19] there was no sufficient reason for this.[20] If, however, Athenian tragedy and *satyr-drama* developed from rituals of the Dionysiac *thiasos*, then they would share the use of masking and impersonation in those rituals for the assumption of the identity of the god, his satyrs, and his male and female human companions. The birth of tragedy was a

[16] Seaford (ed.) 1984, 12–13.

[17] Seaford 1994, 242–3.

[18] It also explains another fundamental feature of tragedy, which, as Seaford rightly notes (1994, 272), has attracted less attention than it should; the impersonation of females by masked and costumed males. There was in classical Greece no social convention, as there was in Elizabethan and Jacobean England, that it was indecorous for females to perform in public; on the contrary, both solo and choral performances by girls and women are widely attested. However, there is strong evidence of male transvestism – males dressing themselves as female *mainades* – in Dionysiac cult (Seaford ibid.).

[19] This is the picture implied by Horace, *Art of Poetry* 275–7.

[20] The act of impersonation may however be one of the reasons why masks were worn in tragedy, since now for the first time in the Greek 'song culture' was the singer consistently pretending, for the duration of the performance, to be someone else. Cf. the anecdote about Solon and Thespis cited at Ewans 1995, xix.

creative leap only in that the first tragic *poiêtes* – tradition gives him the name Thespis – added a solo actor, speaking iambic and tetrameter verse, and playing a number of different parts, to the traditional sung performances in praise of Dionysos.[21]

Competitions for tragedy became established at the City Festival of Dionysos Eleuthereus – Dionysos the god of freedom or liberation – seven years after the constitutional reforms of Kleisthenes at Athens provided the city with a firm political foundation on which to develop democracy. Nearly thirty years of tragic performances followed before the first surviving drama, Aischylos' *Persians* of 472. By that time the genre shows no traces of its birth in 'slight plots and comic diction', and the evidence of improvisatory beginnings is confined to *satyr-drama*.[22] Tragedy had become a medium in which the democratic *polis* could celebrate its achievements, define itself and the boundaries of its culture against 'others', both Greek and barbarian, and explore the darker conflicts and tensions implicit in human nature, and in the political and social structure of Athens.

Tragedy and Society

The Great or City Festival of Dionysos was the largest and most inclusive gathering of the citizens and other inhabitants of Attika. Since it took place shortly after the start of the sailing season, the performances were also seen by travellers from other parts of Greece. During the last ten years scholars have increasingly emphasized the role played by this festival and its tragic performances in the ideology of the *polis*.[23] The citizens

[21] Cf. Webster in Pickard-Cambridge 1962, 130. The masked *choros* was more likely to attract the invention of a speaking actor than the unmasked *choros* of *dithyramb*; Ley 1993, 116–24.

[22] The surviving fragment of *Fishermen* has free-form, quasi-improvisational lyrics without *strophic* responsion. Cf. also Euripides *Kyklops* 607ff.

[23] Cf. esp. Goldhill 1987/1990, which gathers the evidence for the ceremonies mentioned in the next paragraph. This emphasis is pursued further by the other essays in Winkler and Zeitlin (1990); cf. especially Winkler's own paper on the 'ephebes', the young men just reaching manhood (ibid. 20–62). Winkler revives – without acknowledgement – some aspects of Tanner's argument (1975), that ephebes formed the choroses of tragedy, because tragic performance succeeded to the role of initiation ordeals, and formed part of their rite of passage into full participation as citizens and warriors in the Athenian social order.

assembled, as they did for battle and for the Assembly on the Pnyx, in ten separate sections by tribe; their more prominent *agathoi*, and their fifty Council members, were towards the front in separate places of honour.[24]

By the late fifth century Athenian tragic performances were preceded by ceremonials which celebrated the achievements of the *polis*. These included libations poured by the generals, a parade of the silver talents which were the annual tribute by the subject allies, recitals of the names of benefactors to the city, and a parade in full *hoplite* uniform (donated to them by the *polis*) of those male children of war dead who had been brought up to manhood at state expense, and were now ready to contribute their abilities to the *polis* in return. Such ceremonies reasserted the norms of society – in particular, the centrality of military excellence to male achievement;[25] against this background, tragedy can be seen as 'problematizing' those norms, seeming 'to question, examine, and often subvert the language of the city's order'.[26]

However, a focus on the opening ceremonies results in too simple a characterization of the contrasting energies which were released at the festival. Dionysos is a complex, paradoxical god; there are elements in him and in his worship which affirm, as well as those which negate, the order of the *polis*. Similarly tragedy, like the myths on which it drew for its subject-matter, affirms aspects of civic order as well as questioning it.[27] The outcome in the surviving tragedies frequently displays the destruction or self-destruction of the royal family;[28] but this may be balanced with hope for the future of Athens, as the disaster leads by contrast to the foundation of a cult whose religious function is to avert such disasters in the future, if a democratic *polis* continues to observe and practise the appropriate ritual.[29]

---

[24] Winkler 1990, 21ff. and 38ff.

[25] For these norms in Greek society in general, cf. Adkins 1960; on the *polis*, Winkler 1990, 20.

[26] Goldhill 1987, 68/1990, 114.

[27] Cf. Seaford 1994, 363–7.

[28] Almost never at Athens itself – but often at Thebes, which as Zeitlin has shown (Winkler and Zeitlin 1990, 144ff.) is figured in the surviving tragedies as anti-Athens, the quintessential 'other scene'.

[29] So e.g. Euripides' *Hippolytos*, Sophokles' *Oidipous at Kolonos*. Seaford's impressive argument (1994, *passim*) must be qualified by the fact that none of

On the evidence of the dramas which have survived, the
tragedians did not primarily question society, or explore ambiguities in language or ideology; their role was to illuminate
through dramatic enactment the central tensions and sufferings
of human existence – in particular those of human existence in
their own time and place.[30]

Only six of approximately eighty tragedies and *satyr-dramas*
composed by Aischylos survive. These dramas reflect all the
major political issues which confronted Aischylos and his fellow-
citizens during that period: the aftermath of the Persian Wars,
and the need to retain and develop the Delian League;[31] the shift
in foreign policy from alliance with oligarchic Sparta to alliance
with democratic Argos;[32] and in domestic politics the intense
debate on how far the democracy should develop beyond the
reforms of Kleisthenes, which became crystallized towards the
end of Aischylos' lifetime around the attempts by Ephialtes and
Perikles to reform the ancient, and aristocratic, court of the
Areopagos.[33]

There are also larger concerns, which have ensured the
continued study of Greek tragedy in every generation since the
rediscovery of these dramas in the Renaissance. Aischylos
addressed aspects of human life which have preoccupied western
humanity, from the first poets whose contributions are preserved
in the *Iliad* right down to our own times: the causes and
consequences of war; the ways in which wrongdoing is first
created and then inherited; the conflicts between races, nations,
genders, and generations.

In dramatizing these universal aspects of human existence,
Aischylos and his successors expressed their vision in terms
which made the predicaments, the dilemmas and the sufferings

the surviving dramas of Aischylos conforms to this pattern. No cult is founded
in *Persians*; Seaford has no right to assume (139) that a lost ending founded one
at the end of *Seven*; there is no evidence that the Danaid trilogy ended with the
inauguration of a festival or cult; and while the cult of the Solemn Goddesses is
indeed founded at the end of *Eumenides*, to the great benefit of Athens if it
continues to observe their worship, the royal house of Argos is not destroyed,
but restored to life by the acquittal of Orestes.

[30] Cf. Seaford 1994, 365 and Ewans 1977, 13–14 and 26–33.
[31] See Notes on *Persians*.
[32] See Notes on *Suppliants*; also Ewans 1995, 215 on *Eumenides*.
[33] See Ewans 1995, 212 on *Eumenides*.

of their legendary (or, in *Persians*, barbarian) protagonists intensely real and emotionally moving to the Athenian audience. These three dramas engage directly with some of the most powerful values, and therefore the greatest tensions, within Greek society. Aischylos' characters feel emotions, and make decisions, which turn out to have inevitable, binding consequences; we see a *moira* gradually taking shape. As this process unfolds, the outcome turns on issues which were central to the lives of members of the audience;[34] the need for the *agathos* to preserve and increase his inherited *timê* and to avoid incurring *aischron*, regardless of potential cost and danger[35] (Xerxes, Eteokles); the need to avoid indelible *miasma* (Eteokles, Pelasgos); the obligation, imposed by Zeus himself, to accept a *xenos* – again, regardless of cost or danger (Pelasgos). Aischylean tragedy brings no easy answers; the dramatist confronted and illuminated the dilemmas, the choices – and the results, uniting his vast, open-air audience in their contemplation of tragic actions and their horrific consequences.

Here are three dramas of burning economy, powerful both in their emotional impact and in the intellectual strength of their dramatic structure, totally assured in their creative use of words, movement, music and almost minimal theatrical resources. My hope is that this translation, which is designed to be as far as possible both accurate and actable, may make them fully accessible to modern performers and students.[36]

---

[34] Adkins (1960) inaugurated awareness of the centrality of the 'value-terms' which follow to Greek society.

[35] This crucial aspect of Greek values has often been ignored, because of the emphasis on humility in Judaeo-Christian ethics, and the belief that it is an absolute good in itself to renounce worldly wealth. Precisely the tragic dimension of Xerxes' position – and of Agamemnon's – is that in pursuing the goals which an *agathos* had to pursue *qua agathos*, they were obliged to cross limits beyond which there is danger (crossing the Hellespont, sacrificing Iphigeneia to Artemis), and so chose paths which led to disaster.

[36] There is a fuller statement of the principles behind this series at Ewans 1995, xxxiv–xxxvi. This book makes some mildly controversial assumptions, which are argued for ibid. xxiff. *Choros* and actors interacted on equal terms in the *orchêstra*; the *choros* played a collective character, rather than being in any sense the playwright's mouthpiece; individual *choros* members were equally important, and both dialogue and lyrics were normally subdivided between them; the movement and action of Greek tragedy were lively and often realistic, rather than static and stylized.

Performance

Aischylos dramatized human experience by making sophisticated use of a very simple space, blending spoken words
accompanied by blocked movement with lyric *choroi* – songs
and dances which were far more complex in their metre and
range of emotions than the *dithyrambs* which preceded the
tragedies in the festival. Performances of tragedy, *dithyramb* and
satyr-drama probably began in the *agora*, but were soon trans-
ferred to a purpose-built theatre hollowed out of the slopes on
the southern side of the Akropolis, next to the precinct of the
god Dionysos himself. At the time of these three dramas the
spectators sat on wooden seats in five or six straight rows rising
in terraces on a steep, hollowed-out slope; they surrounded two-
thirds of the circumference of a circular, level *orchêstra* around
20m in diameter;[37] and this was supported by a retaining wall,
since the ground continued to slope away behind it, and the
level surface had been created by infilling.

No permanent structure was erected behind the *orchêstra*.
Athenian dramatists almost certainly did not use a *skene*, in the
sense of a wooden building which could represent the façade of
a palace, temple, tent or other building, before the *Oresteia*. For
these earlier dramas the actors used a *skene* in the earlier sense
of a changing tent; but it is argued in the Notes that this could
only usefully have been placed on the level of the *orchêstra* for
the performance of *Seven against Thebes*; for *Persians* and
Suppliants it needs to be placed out of sight of the spectators,
perhaps immediately behind the retaining wall on the lower
level. Aischylos used no technical devices, and very few properties, to create his dramatic effects; the focus of the audience is
constantly directed to the costumes and masks, movements and
gestures of the solo actors and *choros* members in the *orchêstra*.

As with the *Oresteia*, Aischylos' dramatic technique in these
earlier dramas has been obscured by the obsessive modern

[37] The theory that the early *orchêstra* was trapezoidal, like some seventh- and
sixth-century village assembly places elsewhere in Greece, is rejected at Ewans
1995, xviii–xix. My view is further supported by Read's comprehensive survey
of theatre remains (1993), by Scullion's demonstration (1990, 3–98) that
Dindorf's original excavation of the Theatre of Dionysos was correct, and by
Seaford's reminder that circularity is appropriate both to the dances for
dithyrambs, and to sacrifice (1994, 242).

conviction[38] that there must have been some kind of raised
playing space behind the *orchêstra* – a separate performance
area like the stage of the modern proscenium arch theatre, which
many writers[39] believe was normally the performance area for
solo actors, and was also used in *Seven* and *Suppliants* to
represent the place where the altar, and the images of the gods,
are located.

In *Seven*, the Women of Thebes sing an extended choral ode
while huddled close to the images of their native gods; similarly
in *Suppliants* the Daughters of Danaos sing a number of lyric
interjections in Scene 1, culminating in Choros 2, when they are
under the protection of the gods and therefore 'up on' the
'mound' by the altars. If a *choros* sings, it also dances; there is
no space for this on a raised wooden stage.[40]

The references to areas which are 'up' and 'down' in a number
of surviving tragedies, from the second earliest (Aischylos' *Seven
against Thebes*, 467 BC) to the last (Sophokles' *Oidipous at
Kolonos*, 405 BC) reflect a dynamic of interaction between an
'outer' area, further away from a prop or props at the rear of
the *orchêstra*, and an 'inner' area, 'up closer' to it. (The props
are images of the gods in *Seven*, and the entrance to the Furies'
grove – represented by the open doors of a practicable *skene*
façade – in *Oidipous*.)

In the modern proscenium arch theatre the terms 'upstage'

[38] It begins with Horace (*Art of Poetry* 279); Aischylos was 'the first to raise
a stage of modest planks'. In the same sentence, however, he ascribes to
Aischylos the elevated buskins of Roman drama, which we know were not used
in fifth-century Athens.

[39] To the list of scholars since 1960 at Ewans 1995, xx note 14, add Friis
Johansen/Whittle (1980, 3–4), Warren and Scully (1995, esp. 65–6), and Green
and Handley (1995, 35). The case against a raised stage was fully established by
Pickard (1893); I reargue it with further references ibid., xx–xxiii.

[40] There would be even less space on a rock. Hammond (1972) and
Melchinger (1974, 20ff. and 82ff.) believed that a rocky outcrop to the right of
the *orchêstra* circle was left intact until just before or after the production of the
Oresteia, and used in *Suppliants* to represent the area to which the women
retreat. There was always an obvious objection to this on sightline grounds
(noted e.g. by Garvie 1986, xliv); major parts of the performance would be
marooned in a place where over a third of the spectators would have impaired
vision of the action; and Scullion (1990, 68–9) demonstrates conclusively that
Hammond has simply misread the archaeological reports; the top of the rock in
question lay well below the level of the *orchêstra* surface.

and 'downstage' refer not to a differentiation in physical height but to the distance at which the actor, on a level stage, is performing away from the front row of spectators. I believe that the references to different heights in Athenian drama refer similarly to areas of the level *orchêstra*; and that the convention did not evolve, but was the same throughout the fifth century. All these dramas can be played intelligibly if the actors establish by their use of space a curved mental line dividing the rearmost third of the *orchêstra* from the remainder. In *Suppliants*, this imaginary line marks off an area close to the images, 'the mound' which is regarded as being directly under divine protection, from an outer zone, referred to as 'the grove'. Fluid movement by both actors and *choros* was possible in both areas – as the scripts require.

Persians

In the first quarter of the fifth century the Greeks were confronted by the military power of an expansionist Persian empire; in consequence a small number of dramas were created with plots based on recent events. Miletos led an Ionian revolt against Persia in 499 BC, which was finally crushed by Dareios' commanders in 494; in the following year Aischylos' older contemporary, Phrynichos, exhibited *The Sack of Miletos* at the Festival of Dionysos, but was heavily fined for playing too much on the emotions of the audience, since Athenian troops had supported the unsuccessful rebellion.[41] Nearly twenty years later Phrynichos attempted historical material again; in 476 he won the competition with *Phoinikian Women*, a drama about the defeat of Xerxes. Aischylos emulated its subject, and deliberately echoed its opening lines at the start of *Persians*.[42]

In Aischylos' time there was no genre or concept equivalent to our modern prose 'history'. When Sophokles' contemporary and friend Herodotos embarked on his 'historiê', the word still

---

[41] Herodotos 6.21. The drama was also banned from subsequent production.

[42] Cf. Notes on Choros 1. *Persians* is the only surviving drama by Aischylos which was not part of a connected trilogy of dramas using the same myth and characters. (Attempts have been made to suggest that *Persians* was linked thematically with the lost *Phineus*, *Glaukos* and the *satyr-drama Prometheus the Fire-Kindler* which Aischylos also exhibited in 472, but this is unlikely.)

meant, primarily, 'research' or 'inquiry'; his account of the
conflict between Greeks and Persians includes much material
which we would regard as ethnographical and geographical,[43]
as well as a loosely chronological, often discursive and sometimes palpably fictitious account of historical events leading up
to the battles of Salamis and Plataia. For Aischylos and his
audience, a generation earlier, there was no firm dividing line
between 'history' and 'myth'; the events of the Persian Wars
were as available as potential subjects for tragic drama as the
early history of Thebes or Argos; and to judge from the drama,
Aischylos had licence to treat recent historical material with the
same freedom as myth. As with myth, he was not able to change
the basic features of the story, but he could select, compress,
expand, and even distort all but the most central details in
pursuit of his dramatic aims. Why then was historical subject-
matter not used later in the century?

The answer is not to be found in Aristotle's suggestion that
poetry deals with more universal subject-matter than history.[44]
While this is a useful generalization, its application has led to
dangerous underestimates of the extent to which Athenian
playwrights used dramas based on myth to discuss contemporary concerns. Aischylos (and perhaps before him Phrynichos)
chose to write about the fall of Persia because the vast power of
Xerxes, his overreaching and consequent defeat, provided
material analogous in scale and kind to the legendary events of
myth, where other, less exalted moments in contemporary Greek
politics did not. The success of the Athenians in defeating first
Dareios and then Xerxes against overwhelming odds provided
Aischylos with a striking illustration of a recurrent motif in
sixth- and fifth-century thought;[45] the idea that excessive wealth
and prosperity may invite the jealousy of the gods, and those
who go beyond their natural limits may be struck down.[46]

Aischylos portrays Dareios (outrageously, given that in 490

[43] Aischylos drew on Hekataios and other ethnographers before Herodotos,
as well as on his own inquiries, to create his portrait of Persian society. Cf. Hall
1989, 74.
[44] *Poetics* 51b3ff.
[45] Cf. e.g. Solon *Poems* 6, and 13.9–25.
[46] *Persians passim*, esp. 739ff., 821ff.; *Ag* 914ff.; *Niobe* (frag. 13), 15–20.
Herodotos, like Aischylos, saw this moral in the defeat of Xerxes; cf. esp.
Histories 7.10.

he too had bridged the Hellespont to invade Europe) as a monarch who confined his territorial ambitions to Asia; the role of Athens is highlighted, not so much to please the audience (though Aischylos, remembering Phrynichos' fate in the competition of 493, must have found this prudent) as to show how a small *polis*, deprived even of its territory, was able to defeat the Persians by cunning and tenacity.[47] The battle of Salamis becomes the main feature of the Messenger's narrative for a parallel reason; there the magnitude of the Persian losses, and the discrepancy with those of the Greeks, could be dramatized at their most stark and most vivid. The drama emphasizes the success of the free Greek fighters and the failure of the Persian monarchy, when it went beyond its natural, Asian territory and fought at sea in Greek waters.[48]

Scholars in Victorian and Edwardian England responded to the patriotic aspects of *Persians*; perhaps this drama echoed their own vision of a small state's naval success.[49] Some even criticized Aischylos for narrow jingoism. This is however hardly plausible, given the sympathy with which the Persians are treated, and in the second half of the twentieth century a humanist consensus has developed,[50] which invites us to see Xerxes as a universal human figure, as pitiable in his fall as Oidipous, an example to the Athenians of the pattern of excess and violence leading to destruction; perhaps even as a warning to them that they too must beware of breaching moral laws.[51]

[47] The stratagem to which the Messenger refers at 355ff. was Themistokles'; Herodotos 8.61. Podlecki (1966, 20) notes that Themistokles had sponsored Phrynichos' *Sack of Miletos* – perhaps hoping to make the Athenians see the need to continue to resist Persia. During 472 Themistokles was embroiled in a serious political confrontation with the pro-Spartan Kimon, who was raising questions about his patriotism in a sequence of political manoeuvres, which were shortly to lead to Themistokles' ostracism. Aischylos was aligned politically with Themistokles; his sponsor for the production of *Persians* was the young Perikles, who continued Themistokles' opposition to the conservatives led by Kimon; and Aischylos' approval for Periklean foreign policy is overt in *Eumenides* (Ewans 1995, 215). This does not however imply that the main aim in *Persians* of the reference to Themistokles was to assist his political position.

[48] Winnington-Ingram 1983, 10–11; cf. lines 181ff. and 762ff.

[49] Cf. e.g. Sidgwick 1903.

[50] Best expressed by Broadhead (1960), Kitto (1966; see esp. 107) and Conacher (1974).

[51] So e.g. Melchinger 1979, 39; Raphael and McLeish 1991, xviii.

Hall challenges this modern orthodoxy with a revisionist reading; she proposes to read the drama once more as a 'celebration of the victory over Persia'[52] – but from a new perspective. Her chapter offers a detailed analysis of the ways in which Aischylos effectively 'invents the barbarian' in *Persians*, building on the heightened Greek sense of ethnic self-consciousness after the Persian Wars. She draws attention[53] to the use of barbarian names to establish 'otherness'; the Persians' cruelty, fear of regal authority, and chaotic flight after defeat; and above all the hierarchic structure and absolute, god-like monarchy, luxuriousness and unrestrained emotionalism displayed by Aischylos' barbarians. The conclusion[54] is that Aischylos sees Persia's greatness as containing the seeds of its own destruction, because it was built on despotism, slavish subservience to the king and other excesses; the drama therefore celebrates the contrasting greatness of the Greeks, especially the Athenians, which is built on freedom, equality and austerity.

These readings are not mutually exclusive; they can and should be reconciled.[55] Drama is a complex medium, capable of evoking simultaneously emotions which in a strict logical analysis would be incompatible. Even if his sole aim had been to celebrate the military excellence of the Greeks, defining it by contrast with that of the Persians, Aischylos would still have needed to create some degree of emotional involvement with the defeated enemies. The extraordinary feature of *Persians*, and the one which legitimates the humanist reading, is the extent to which this is done. The Elders and Queen possess a quiet dignity, which sustains them even through this disaster. Aischylos uses as a focal point, to crystallize the horrors of warfare, the suffering of the young Persian women who have lost their men[56] – just as he was to do five years later, with Theban young women, in *Seven*; and the rehabilitation of Dareios leads to a climax in which he, and the Elders and Queen who are of his generation, are unequivocally portrayed as moderate *agathoi*, deserving of respect because they are fully aware of mortal

[52] Hall 1989, 57.
[53] Ibid. 77ff.
[54] Ibid. 100.
[55] Cf. Gagarin 1976, 51–4.
[56] 11ff., 132ff., 536ff.

limits. The contrast with Xerxes – rash, impetuous, capable of being played upon by bad advisers – loses its force if all that is Persian is to be regarded as inferior. Indeed, the enormity of Xerxes' loss, the extent to which he has abased himself – justifying the almost hysterical terms of the lament in the Finale – depends absolutely on the perception that his father's Persia had justifiably gained its rule over the continent of Asia.

In *Persians*, Aischylos has achieved a remarkable feat. Imagine, perhaps, a lyric dance-drama performed in Hanoi ten years after the fall of Saigon – set in Washington, and portraying the impact there of America's humiliating defeat in South Vietnam. For such a drama to celebrate the tenacity which enabled the Vietnamese to expel from their country an occupying force of vastly superior technology and power would be expected; for it also to portray, with sympathy and compassion, the impact of their losses upon American civilians, and the bitter self-reproaches of a defeated President, would be astonishing.

Dramatic Technique

Aischylos places his audience totally inside the world of his Persians at Sousa – a world which was partly imagined, and partly developed from knowledge. The Persians' recital of the strange names of their commanders, the style of their speech, lyrics, movement[57] and dance all establish the 'otherness' of the culture in which the drama is set.[58] So too do the props – the elaborate, exotic costumes of all the characters, especially that worn by the Queen on her first appearance, and the ornamented vehicles on which both she and Xerxes[59] enter the *orchêstra*. All this is designed for powerful contrast with the final spectacle when Xerxes, humiliated and in rags, joins his Elders in the ritual self-punishment of the *threnos*.

Persians has been condemned for lacking plot and structure. If by plot you mean an exciting sequence of twists and turns, the recognitions and reversals beloved of Aristotelian theory and of Hellenistic comedy, *Persians* will disappoint, since it gradually unfolds a sequence of revelations not of the previously

[57] Even the special running style of the Messenger (247–8).
[58] Hall 1989, 76ff.
[59] See Notes to Scene 1 and Finale.

unknown but of the deeply expected.[60] Aischylos' fundamental decisions were to place the action of the drama in time after Salamis and before Plataia – during the return of Xerxes; and to begin, in contrast to Phrynichos, before the news of defeat has reached Sousa. As the drama opens, the Elders are stranded in a no-man's land; to their left the retreat to the palace, to their right the menacing road to the coast. 'The Persians have gone/to Greece . . .'; and already in the first two lines the poetry carries the implication of disaster, since the line-break after 'gone' implies for a moment that they are dead as well.[61]

As he was later to do in *Agamemnon*, Aischylos arranges past events to virtuoso effect around the framework of the homecoming of a king from war.[62] Like all his surviving dramas, *Persians* is shaped around the gradual development of our understanding of how a *moira* takes shape; the key decision was to reserve the battle of Plataia for Dareios' prophecies. First come the uncertainty and fear of the Elders in Choros 1; then the crystallizing certainty which the Queen's dream conveys;[63] then the Messenger, who in three intense narratives delivers a cumulative series of blows to the body politic of Persia: Salamis, Psyttaleia and Strymon.

At this point, for some commentators,[64] the drama falls apart. They are not attuned to Aischylos' psychological insight; the shock of the defeat at first misdirects the Queen's response, and only afterwards does she recover enough to see her way clear. This leads by a fine dramatic strategy to a surprise new direction – the summoning of Dareios – which swiftly takes the drama to its climax. Dareios places the events in a perspective which makes even this unparalleled disaster comprehensible, showing how Xerxes has brought down upon his own head a *moira*

---

[60] Cf. Ewans 1995, xxixff.

[61] This implication is developed by repetition (1, 12, 25, 60); the Messenger's first sentence, 252, brings out the full meaning.

[62] Aischylos' handling of what are now termed flashback and flashforward is rightly praised by Raphael and McLeish 1991, xxi–ii. There is however the important difference (cf. Conacher 1974, 167) that in *Persians* we see only the impact of past events on the capital city, while in *Ag* we see as well how these past events shape a deed of violence which is enacted during the drama.

[63] The Elders' reaction to her narrative is a telling insight into the extent to which self-deception can triumph over plain indications of truth.

[64] See Notes on Scene 2.

which could have been postponed (740–42), and sealing the impact of his words by prophesying, in his vision of Plataia, even worse consequences than the Queen and Elders have already absorbed. After which the Elders can only hang on to their muted summary of 'the glory that was Persia'; all that remains is for Xerxes to return, and suffer the reproaches he deserves, as both he and his Elders try to absorb their catastrophic losses through lamentation.

Aristotle denied that it is true tragedy to see a wicked or stupid man receiving his deserts.[65] Winnington-Ingram argues that 'morally, [*Persians*] is a study in black and white, and so lacks subtlety. The theological doctrine is fundamentally the same as that of Aeschylus at his greatest, but it is not put to the severer tests – that is to say, it is not developed in a context which, like those of the *Oresteia* or the Danaid trilogy, raises wellnigh insoluble problems . . . the victims are all guilty!'[66]

Aischylos is not a theologian, exploring 'the nature of Zeus and his justice'[67] in a series of progressively more deep dramatic meditations; he takes a philosophically simple aspect of human existence, the 'tall poppy syndrome',[68] and invests it with dramatic depth by the sheer power with which the spectacle of the watching, waiting and progressively more defeated Persians affects the audience. He exhibits the Persians as 'other', with weaknesses which explain to culturally biased Greek eyes why they were defeated; he also shows them as suffering human beings, forcing even an Athenian audience to respond with empathy. As Aischylos was to show in later dramas, Greeks as well as Persians could go beyond their *moira* and bring down disaster upon themselves. The Athenians themselves, after his death, confirmed the truth of his vision.

Seven against Thebes

Seven against Thebes was the third drama in Aischylos' Theban tetralogy: *Laios, Oidipous, Seven against Thebes* and the *satyr-*

---

[65] *Poetics* 52b 36ff.
[66] 1983, 15. Cf. Lattimore 1958, 38.
[67] Ibid.
[68] This English idiom goes back to a story from Ionian Greece in Aischylos' lifetime; cf. Herodotos 5.92.

drama Sphinx. These dramas won the first prize for tragedy at the Festival of Dionysos in 467.

Earlier scholarship patronized *Seven.* Judged by the standards of Sophokles' *Oidipous the King* – itself misinterpreted as being primarily concerned with how the character of Oidipous caused his downfall – Aischylos' apparent lack of interest in the character of Eteokles, and his fusion of the defence of Thebes with the curse of Oidipous and the Fury of the royal house, struck many scholars as archaic, stylized and undramatic.

Perhaps our main difficulty in approaching this drama today is that in the more civilized and affluent nations of the west warfare has become separated from normal civilian experience, either by time or by distance. It is over fifty years since Hitler attempted to conquer the United Kingdom; and although the United States and Australia have fought wars on foreign soil since 1945 to defend their perceived national interests, neither has come under serious threat of invasion in the twentieth century. In many countries only volunteer soldiers, aid workers and reporters have any first-hand experience of war – though graphic television images now bring the conflicts even of the most distant parts of the globe into our homes.

Warfare was a fundamental condition of ancient Greek life. During Aischylos' lifetime the Athenians had twice repelled an invasion by overwhelming forces from Persia; on the second occasion, they had been obliged to evacuate, allowing their whole territory to be ravaged and their city to be sacked. In his boyhood the city had also been racked by internal conflict leading up to the expulsion of the tyrants, and this was followed by Theban and Spartan attempts to meddle in the internal affairs of the newly formed democracy, and reimpose autocracy. After that there were political manoeuvres, framed around the success and failure of military expeditions and the development of the Delian League, headed by Athens, initially to contain Persia; in Aischylos' last years these culminated in a major shift of foreign policy when Athens allied herself with Argos in 461. This led almost inevitably to the outbreak in 460 of the 'First Peloponnesian War' between the new alliance and an anti-democratic, Dorian coalition headed by the Spartans.

The need to be able to fight – to protect a community and its crops, and later its sea-lanes and its allies – was fundamental to Greek life and therefore to Greek values. A man's excellence was from Homer onwards crystallized around his fighting abilities – his capacity to defend his *oikos*, and subsequently his capacity to join with others to defend his *polis*.[69] Aischylos places his central figure firmly within these values; when Eteokles departs to fight his brother at the climax of this drama, he defends his decision to avoid the shame of appearing to shirk battle, even at the cost of possible fratricide, by appealing to the warrior code. At 717 he defines himself precisely, in contemporary terms, as a *hoplite* – one of the fully armed, middle-class footsoldiers who formed by the fifth century the backbone of the Athenian and Spartan military machines.

The one word for peace is relatively rare in surviving Greek literature – especially when set against the incidence of the many words which form the vocabulary of warfare and battle. The first extant Greek poem, the *Iliad*, is an epic of almost unparalleled length; much of it consists of close narrative description of battle and hand to hand combat.

Warfare is rarely far from the concerns of subsequent Greek literature. More specifically, the theme of the city under siege, so brilliantly realized in *Seven* that Aristophanes was more than justified in describing this drama as 'brim-full of the War-god',[70] receives emphasis from the *Iliad*, where the scene is twice set on the city walls to bring out the pathos of the plight of the besieged Trojans, via *Seven* itself through to Euripides' later treatment of the same subject in *Phoinikian Women*.[71]

Aischylos evokes the terror of a siege by every theatrical means at his disposal – in the Scout's accounts of the Argive champions, in the almost hysterical reaction of the women to the imminent advance of the Argive army, and in the intense internal combat within Thebes, as Eteokles struggles to subdue their terror.

[69] Military, 'competitive' virtues were central to male excellence in Greek society and thought before Sokrates; see Adkins 1960, *passim*. Later demonstrations that the 'co-operative' excellences also played a role (e.g. Long 1970) have not undermined his argument. Cf. Vernant 1980, 23; 'marriage is to a girl what war is to a boy'.

[70] *Frogs* 1021.

[71] Euripides also set two of his most powerful dramas, *Hekabe* and *Trojan Women*, in the no-man's land outside the destroyed walls after the sack of Troy. *Trojan Women* is a searing denunciation of the Athenians' cynicism and ruthless immorality in the sack of Melos the previous year.

Trilogy

We know very little about Aischylos' version of the earlier phases of the story;[72] what little we do know differs in significant respects from previous versions of the Theban legends, and from Sophokles' famous version in *Oidipous the King*. For example, the oracle that if Laios had a son, it would kill its father and marry its mother, was clearly not present in Aischylos' trilogy.

Laios had committed some crime – perhaps, as in other traditions, the abduction and homosexual rape of Pelops' son Chrysippos, who committed suicide in shame. In retaliation, Pelops cursed him 'that the evil should descend to his children'.[73] After Laios became king of Thebes, Apollo's oracle told him that he must die childless to keep the city safe.[74] However, his wife[75] conceived Oidipous. At birth he was exposed in a jar on a mountain to die, but was somehow saved.

In *Laios* the king (who is known to have spoken Scene 1 of the drama) went on a journey. At Potniai he became involved in a quarrel with a stranger; Laios was killed, together with most of his retinue. A survivor comes back to Thebes and reports the crime – but the murderer's identity is unknown.

In *Oidipous*, Oidipous has arrived at Thebes, and has rescued the city from torment by the Sphinx, which had been devouring the inhabitants. His reward was the hand in marriage of the former king's widow, and he had children by her.[76] Oidipous subsequently discovered who he is and what he has done, blinded himself, and cursed the sons of his incestuous marriage, that they will divide their inheritance with iron.[77]

[72] There is a good discussion in Baldry 1956; for more detail cf. Hutchinson 1985, xvii–xxx. See also Thalmann 1978, 8–30.

[73] Thalmann 1978, 16, citing a scholiast's comment on Euripides *Phoinikian Women* line 60.

[74] *Seven* 748ff. Hutchinson 1985, xxviiff. notes that we cannot know the full dimensions of the prediction. Did Apollo foretell Laios' death, as in Pindar *Olympian* 2. 38ff.?

[75] She is not named in *Seven*; perhaps her name in epic, Epikaste, had by now been replaced by 'Iokaste', which is used by Sophokles and Euripides.

[76] This development is crucial to the story as dramatized by Aischylos and Sophokles; it appears to be Aischylos' own creation. Earlier versions either imply that Oidipous had no children at all, or state that he remarried after Epikaste's death, and had children by his second wife, Eurygeneia (cf. Pausanias 9.5.110).

[77] All three elements are new in Aischylos. In Homer (*Odyssey* 9.271–80) he discovered what he had done almost immediately; Epikaste hanged herself, but

It is apparent from *Seven* that after Oidipous' death Eteokles and Polyneikes quarrelled over who should rule Thebes, and Eteokles drove Polyneikes from the city.[78] Polyneikes took refuge in Argos, married the daughter of the Argive King Adrastos and returned from there to attack Thebes with an army led by himself and six other champions.

We cannot know whether *Laios* and *Oidipous* had a formal symmetry with each other, a fundamental pattern which was altered deliberately for dramatic effect in the third and last drama.[79] However, it is safe to conjecture that the three dramas showed catastrophe coming upon the royal house in each of three successive generations.[80] The Women's ode after the fatal exit of Eteokles sounds like a summary, linking back what we have seen in this drama to the events before; and in that summary Laios' defiance of Apollo is clearly established as 'the first-beginning crime' (*Ag* 1192) – 'soon punished, but still lasting/to the sons of sons' (*Seven* 744–5).

Oidipous' discovery, self-blinding and Curse were presumably seen as consequences, growing organically from the moment when 'thoughtless desire for children conquered [Laios]' (750) through to the Curse laid by Oidipous on the children of his incest, which precipitated the fratricidal climax of *Seven against Thebes*. Only after that climax is the full pattern visible; the fate of the royal *oikos* of the Labdakids is suddenly and violently detached from that of the *polis*; when all the offspring of Laios have been destroyed, the safety of the city is restored again.[81]

Structure

Thalmann saw *Seven against Thebes* as a drama in three parts; Scene 3, he argued, forms a long and predominantly spoken

he lived on. Aischylos' second creative invention (also imitated by Sophokles in *Oidipous the King*) is Oidipous' long period of prosperity before the discovery. He also innovated in having his Oidipous curse his sons not, as in the epic cycle, for a subsequent relatively trivial act of neglect, but at this same moment, because they were the offspring of an incestuous union. The self-blinding is also new in Aischylos; Baldry 1956, 25–30 (*contra* Winnington-Ingram 1983, 47–8).

[78] In the standard version of the myth, the brothers agreed to rule for one year each – until Eteokles refused to let Polyneikes have his turn. Apollodoros 3.6.1.

[79] This was Aischylos' strategy in the *Oresteia*; Ewans 1995, xxxiiff.

[80] Hutchinson 1985, xxx.

[81] This is established by the Scout's words in Scene 4, and echoed strongly in the question which opens the Finale, 820ff.

plateau between a more lyric-dominated introduction and Finale, in which the panic of the Women and their final lamentation are the main elements.[82] This isolation of the long spoken scene of the pairs of speeches has been encouraged by the false view that it is the most profound part of the drama, because it has less action. There has been a tendency to underestimate the theatrical power of Scene 3, together with an equal and opposite tendency to underestimate the amount of meaning communicated in the earlier and later sections of this drama, because they contain lyrics and vigorous, exciting action.

Once this prejudice has been overcome, the underlying shape becomes plain. *Seven* conforms to the pattern familiar elsewhere in Aischylos – a steady build-up to a climax around two-thirds of the way through the playing time,[83] followed by a Finale in which characters shattered by that climax attempt to come to terms with its consequences. In *Seven* the climax is the moment when Eteokles discovers that he must meet Polyneikes at the seventh gate, and recognizes in this the power of his father's curses and Apollo's hatred of the race of Laios.

For the great German scholar von Wilamowitz, the sudden appearance here of a Curse, which has been mentioned only once before (line 70) was evidence of Aischylos' dramatic incompetence – an imperfect welding of material from epic poetry about the siege of Thebes with material concerning the fall of the house of Labdakos.[84] For more recent critics with a higher view of Aischylos' 'dramatic art',[85] the central feature is the surfacing of the Curse at the climax to defeat Eteokles.

However, the curses of Oidipous on his sons, and the anger of Apollo at Laios' attempts to defy him, should not be seen as inexorable, pre-existing forces, which suddenly surface to create Eteokles' downfall.[86] In Aischylean drama, as in real life both ancient and modern, curses uttered by human beings do not

---

[82] 1978, 26ff.

[83] On this pattern in the *Oresteia*, cf. Ewans 1995, xxxii.

[84] 1914, 66ff.

[85] The title of Thalmann's book-length study of this drama (1978; cf. 27ff.).

[86] This reading legitimates a dangerous line of interpretation, in which Eteokles can be psychoanalysed, as if he were a real person and not a character in a drama, and castigated for suppressing knowledge of his inheritance and of the curse, as he attempts to direct the city's strategy; cf. e.g. Caldwell 1973.

automatically come true.[87] Nor is Apollo's oracle fulfilled in a
way which responds to the natural interpretation of its words –
for although Laios did have offspring, the *polis* was (eventually)
saved.

The curses of Oidipous, and the Fury of the royal house, are
not underlying forces which suddenly surface in Eteokles' mind
at the climax and drive him to fratricide. On the contrary – and
this is the connexion between the earlier parts of the drama and
the climax, which von Wilamowitz could not discern – the
action of Scenes 1–3 shows the gradual taking shape of Eteokles'
moira through human choices – on the Argive side, the decision
to attempt to storm the city, to place seven champions at each
of Thebes' seven gates, and to select those champions by lot; on
the Theban side, Eteokles' successive decisions – first to resist at
all costs, conscripting even the very old and the very young, then
to use the Women to evoke firm support from Thebes' native
gods, and finally to select seven champions (including himself)
to answer the Argive threat. Each of these choices and actions
leads closer towards the moment at which Polyneikes is revealed
at the seventh gate, and Eteokles – like other principal figures in
Aischylos at moments of crisis[88] – faces a free choice between
two alternative courses of action, which are both appalling, but
of which only one can and therefore must be done. He is faced
with either backing down before his brother's challenge, so
incurring *aischron*, or else incurring the 'indelible' *miasma*
consequent on shedding kindred blood. He must choose to
confront Polyneikes;[89] and when he does so, the house is
destroyed. This fulfils Oidipous' curses, and satisfies Apollo. The
city is then saved (as Eteokles correctly expected) by the superior
excellence of the champions at the first six gates.

Dramatic Techniques
As in *Persians*, the playing space required for *Seven against
Thebes* is simply an *orchêstra*, preset with images of the gods.[90]

[87] Cf. e.g. Thyestes' curse on all the descendants of Pleisthenes, reported by
Aigisthos at *Ag* 1602 but not fulfilled.
[88] The closest parallels are with Agamemnon at Aulis, and Orestes in Scene 6
of *L B*. Cf. Ewans 1995, xxxii and 162.
[89] See Notes on Scene 3.
[90] The 'set' is identical with that for *Suppliants*, except that in *Seven* no altar
between the images is required; Canavan 1972, 97–8.

These need to be placed just outside its rear circumference,[91] so that the Women can take their song and dance of supplication close to the images during Choroses 1 and 2.[92] This encourages a blocking pattern which, at several points in the drama, works by establishing an interaction between a smaller, 'up-*orchêstra*' section of the playing space and a larger 'down-*orchêstra*' section which represents being away from the images.[93]

The attack of the Argives is not represented to the audience except through the characters' differing reactions to it; it is therefore inappropriate to suggest that a representational *skene* building was used in this drama.[94] However, there is point here – as there is not in *Persians* or *Suppliants* – to the hypothesis that a *skene*, in the earlier sense of a non-representational tent inside which the actors could change masks and costumes – might have been placed for *Seven* in a visible position at extreme back centre, between and just behind the images.[95] Eteokles' first two entries are far more effective if they are sudden, than if he comes in down the left *parodos*.

The power of *Seven* lies in the contrasts which Aischylos deploys; female against male, lyric against spoken verse, reason against emotion – and the corresponding use of the *orchêstra* to

[91] Cf. Canavan 1972, 82 and 102–5.

[92] A raised stage is no more desirable in *Seven* than in any other surviving drama of Aischylos; cf. Canavan 1972, 103 n. 47.

[93] Since *Suppliants* makes complex and sophisticated use of this same pattern of blocking, it is worth conjecturing that Aischylos in 467 was beginning to experiment with a new pattern of theatre dynamics which he exploited further in 463.

[94] The main arguments against a representational *skene* in 467 are (1) that it is not used in *Suppliants*, a later drama; and (2) that when it is first used in surviving drama – in the *Oresteia* – Aischylos uses all its facilities, with sudden entries and exits, two uses of the *ekkuklêma* and even a speech from the roof, in a way which has the feel of a dramatist exploiting to the full a new theatrical resource (whose installation he might even have suggested himself). Neither argument is particularly strong, given the small number of surviving dramas. *Aigyptians* and/or *Danaides* might well have been set in front of the lodgings in Argos of Aigyptos' sons; the representational *skene* may therefore have been inaugurated in the 460s, but Aischylos only felt free to exploit the new facility to the extent seen in the *Oresteia* after several years of relatively cautious experiment.

[95] This position was occupied in *Persians* by the tomb of Dareios, and in *Suppliants* by the central altar.

portray the fluctuations in the relative power of the characters. The siege of Thebes is not a Hollywood spectacular; the presence of the invaders is the greater because they are unseen – evoked by verbal and lyric means,[96] and realized in action through choreography and blocked movement. Commentators have too often paid more attention to what Aischylos does not provide, because he had no wish to, than to the enthralling series of confrontations through which Eteokles is brought face to face with his tragic choice, and the Women of Thebes are left not to celebrate the survival of their *polis*, but to mourn, in an extended closing *threnos*, the process which has destroyed the last two descendants of Laios.

Suppliants

For me, as for an increasing number of students, *Suppliants* is Aischylos' greatest surviving drama outside the *Oresteia*;[97] the loss of *Aigyptians* and *Danaides* is one of the most serious gaps in our knowledge of ancient Greek drama.

Most scholars and critics in the last hundred years would have regarded that judgement as wildly eccentric. Friis Johansen and Whittle[98] cannot understand why late Roman scholars ever chose to include *Suppliants* in the canon of seven Aischylean tragedies preserved for posterity; a characteristic nineteenth-century judgement was that 'there is no thrilling action in the piece'[99] [!]; its only saving grace was that 'the scene is eminently spectacular, and is therein suited both to Aeschylus' natural taste for pomp and also to the comparatively inartistic character of the early drama'.[100] Since *Suppliants* contains long choral

---

[96] I doubt whether even sound effects were used; they would distract from, rather than add to, the power of the hysterical individual outcries in song and dance at 78ff.

[97] Hence the title of this book.

[98] 1980, 55.

[99] Tucker 1889, xvi.

[100] Ibid. The view that Aischylos was more addicted to pomp and spectacle than his successors goes back to the ancient *Life of Aischylos*; it is demolished by Taplin 1977, esp. 202–3. Tucker adopts from Aristotle (*Poetics* 50b 15–20) the equally false, literary-biased view that the use of spectacle is in itself inartistic and relatively primitive. For a long overdue counterstatement cf. Burian 1991, xi–xii: 'a world at once remote and exotic, yet primal in its evocation of the

odes, and late nineteenth-century taste expected dramas from a developed tradition to concentrate on individuals, most scholars ignored the political and other indications which had led a few to suggest a date in the 460s, and placed it as early as possible in Aischylos' career – in the 490s.[101]

Gilbert Murray developed this position.[102] He viewed *Suppliants* as primarily a spectacular work, with no actors in the normal sense of the word but simply three *choros* 'directors' – Danaos, Herald and Pelasgos – each leading a *choros* of fifty (Danaides, Aigyptians and Argives), since he believed that the legendary number of the daughters of Danaos must have been realized literally in the theatre.[103] On Murray's calculations, this yields a total of 153 people massed in the *orchêstra* – or perhaps, if the Danaides all have Handmaidens[104] and they are visible throughout, there are a hundred female characters present and must therefore, for balance, be one hundred Aigyptians and one hundred Argives.

In a 20m diameter *orchêstra*, 153 people would give each player two square metres of space; 303 people would give each player one. Dancing – or indeed movement of any kind to accompany the text – would have been impossible; but then, it is readily apparent that these scholars had little or no idea that there is any dramatic content to *Suppliants* which might require complex and subtle movement for its realization in performance. For them and many others, *Suppliants* was solid evidence for the original, primitive form of Greek tragedy – more like a spectacular, but theatrically static oratorio-ballet than any normal conception of drama.

struggle of male and female, its enactment of terror, cunning, and lust, its insistence on the presence of the sacred in the world. And . . . a gripping drama of civic crisis, of ideologies in conflict and clashing forms of power.'

[101] Tucker 1889, xxi–ii. Other similar views between 1890 and 1920 are cited at Garvie 1969, 107 note 5.

[102] 1949, 48ff.

[103] It was however clearly a convention that the *choros* – whose number was twelve in Aischylos' time, later increased to fifteen – could represent groups of people both smaller than that number (the three Furies, in *Eumenides*, and the seven mothers of the champions in Euripides *Suppliants*) or, as in this trilogy, a larger number, the fifty Danaides of this drama and the fifty sons of Aigyptos in the sequel.

[104] Against the traditional introduction of Handmaidens to solve alleged problems in the Finale see Taplin 1977, 230–8.

A papyrus fragment was discovered in 1951 which demonstrates beyond reasonable doubt that Aischylos must have presented the Danaid trilogy at a festival after 467 BC, almost certainly in 463. As John Jones noted, commenting in 1962 on the first ten years of scholarly reaction to the discovery,[105] this fragment demonstrates the extreme danger of generalizing about Greek tragedy – and in particular, of assuming (or trying to prove, from the fraction that survives of the known tragic dramas performed at Athens in the fifth century) that it evolved during that period from some kind of primitive, *choros*-centred performance through to a drama focused on individuals, simply because modern western culture, unlike the Athenians, regards as the most interesting aspect of tragedy a focus on the character of individuals, seen in isolation.[106]

However, evidence can always be played down, if not completely ignored; and the vigour of the rearguard has been remarkable. Sir Denys Page reasserted the 'spectacular' *Suppliants* six years after the discovery of the fragment;[107] and Jones himself suggested that 'Of course [Aischylos and his audience] must have thought it old-fashioned – and chiefly because of the prominent Chorus'.[108] Only in 1969, with the publication of Garvie's painstaking stylistic and structural analysis, were most doubters effectively silenced. Even after that two admirers, Arrowsmith and Lembke, could still write about the 'antique strangeness' of *Suppliants*, and liken the piece to an 'archaic oratorio'.[109]

This drama has more choral lyrics than most other tragedies for two reasons: neither of them has much to do with its date of composition. The central character is a group of people, not an individual – as in *Eumenides*, but in no other surviving drama;[110] and the Danaides are in a state of heightened emotion for most of its length, and therefore naturally express themselves through the medium of lyric. The pervasive modern assumption (usually

[105] 1962, 65ff.
[106] Cf. Ewans 1995, xxiff. Strong objection was rightly made to the evolutionary theory, and the damage it has done to our view of *Suppliants*, by Garvie 1969, 140 and Lloyd-Jones 1974, 372–4.
[107] 1957, xxx.
[108] 1962, 69.
[109] Lembke 1975, 5 and 19.
[110] Cf. Garvie 1969, 138; Friis Johansen/Whittle 1980, 26.

among scholars unfamiliar with opera) that lyric expression can never be socially and politically subtle, and must therefore necessarily be early and archaic, will not stand sustained examination in the context of early fifth-century Greece. Aischylos performed his tragedies in the same culture in which complex, allusive odes composed to celebrate victories in Olympic and other games made Pindar a millionaire.

The other principal barrier to appreciation of *Suppliants* has been incomprehension or ignorance of the importance to the Greeks of the issues which it dramatizes, together with prefeminist male indifference to a woman's right to dispose of her own body as she wishes.[111]

Suppliants is interpretation as well as translation of the title. Literally, 'Hiketides' are 'women who have come' – to a place away from their homeland.

Travelling was hazardous even for groups of armed males in the early Greece where this drama is set; it still remained so, though to a lesser extent, in Aischylos' own time. There were no universal human rights, and 'Hellas' (Greece) was not a single political entity, with a nationally recognized legal system; to travel outside the protection of your own *philoi* was to risk your life.

Accordingly arrival, coming to a new place, was automatically an act of supplication, and the rights of the newcomer were given the strongest possible divine sanction, that of Zeus himself.[112] Suppliants demonstrated their complete dependence; they prayed to the gods of the city, holding suppliant wands – olive branches, wreathed in wool – and clung to the protection of

[111] A remarkable number of male interpreters have diagnosed the Danaides as suffering from a pathological aversion to marriage, because they assert their right not to marry men they do not want. Belfiore (n.d. 2) collects these comments, which say much about modern scholastic life but nothing about Aischylos' characters; cf. e.g. Murray 1958, 28 and even Winnington-Ingram (normally a sensitive and far from sexist critic) 1983, 60.

[112] His authority was, of course, acknowledged by most civilized (i.e. Greek) human beings and gods; but Odysseus' discourse with the Kyklops, when he and his crew are at that creature's mercy in the *Odyssey* (9.266ff.; contrast e.g. Eumaios at 14.48ff.), reveals how accepting the god-protected rights of strangers was a precise marker of the boundary between civilization and barbarism. Cf. *Suppliants* Scene 4, where the Aigyptian (i.e. barbarian) Herald refuses to recognize the authority of the Greek gods, and proposes simply to seize the suppliant Danaides by force.

their altars, or knelt in a submissive posture before a significant individual, touching his or her knees, hand or beard, until the people of the place acknowledged their supplication and responded by leading them from the altar, or raising them from the suppliant posture, and granted protection.[113] In this way ritual was used to convert 'outsiders' into people with a *xenos* relationship to the city and/or its individuals, entitled to settle there with the same *time* and protection as members of the *polis* themselves.[114]

The arrival of suppliants seeking protection was a basic feature of Greek life, and is therefore naturally reflected in the surviving Athenian dramas.[115] The suppliant, showing by ritual self-abasement that he or she has no personal *time* in this place, invokes the *time* of the gods for protection.[116] Although the arriving person is weak and the host nation strong, the ritual of supplication is double edged: 'a plea for the protection of an acknowledged and magnanimous superior (and thus an acceptance of harmless inferiority), but also a threat to the integrity of the person supplicated'.[117]

A fictional situation can therefore be developed in drama which exploits the ambiguities of the two roles, the power struggle innate within the act of arrival and supplication, and the choice between reception and rejection which confronts the host country. Aischylos did this in *Suppliants*, and sharpened Pelasgos' dilemma in four ways.[118]

1 If he accepts the Danaides, there will inevitably be war with a large and well-armed Aigyptian force. If he does not, the young women will – as they reveal when he continues to waver – place an indelible *miasma* on Argos, using the ultimate weapon of the truly defenceless by hanging themselves on the images of its

[113] The appropriate rituals are fully analysed and discussed in Gould 1973, 74–103; see also Vickers 1973, 438ff.

[114] Gould 1973, 94.

[115] Cf. especially Aischylos *Eumenides*, Sophokles *Oidipous at Kolonos*, Euripides *Suppliants*, *Herakles* and *Andromache*. Good discussion in Lattimore 1964, 46ff. and Rehm 1988 *passim*.

[116] Cf. Cairns 1993, 185.

[117] Gould 1973, 100.

[118] For Pelasgos' reluctance cf. e.g. the Kymeans in Herodotos 1.157–61. Cf. also the dilemma which Orestes' refuge at her image creates for Athena and the Athenians in *Eumenides* (Ewans 1995, 191ff., esp. 201).

gods (619ff.; Argive prehistory already contained an incident of near-indelible *miasma*, of which Aischylos' Pelasgos is well aware; 26off.).

2 The Danaides are not simply strangers; during the course of Scene 2 they establish that despite their exotic appearance, they are *philoi*, blood-relatives of Argos and therefore far more entitled to refuge there than ordinary *xenoi*.

3 The Danaides frequently appeal and pray to Zeus because, almost uniquely among characters in tragedy,[119] they are direct blood-descendants of the most powerful god and therefore have a strong claim to his support. To hand them over to their pursuers would therefore be exceptionally hazardous.

4 Most importantly, these suppliants are female. As women, in a world dominated by male physical violence, they need the protection of men; but equally, as women also, a Greek society could regard them as inferior, and therefore not worth fighting – losing men – about (477). Pelasgos correctly anticipates (386ff.; cf. 918) that the sons of Aigyptos will claim legal ownership of their female cousins, and therefore the right to do what they please with their bodies. There are other issues in the drama; but here Aischylos asks the Athenians directly whether even their male-dominated society could foreswear its obligations, allowing expediency and barbarism to triumph over a fundamental institution of Greek civilization, simply because the suppliants are female.

Dramatic Technique

As always in Aischylos, the ebb and flow of power relationships is at the heart of the drama,[120] and the characters and situation in *Suppliants* place in confrontation some of the most fundamental polarities of Greek society: suppliant against citizen, male against female, Greek against barbarian, white against black, *philos* against *echthros*, *nomos* against violence, young against old. The only hand props are weapons – the swords and armour which literally embody the male power of the Argives and Aigyptians, the wands which the Danaides correctly describe as

[119] Cf. only Herakles in Euripides *Herakles* and Sophokles *Women of Trachis*. In Sophokles' drama, Herakles' direct kinship with Zeus, who appears to have acted completely contrary to his obligation of *philia* to his own son, legitimates the bitterness of Hyllos' complaint (1264ff.).

[120] On this aspect of the *Oresteia* cf. Ewans 1995, xxiff.

'the weapons of a suppliant' (21), and above all the waistbands, tokens of their femininity, which they threaten to remove, not to give their virginity to men but to hang themselves on the images of gods and so cause indelible *miasma* to Argos.

Realization of this drama in a performance space depends on understanding Aischylos' use of the two axes of the *orchêstra*; back/front ('up'-/'down'-*orchêstra*), and left/right. The images of the gods must be placed around the rear perimeter of the *orchêstra*, fanning out from an altar placed at extreme back centre.[121] This enables the Suppliants to foreshadow in Choros 1, and establish in Scene 1, a convention that the rearmost third of the *orchêstra* represents the area close to the images, which is regarded as being directly under divine protection, in contrast to the remainder of the *orchêstra*, an outer zone which the audience was required to imagine as being a leafy grove.

Together with this front/back dichotomy Aischylos also makes a particularly strong use of the Athenian convention that the right *parodos* leads to the country, left to the downtown area of the city where the action is set. In *Suppliants* right is the place from which the Danaides have come – the road to the sea, from which they will be pursued; left is the path to Argos, which at first is almost equally perilous but later becomes the path to safety.[122] The *orchêstra* is thus polarized L/R as well as B/F; and the movements along and across these axes take on a particular intensity in production. The Notes try to bring out the ways in which Aischylos shows his absolute mastery of the performance space in this drama of his late maturity; the patterns of advance and retreat, confrontation or reflection complement the verbal meaning of the lyrics and dialogue to make full sense of the unfolding predicament of the characters.

In all the other surviving dramas with a suppliant story-pattern, the arrival and reception of the suppliant individual or group only occupies about a third of the action. In *Suppliants*, Pelasgos raises the Danaides from their place of supplication at

---

[121] Practical experiment rapidly rules out any position inside the *orchêstra*; other positions on the perimeter make the drama almost impossible to block.

[122] Taplin 1977, 239 notes the importance of the different directions from which the Suppliants arrive at the start and to which they go at the end; characteristically, however, he fails to note the many ways in which the polarization is important during the action.

506, and takes on the role of their 'proxenos', their supporter and champion at Argos. However, the supplication is not complete until after the vote of the Argive people;[123] the drama ends only when the Danaides leave for their new residences in the city of Argos. This comes after the climax, when Pelasgos confronts the Aigyptian Herald, rescues the Suppliants and accepts the consequences. The supplication and reception of the Danaides at Argos is shown at length because it realizes an almost archetypal pattern of enmeshment, in which a reluctant host nation finds itself drawn into a situation where – as Pelasgos comes to recognize, 468ff. – there are 'seas of evil' surrounding him and his city whatever they do. The drama only concludes when the consequences have been established as inevitable, and Pelasgos' *moira* has taken shape; in the sequel the reception of the Danaides led the Argives into a war, in which their king probably paid with his life.[124]

There is therefore a steady development over the first half of the drama, up to the moment at which Pelasgos commits himself to accepting the Suppliants; then, in a formal pattern which Aischylos later echoed in *Agamemnon* and *Libation Bearers*,[125] there is a further movement onwards and upwards to the climax, which occurs two-thirds of the way through – the re-entry of Pelasgos to rescue the Suppliants from the Aigyptians in Scene 4. This is followed by a calming movement down to the conclusion. After the rescue Aischylos allows the Danaides to celebrate their deliverance in the Finale – but also (as at the close of each of the first two dramas in the *Oresteia*) he injects into the closing phase a note of apprehension. This directs the audience's attention to certain unresolved issues, which will be addressed in the next drama.

Trilogy

Far too much has been written about the possible content of the two lost dramas[126] (and too little about *Suppliants* itself). From

[123] Cf. Belfiore n.d. 8 against Gould 1973, 88–9.

[124] By contrast in *Eumenides*, Euripides' *Suppliants* and Sophokles' *Oidipous at Kolonos*, the hosts (all Athenian) overcome the dangers involved in accepting suppliants, and live on to receive blessings because they did so.

[125] Ewans 1995, xxxii–iv.

[126] There have been some outrageous reconstructions. Even Winnington-Ingram (1983, 55ff.) ventures well beyond his normal caution.

the fragmentary hypothesis it seems almost certain that the sequence of the dramas, with which Aischylos won the prize (probably) in 463 was *Suppliants*, *Aigyptians*,[127] *Danaides* and the *satyr-drama Amymone*.[128]

Other ancient sources provide a variety of different accounts, and the surviving fragments of Aischylos' dramas[129] tell us almost nothing. It is important to remember that we can only make conjectures, based on the way the story is begun in *Suppliants*. Even the common assumption that the famous fragment from *Danaides*, spoken by Aphrodite (frag. 6), must have been delivered at a trial, and resolved the issues of the trilogy, is wishful thinking based on an assumed parallel with *Eumenides*. Garvie rightly asks[130] why there should be a trial. If there was one, who was the defendant – Hypermestra, or the other Danaides?[131] We may cautiously assume that in a trial this

---

[127] Presumably the *choros* played the sons of Aigyptos, though if so this imprecise title (which may not be Aischylos' original, cf. '*Eumenides*') is strange, especially since the third drama was explicitly 'Daughters of Danaos'. Winnington-Ingram (1983, 64) is reluctant to accept that Aischylos might have desired to present in the second drama a full portrait of the aggressors to set against the Danaides' highly emotive view of them as nothing but villains. However, allowing the sons of Aigyptos to show that they are (perhaps literally as well as metaphorically) not as black as they have been painted, and make their own legitimate claim of kinship to the Argives, is exactly the kind of next move that Aischylos (who constantly shifts his audience's moral perspective in the *Oresteia*) might have made; and it would have allowed him to portray them as sympathetic figures just before they are murdered. Cf. Garvie 1969, 196 and Robertson 1924, 51ff.

Taplin (1977, 197–8) proposes *Aigyptos* as the title; but *Suppliants* significantly does not use the later story that the Danaides' flight began after a quarrel between Aigyptos and Danaos; Aigyptos is therefore unlikely to have been a character in this trilogy until *Danaides*, if at all.

Cunningham (1953) ascribes fragment 29, in which a female *choros* laments the death of someone who has received strangers, to this drama. Like Garvie (1969, 200–202) I cannot accept this attribution as established, or even probable.

[128] Some scholars would place *Aigyptians* first; they are convincingly refuted by Garvie (1969, 185–6). What could we need to know about the events before the action of *Suppliants*, which we are not already told in the surviving drama?

[129] Frags. 5 and 6, together with a few individual words.

[130] 1969, 184, 206 and 210. Cf. Winnington-Ingram 1983, 58.

[131] Danaos puts Hypermestra on trial in Ovid, *Heroides* 24. But if anyone was put on trial in this trilogy it is more likely to have been the other Danaides, given the stress on *miasma* in *Suppliants* and the concern with the horror of

speech would support Hypermestra; but what if Aphrodite's case were effectively counterbalanced, for example by Artemis?

On the basis of the other ancient sources for this myth,[132] it is probable that:

(1) War broke out over the suppliants. Pelasgos, who has no son, was killed in the fighting, and the Argives made Danaos their king.

(2) In *Aigyptians* the outcome of the war was dramatized. The sons of Aigyptos claimed the daughters of Danaos as their brides, perhaps as one of the terms of a peace treaty. Possibly they were received as guests by Danaos into what is now his royal palace.[133]

(3) In *Danaides* it is discovered that all the daughters murdered their husbands on the wedding night except Hypermestra, who saved her husband Lynkeus.[134]

(4) Possibly Aigyptos demanded that the daughters of Danaos stand trial for the murders of his sons; but in some way a reconciliation was achieved.

(5) The goddess Aphrodite herself appeared, and gave a powerful speech in praise of the force of Eros – perhaps defending Hypermestra from the anger of her father and/or sisters, perhaps freeing the other Danaids from the *miasma* of kindred murder and persuading them to accept new husbands.[135]

---

shedding kindred blood which Aischylos evinces in the *Oresteia*. Cf. Euripides, *Orestes* 871ff. + scholion. However, a trial scene is unlikely, simply because too many characters would need to be in the *orchêstra* at once; Friis Johansen/Whittle 1980, 54.

[132] Listed in full at Garvie 1969, 113, and discussed ibid. 163–233 and Friis Johansen/Whittle 1980, 47ff.

[133] As Burnett notes (1971a, 60), they cannot have won the war and occupied Argos after Pelasgos' death; the Danaides could not then have murdered them without immediate revenge from other Aigyptians.

[134] The murders were committed on the wedding night because, as Sissa correctly suggests (1990, 133), only once their own blood has been shed in defloration can it be avenged by shedding male blood. Also, as a matter of practicality, the marriage-bed was one of the few places (apart from the bath, as in *Agamemnon*), where a Greek woman could find her man naked and unarmed, and therefore at the mercy of a concealed weapon, if wielded with sufficient swiftness and determination.

[135] The tradition that Danaos betrothed them (except for Hypermestra and Amymone) to the winners of a footrace (Pindar *Pythian* 9.112) is not compatible with Aischylos' *Suppliants*. It is inconceivable that his Danaides would accept

(6) In many accounts Lynkeus and Hypermestra became the next king and queen of Argos.

Even inside the span of the surviving drama, Aischylos obliged his spectators to change their perspective both on people and on actions, as the story unfolded. The Danaides speak with different individual voices, and react successively in different ways: as frightened virgins, enfeebled by self-pity – and as ruthless manipulators of a suppliant's power; justified pleaders to Zeus and outrageous over-optimists; utterly right in demanding power over their own bodies, and vainly resisting the inevitable demands of Aphrodite. Their characterization in *Suppliants* foreshadows rich possibilities for further manipulation of the audience in the sequels – their dialogues, both with each other and with the other characters, foreshadow a divergence between their individual attitudes to marriage in general, to marriage with the sons of Aigyptos in particular, and above all to murdering them.[136]

Hypermestra spared Lynkeus, according to the tradition, either because she loved him, because she wanted to have children, or because he did not attempt, like his brothers, to take her virginity by force.[137] Perhaps – to offer a conjecture which is compatible both with *Suppliants* and with the *Danaides* fragment – Aischylos' Hypermestra felt desire for Lynkeus, and spared him, because he loved her and *therefore* would not take her against her will.[138]

The *satyr-drama Amymone* continued the theme of sexual union, voluntary and involuntary. While the Danaides were out

marriage to anyone whom they did not choose themselves (cf. Friis Johansen/ Whittle 1980, 52). The case for a voluntary remarriage is strengthened by Seaford's demonstration (1987, 116–17) of the relationship between Aphrodite's words in frag. 6 and her role in Greek wedding ritual.

[136] As we subdivided the dialogue, and some lyrics, during the workshops, it was possible to identify passages which express a 'softer' attitude to marrying the sons of Aigyptos. If these are all assigned to one *choros* member, this foreshadows the probable emergence of Hypermestra as an individual character in *Danaides*.

[137] Horace's *Odes* 3.11; *Prometheus Bound* 864ff.; 'Apollodoros' 2.1.5, cf. scholiast on Pindar *Nemean Ode* 10.10. The *Prometheus* passage is ambiguous; it could literally mean 'desire for children will overcome one of them . . .' – but also, more probably 'desire will overcome one of the children . . .'

[138] Cf. Sissa 1990, 133; Lynkeus 'did not avail himself of his legitimate right to commit rape, and Hypermestra therefore did not slit his throat'.

looking for water, Amymone was assaulted by the satyrs. She resisted their attempts to violate her, and was rescued by Poseidon. He revealed the springs of Lerna to her, and then seduced her – resulting in the birth of Nauplios, founder of a distinguished line. This must clearly have been the theme which carried over from *Suppliants* into *Aigyptians* and *Danaides*; the Suppliants' attempt to escape from the sons of Aigyptos is morally right, but further resistance, after their deaths, to marriage would become opposition to a biological necessity, procreation. For many in the overpopulated modern world, human reproduction can and should be limited; but for the Greeks, marriage and childbirth were the essence and goal of womanhood. Indeed, virginity after menarche was viewed as a potentially dangerous transitional state, and 'the health of the female body was essentially linked to sexual relations';[139] some Greek doctors regarded immediate marriage and childbirth as necessary, to release women from the literally hysterical excesses in which girls might indulge during puberty.[140]

Aischylos regards the problems, and the sometimes aberrant behaviour, which their own physical development and the desires of adolescent males inflict on young women, with rather more insight and sympathy than were apparently shown by the ancient medical profession. Aphrodite's speech provides the basis for resolution of the Danaides' situation in voluntary marriages; even in *Suppliants*, where their fear and anxiety are sometimes extreme, they are not opposed to sexuality and marriage in themselves, only to being taken by partners whom they do not want.[141]

Fragments: Tragedy

Aischylos wrote at least seventy, perhaps as many as ninety, tragedies and *satyr-dramas*; of these only six survive complete. The 'fragments' are the portions of his otherwise lost dramas

[139] Sissa 1990, 51.
[140] The relevant medical treatises are cited at Sissa 1990, 121.
[141] N.B. esp. 1063. Cf. Winnington-Ingram 1983, 61 and Friis Johansen/ Whittle 1980, 32–3. The famous later story that the Danaides were eternally punished in the underworld, filling leaky sieves with water, is unlikely to date back to Aischylos. Cf. Garvie 1969, 234ff. and Winnington-Ingram 1983, 59.

which are preserved either in quotations by later writers, or in the scraps of papyrus discovered at Oxyrynchos in Egypt.

Ancient readers in and after the fourth century BC had no sense of the performance idiom and dramatic style of these dramas; their interest was purely in words. As the caricature in Aristophanes' *Frogs* makes abundantly clear, Aischylos' style of writing already seemed remote, fantastic and bombastic to many ears at the end of the fifth century; later taste continued by and large to favour the easier, more comprehensible idiom developed by Euripides. As a consequence, many citations from Aischylos consist merely of isolated words and phrases, quoted to illustrate particular exotic coinages or idioms; even some of the more substantial fragments were cited to criticize the playwright for his rhetorical excesses.[142]

None the less, what remains is better than nothing; for the classical scholar, intimations of Aischylos' greatness as a verbal craftsman shine even through isolated words.[143] In this book I have translated only fragments of three or more consecutive lines, since small extracts in translation induce nothing but frustration. The fragments from tragic drama tell us very little about the ways in which the lost dramas worked as theatre; but the glimpses are fascinating. Two pairs of fragments, from *Summoners of Dead Souls* (frags. 21–2) and *Bone-Gatherers* (frags. 2–3) came from a trilogy based on the *Odyssey*. Odysseus sacrificed to the gods of the underworld, and summoned up dead souls; later we hear him in triumph over the dead suitors, repaying them with words for all the abuse he suffered in his own halls.[144] Two short extracts (frags. 5 and 6) come from *Danaides*, the third drama of the trilogy begun in *Suppliants*; there are two pieces (frags. 8, 23) which remind us that Aischylos wrote at least one trilogy about the origin of tragedy itself – the rites of Dionysos, and the sufferings of those who denied his greatness and his divinity when he first came to Greece; and two solo speeches are preserved from dramas

---

[142] E.g. frag. 18 from *Oreithyia*, cited by [Longinos] 3.1 to illustrate the turbid expression and confused imagery characteristic of pseudo-tragedy.

[143] Cf. Herington 1986, 45–57. Some theatrical implications of the surviving fragments are discussed in Ley 1993, 118ff.

[144] Did Aischylos actually enact the sacrifice, or the slaughter of the suitors? Both are implied by the text, and would radically change our view of the kinds of action Aischylos felt able to represent in the *orchêstra*.

focused upon the anguish of women who suffered by close contact with the gods, one spoken by Europa (frag. 9), and one (frag. 13) almost certainly by Niobe's old nurse.

Three extracts from *Myrmidones* (frags. 10–12), and one from *Phrygians* give us glimpses of how Aischylos – who once, it is said, modestly referred to his dramas as 'slices from the great banquet of Homer'[145] – dramatized the story of Achilleus.[146] Three short citations from Achilleus' speech over the mangled body of Patroklos[147] show that in Aischylos' version the relationship between Achilleus and Patroklos was passionately homosexual, bringing out an emotional intensity which is only implicit in Homer; and if frag. 32 is from this trilogy, Aischylos exploited the pathos of Thetis' loss of her son as well as that of the death of Patroklos, and the misery of Priam when Achilleus killed his son Hektor (frag. 20).

Fragments: Satyr-drama

There was a tradition in later antiquity that Aischylos was the finest writer of *satyr-drama*.[148] Until the excavations at Oxyrynchos, this could not be tested; the genre was unpopular with later ancient scholars, and the sole example was Euripides' *Kyklops*, which survives by accident. However, *satyr-drama* was read and copied in Egypt in the second century BC, and the sands of Oxyrynchos have given us around half of *Trackers*, a previously unknown *satyr-drama* by Sophokles,[149] together with around one hundred lines each from Aischylos' *Fishermen*

[145] Eustath. *Il.* 1298, 59 = frag. 112b Radt.

[146] Later tragedians avoided writing dramas which included episodes directly treated in Homer's *Iliad* and *Odyssey*. With characteristic boldness, Aischylos dramatized both, devoting a trilogy to his reinterpretation of episodes from each epic.

[147] 'Did you show no respect for all the glory of our thighs;/are you not grateful for my many kisses', '. . . also my reverent closeness to your thighs . . .', and 'I love him; they are not revolting to my sight' (frags. 135–7, Radt 1981).

[148] Pausanias 2.3.16, Diogenes Laertius 2.133.

[149] This fragment inspired Tony Harrison's robust verse comedy *The Trackers of Oxyrhynchus*; the London version develops towards the end a rueful contrast between ancient Greece, which found a central role for the energies represented by satyrs, and the divisions in contemporary Britain between culture and the common people.

(discovered in 1933 and 1941) and *Ambassadors to the Isthmian Games* (1941).

Satyr-drama was performed at the Festival of Dionysos from very early in the fifth century. Many scholars believe that it was added to the Festival because of the complaints about tragedy preserved in the expression, 'nothing to do with Dionysos', which later became proverbial. However, it is far more likely that each competing *poiêtes* had to provide both tragedies and a *satyr-drama* from the first competition in 501 onwards; tragedy and *satyr-drama* go naturally together, since they are both direct developments out of the celebration of Dionysos. In myth, in iconography, and in cult, Dionysos' followers include both human beings and satyrs. Satyr *choros* members wear a bearded, slightly balding mask, with pointed ears and a snub nose; they are naked except for a furry loin-cloth, from which a phallos protrudes at the front and a horse-like tail from the rear. They invariably accompany their father, Silenos;[150] his features are similar, and he wears a body-suit of white hair.[151] The satyrs are as contradictory in character as Dionysos, the god whom they follow and serve; utter hedonists (especially in the pursuit of wine and sex), they are also incarnations of superhuman wisdom.[152]

In the known *satyr-dramas* opposition to the types of wisdom and insight associated with Dionysos (which was elsewhere[153] a subject – perhaps at first the only subject – for tragedy) is handled with techniques which we would associate with farce and burlesque. A tension is set up between the *thiasos* of satyric worshippers of Dionysos and other, more normal gods and goddesses, heroes and heroines who have to survive their mockery, abuse, deception and (if female) sexual harassment. Some themes recur in the four dramas of which part or all

---

[150] The satyrs of Athenian tragedy are an amalgamation of Attic or Ionic 'silenoi' with Dorian 'satyroi' from the Peloponnese. Seaford 1984, 6.

[151] The physical appearance of performers in *satyr-drama* is known from a late fifth-/early fourth-century vase depicting an acting company, the 'Pronomos vase'. Illustration e.g. in Green and Handley, 1995, plate 5.

[152] Cf. Seaford 1984, 6–7.

[153] E.g. in Aischylos' trilogies on the arrival of Dionysos in Edonia and Thebes (frags. 8 and 23), in which the king (Lykourgos, Pentheus) defies the god and was destroyed. The theme was rehandled at the close of the century in Euripides' last masterpiece, *Bakchai*.

survives;[154] the satyrs leave the service of Dionysos, either voluntarily (Aischylos, *Ambassadors*) or under compulsion (Euripides, *Kyklops*), and return to him at the end of the drama. They encounter some marvellous discovery (Danaë's chest, Hephaistos' 'new toys', and Hermes' new invention, the lyre in Sophokles' *Trackers*); they may also be confronted by someone emerging miraculously from under the earth or the sea (Danaë, and Kyllene in *Trackers*). They pursue women or nymphs, who have to be rescued from them by a god (to Danaë and Kyllene add others in lost dramas, e.g. *Amymone*); they find themselves temporarily caring for divine or heroic male infants (Perseus in *Fishermen*, Hermes in *Trackers*); they compete in athletic contests. As Seaford has shown,[155] each of these activities is grounded in some aspect of Dionysiac ritual; each also provides an opportunity for a drama of fun, surprise and entertainment, making an ideal contrast with the three tragedies which had preceded it.

The two long fragments (33, 35) confirm the ancient tradition of Aischylos' excellence at *satyr-drama*. They reveal the same absolute mastery of dramatic form and space which is evident in his surviving tragedies, allied with a light and racy, but also crisp and incisive poetic style which seems to capture the essence of the genre. This should be no surprise, except to those who insist on reading Aischylos as a solemn philosopher and theologian, instead of seeing him as a dramatist of formidable linguistic range, with a wide-ranging and inclusive vision of human beings and their world.[156]

Prometheus Bound

Prometheus Bound was for Goethe, Byron, Shelley, Hugo and Marx the greatest surviving classical drama. The Titan's defiance of Zeus was a symbol of the Enlightenment, echoing the cherished Romantic dream of the human spirit bringing down

---

[154] Cf. Seaford 1984, 33ff.

[155] Ibid. 40–44.

[156] On humour in Aischylos see Ewans 1995, xxxvi. Even in his tragic dramas, Aischylos was as direct and uninhibited in his approach to sexual and other bodily functions as the vase paintings and sculpture of his time; cf. e.g. *Seven* 363ff., *Suppliants* 1042, *L B* 755ff. and *Eu* 179ff.

despotic tyranny; the drama seemed to anticipate the nineteenth-century yearning to replace God with man at the centre of the universe. However, they lived in a time of unprecedented separation between poetic exponents of drama as high art, and the practicalities of stagecraft in the live theatre. *Faust II*, *Manfred* and *Prometheus Unbound* were written for the imagination of an educated reader. The exotic setting and extravagant scenic demands of *Prometheus Bound* seemed perfectly natural from the pen of a great classical dramatist, especially since early translators had given Aischylos a reputation as a poet of rugged, awe-inspiring grandeur and bold theatrical effects.[157]

Today this is no longer the case. Although later classical tradition ascribes *Prometheus Bound* to Aischylos, it comes down to us without an extract from the Festival records to confirm the date and authorship; internal and external evidence only dates *Prometheus Bound* to somewhere between the eruption of Mt Aitna (either in 479 or 475 BC), and the performance in 429 of Kratinos' comedy *Ploutoi*, which parodied the sequel, *Prometheus' Release*. Doubts about *Prometheus Bound* were first raised in 1861, and Aischylean authorship was denied by several scholars from 1911 onwards.[158]

As the twentieth century unfolded, increasingly careful analyses demonstrated that *Prometheus* contains many features characteristic of the style of writing and intellectual climate of the 440s and 430s. Since Aischylos died in 456, defenders of his authorship tried to suggest that it must have been written in the last two years of his life, under the influence of Sophokles' new style of drama and of the earliest sophists, or even specially for performance in Sicily.[159]

[157] Cf. Ewans 1982b, 26–7. Although he once referred to *Prometheus* (in a phrase lifted from the introduction to Droysen's German translation) as 'the most profound of all Greek tragedies', Wagner did not share the romantic preference for this drama over the *Oresteia*; cf. ibid. 256–60 against e.g. Taplin 1977, 467. The issue is important, since both Aischylos and Wagner have wrongly acquired a reputation for bombast and grandiose spectacle, which has often prevented appreciation of their dramatic economy, their use of stage effects only to complement verbal and musical meaning – for which cf. Taplin 1977, 39–49 on Aischylos, and Ewans 1980, *passim* on Wagner.

[158] See Griffith 1977, 1–7.

[159] Cf. references at Griffith 1977, 3; esp. e.g. Herington 1970, *passim*. Against the Sicilian theory see Griffith 1978, 105ff.

These arguments were never very cogent; and the case against authenticity was firmly established by Griffith's painstaking analyses.[160] His book analyses a wide range of features of *Prometheus Bound*, compares them in detail not only with the six undoubtedly authentic dramas by Aischylos but with Sophokles and Euripides as well, and finds that in almost every aspect *Prometheus* conforms with the writing style of the later fifth century rather than with that of Aischylos.

Unfortunately, most of the material assembled by Griffith is inaccessible to the Greekless reader; many will therefore hesitate to believe that 'one of the grandest poems of Greek literature'[161] was not written by the great author to whom it has been ascribed for over two thousand years. However, continuing to believe that Aischylos wrote *Prometheus* distorts our estimate of his work. In dramatic style and technique, as well as language and poetic style, *Prometheus* is markedly different from, and inferior to, the six other dramas.

Prometheus spends all but the opening minutes bound to a rock. This deprives the action of the ebb and flow characteristic of actor-*choros* interchanges in Aischylos and Sophokles, and makes the patterns of blocking and movement for the other characters largely depend on the individual whims of the director. Much of *Prometheus* consists of extended monologues, rich in word-play and sophistic jargon; their subject-matter is the growth of civilization, and the geography of the furthest limits of the known world – intellectual preoccupations of the Greeks in the period after 440.[162] The author clearly favours extended speeches by a single, static actor; the rhetorical style is simple, often prosaic, sometimes verbose. By contrast speeches in Aischylos are rich in their language, never prosaic or verbose, and always designed to be accompanied by rich and varied movement.[163]

---

[160] Griffith 1977. A book-length attempt to counter his arguments was undertaken by Pattoni (1987); but as West notes (1990a, 51), her qualification of some individual details does not counter the cumulative force of Griffith's analysis.

[161] Sikes and Wilson 1906, xix.

[162] Griffith 1977, 221ff.

[163] West was perhaps unkind when he wrote of *Prometheus*' 'Brucknerian pace' (1979, 133); but no one who has worked closely with this drama can compare the texture of its spoken verse with the dense patterns created by Aischylos in the other six extant dramas.

For his *choros*, the playwright selected the Daughters of Oke-anos. The main thread of the action is their relationship with the protagonist, their oscillation between a timid revulsion from Prometheus' imprudence and a sympathy with his daring, which culminates in a sudden decision to share his fate. Since the drama is set on a cosmic scale, and enthusiasts[164] dwell on the profundity of its theology, it is extremely strange, if Aischylos was the author, that the *choros* sing so little.[165] In the other six dramas the *choros* characters use their lyrics to speculate on the implications of the action at a level equal to or greater than that of the most intelligent solo characters; by contrast the response of the Daughters of Okeanos to each scene in *Prometheus* is brief and facile. Not one ode reflects in depth on the dramatic situation, the moral issues raised by the theft of fire, or the purpose of Zeus in punishing Prometheus so hideously; and in not one instance does the content of an ode advance the action – again, in signifi-cant contrast with all of the other six dramas. There are occasional fine moments, where the visual and verbal elements combine well – as, for example, at the entry of Io[166] – just as there are fine moments in the poetry (e.g. Io's narrative, 640ff.). But the structure clearly diverges from the genuine Aischylean dramas; *Prometheus* lacks their common pattern of a *moira* gradually developing to a culminating revelation.[167]

It also abandons their fundamental realism. In the six authentic dramas, nothing happens which could not be realistically shown by enactment in the Athenian theatre. By contrast *Prometheus* begins with a scene of physical torture[168] so acute that some scholars even suggest that Prometheus must have been repre-sented by a dummy, and his lines spoken by a concealed actor.[169]

---

[164] E.g. Murray 1949, 87ff.

[165] Only 18 per cent of the drama's verses, where the average for the other six dramas is 42 per cent; and there are never more than six consecutive stanzas. The figure for Sophokles is 26 per cent. Griffith 1977, 123; cf. 67.

[166] Taplin 1977, 266–7. She is Clov to Prometheus' Hamm (Beckett, *Endgame*).

[167] West 1990a, 55 correctly analyses *Prometheus* as a long, slowly develop-ing conversation between Prometheus and the Okeanides, framed by the divine interventions at opening and close, and interrupted arbitrarily by the sudden appearances of Okeanos and Io.

[168] I have accepted the transposition of 71–3 proposed by Dyson, 1994.

[169] References at Taplin 1977, 43. The idea was convincingly refuted by Sikes and Wilson; 1906, xliiiff.

The Daughters of Okeanos enter behind Prometheus, and sing that they are flying on aerial chariots (124ff.; 279). Once again, we must either assume that the characters refer to, and require the audience to imagine, actions which they are not representing, or assume a level of technology which was not available in the theatre of Aischylos' time (and probably not in the ancient Greek theatre at any time).[170]

The Okeanos scene is at start and finish ludicrous, and much of the middle is by Aischylean standards irrelevant; even though Okeanos' politically subtle sympathy with Prometheus contrasts effectively with the more naive feelings of his daughters, those who have criticized this disconnected scene, by contrast with the organic growth through successive scenes and choroses of the other Aischylean dramas, are surely justified. It also poses a staging problem for advocates of authenticity; Okeanos' entry was clearly designed to use the *mechane*, which was not used in any known drama by Aischylos or his contemporaries, and is not attested until long after his death.[171]

The most serious production problem in *Prometheus* is of course the ending; for the third time in this drama, the words imply a stage direction which could not have been realized realistically. The Okeanides' sudden decision that they will share Prometheus' fate complicates the problem; to show an individual rock crushing Prometheus at the centre might have been possible, but to obliterate an additional twelve[172] actors realistically was beyond the resources of the Athenian theatre. We apparently have to resort to Taplin's solution of a 'cancelled exit';[173] the actors playing Prometheus and the Okeanides freeze after

[170] Taplin (1977, 252ff.) cites some scholarly conjectures. Favoured alternatives have been a large 12-seat flying chariot, either on the *mechane*, on the *skene* roof, or simply pushed into the rear of the *orchêstra*; twelve individual (dodgem-like?) cars on the *skene* roof, and (West 1979) six swinging cranes for two riders each.

[171] The first datable dramas known to have used it are Euripides' *Medeia* (431BC) and his lost *Bellerophon*, referred to at Aristophanes, *Acharnians* 427ff. and therefore produced *c*. 425 BC.

[172] Or fifteen, if the drama was composed after the increase in *choros* numbers which occurred in the 440s.

[173] Taplin 1977, 274–5 (following Pickard-Cambridge 1946, 38). As Taplin notes, there is no parallel for this in any surviving drama by Aischylos, Sophokles or Euripides.

the last lines, prepared for the worst; the audience are to imagine the cataclysm – and then the drama is deemed to have ended, and the actors rise and depart. (Prometheus presumably cast off his chains before leaving for the interval – unless the long-suffering actor was required to remain in place and in character, while the *choros* changed costumes to re-enter as the Titanes for the start of *Prometheus' Release*.)

These departures from Aischylos' normal dramatic style and technique sharply distinguish *Prometheus Bound* from the six undeniably authentic dramas.[174] The drama is sometimes defended by reference to the grandeur of its themes, and the fact that, with the exception of Io, all the characters are divine. To my mind, the greatest limitations of the Prometheus cycle are the near-absence of human beings, and the consequently abstract presentation of the conflict between Zeus and Prometheus. Aischylean characters, in the other six dramas, are real individuals with real predicaments and feelings.[175] Their world is immeasurably enriched by its close interpenetration and interaction with the world of the divine and the marvellous. That closeness was already receding by the time of *Oidipous the King* and *Antigone*, and the decline of tragedy began towards the close of the fifth century, as philosophers, orators, doctors and historians began to develop a vocabulary for describing humanity in which gods, if they exist at all outside our minds, have no necessary, close or direct relationship to human affairs.[176]

Prometheus belongs to that later period, when the close contact with the divine was being lost. The gods are used as symbols in an allegory of the relationships between tyrant and subjects; the ethics and characterization are simple, by contrast with the complexities of moral judgement in which Aischylos' action and characters normally embroil his spectators. This is a drama of ideas,[177] written by a playwright who lacked the ability to express those ideas effectively in the theatre, and was insensi-

[174] There are also several structural problems; the construction and order of the scenes violate the patterns and conventions which are characteristic of Aischylos. However, Taplin (1977, 245–50) overstates the difficulties.

[175] This applies to the gods and Furies who appear in *Eumenides* as well as to the human characters.

[176] Cf. Ewans 1993, *passim*.

[177] Cf. Griffith 1977, 253.

tive to the fact that in his *Prometheus* – the Io-scene again partially excepted – those ideas are divorced from the human feelings which could give them dramatic life and real theatrical intensity.[178]

Who wrote it? The most likely date is *c.* 440–30,[179] and the most likely author is Aischylos' son Euphorion, who won four times at the Festival with tragedies written by his father, as well as pursuing a modest career of his own as a tragedian. Unless all four occasions were revivals of dramas first produced in Aischylos' lifetime, we are asked to believe that Aischylos left twelve tragedies and four *satyr-dramas* unperformed when he died. It is more probable that Euphorion, when close memory of his father's compositional style was fading and audience tastes had changed considerably, might have taken the risk of passing off three dramas of his own on the theme of Prometheus as posthumous work by his famous father.[180] Perhaps he even revived as the *satyr-drama* Aischylos' *Prometheus the Fire-Kindler* of 472 BC (see frag. 36).

Prometheus Bound can tell us much about the tastes of Athenian audiences in the 430s, and the style of a lesser dramatist under the influence of Aischylos. It says nothing about Aischylos himself – except to clarify by contrast the distinctive excellence of his six surviving dramas.

MICHAEL EWANS

[178] Cf. West 1990a, 57ff.

[179] West 1990a, 65–6 detects the influences of Protagoras, Pherekydes, and Sophokles' *Antigone*, which all suggest this particular decade.

[180] Cf. West 1990a, 67–72. Some alternative possibilities, less likely because they do not explain as well the false ascription to Aischylos, are canvassed by Griffith 1977, 252–4.

NOTE ON THE TEXT AND TRANSLATION

The translation of *Persians* was originally made from the Oxford Classical Text edited by Sir Denys Page; of *Seven* from the edition by Hutchinson, of *Suppliants* from the edition by Friis Johansen and Whittle, and of *Prometheus Bound* from the edition by Griffith. The translations were then workshopped at the University of Newcastle, in 1994 and 1995, and revised in the light of Martin West's Teubner edition and its companion volume, *Studies in Aeschylus*. Fragments are translated from the edition by Radt, in conjunction with that by Lloyd-Jones, which offers supplements where the papyri are deficient.

The attributions of speeches, and all stage-directions in any translation from Greek tragedy, are modern. The directions in this edition are for the Greek theatre shape, and based on experience gained in workshop sessions. Modern directors who need to modify these directions to suit a differently shaped performance space must still be aware of Aischylos' own practice. Only those directions which I regard as certain are printed in the text; further suggestions will be found in the Notes.

A sudden entry could be made, in the early theatre, only from the *skene* (changing hut); in the surviving dramas before the *Oresteia*, this was only located in sight of the audience in *Seven against Thebes*. Entries were normally gradual, down one of the two *parodoi*.[181] A character entering down a *parodos* is in the sight of some of the actors and audience, on the opposite side from where he is making his entry, long before he steps into the *orchêstra*. Presumably the convention was that the actor was in

---

[181] Reflecting the actual topography of Athens, these represented entry either from the downtown district of the place in which the action is located (actor left, audience right), or from the country and from other cities (actor right, audience left). Rehm (1992, 154) questions whether this convention goes back to the fifth century – rightly noting that the evidence is late, but unduly influenced by the orthodox view that Aischylean tragedy was not specific in regard to the geographical location of action.

character from the moment he became visible to any of the audience, but engaged in interaction with the players already there only after he stepped into the *orchêstra*. Accordingly in these texts the direction *Enter X* is positioned at the moment where X enters the *orchêstra*, not when the actor first comes into the sight of some of the audience.

The text is divided into Scenes (predominantly consisting of spoken dialogue), and Choroses (passages sung and danced by the *choros* alone). These are numbered in separate consecutive series for each drama. Two choral odes, which are too short to interrupt the development of a scene as a whole (Choros 2 in *Suppliants* and Choros 4 in *Prometheus Bound*), are numbered as new odes; but the number is placed in parentheses, and the scene is not ended when they begin.

Alternation between Choroses and Scenes is the basic structural feature of fifth-century tragedy; I have therefore not obscured it by importing the later technical terms found in the twelfth, probably interpolated, chapter of Aristotle's *Poetics*.[182]

Transliteration

In this edition, following the practice of an increasing number of classical scholars, proper names are transliterated directly from the Greek original, and the traditional Latinized spellings (e.g. Darius for Dareios, Eteocles for Eteokles) are not employed. Upsilon is transliterated by *y*, not *u*; and chi by *ch*, not *kh*.

Lyric and Spoken Verse

The interplay between lyric and spoken verse is marked in this edition by double-indenting all verses that were sung in the original Greek dramas.

Strophic response in lyrics is denoted by numbering the first *strophe* (A1), its matching *antistrophe* (A2); if there is a concluding *epode* that is marked (A3). The second pair in a system is numbered (B1), (B2) – and so on.

---

[182] *Prologos, parodos, stasimon, epeisodion* and *exodos*. I have also not accepted the over-ingenious theory of Act-dividing and non-Act-dividing odes with which Taplin (1977, 49ff.) sought to replace this terminology.

Line Numbering

For uniformity in referencing, all modern scholars use the line numbering of one of the early editions of Aischylos. However, there has been much research, particularly in the last fifty years, into the nature of Greek lyric verse; this has led to revised arrangement of the line-structure. This edition follows the layout of the most recent editions; accordingly in lyric sections there are sometimes more, sometimes less, than ten lines of English verse between the line-markers.

Notation

Positions in the *orchêstra* are described in the Notes by a combination of letters denoting its parts as viewed by an actor entering the playing space at the opposite side from the spectators: F = front; B = back; L = left; R = right; C = centre; E = extreme (i.e., at the perimeter).

All directions for entry and exit, left and right, are from the actor's not the spectator's viewpoint.

PERSIANS

THE ACTORS AND THEIR ROLES

Elders of Persia	Choros
Queen	Actor 2
Messenger	Actor 1
Shade of Dareios	Actor 1
Xerxes	Actor 2
Maidservants	Silent Faces

Preset the tomb of Dareios, EBC.

CHOROS I

Enter the Elders, left.

1. ELDER   The Persians have gone
            to Greece, and we are the faithful
            Elders, appointed
            to guard their rich and golden halls;
            the King himself, Xerxes our lord,
            the son of Dareios
            chose us to oversee the land.
1. ELD   But will the King come back,
            and will his teeming army?
            I am disturbed
            by premonitions of disaster.   10
1. ELD   All Asia's strength has
            gone, and women weep aloud
            for men they've lost.
            No runner and no horseman comes
            back to the capital of those
            who went from Sousa and Agbatana
            and from the ancient fort of Kissia –
            some on horseback, some by ship,
            and infantry with measured steps
            in dense array for war: 20
1. ELD   men like Amistres and Artaphrenes
            and Megabates and Astaspes,
            leaders of Persia,
            kings, and vassals of the greatest King.
            They've gone in haste, commanders of

our mighty army; bowmen, horsemen,
fearful to see and terrible to fight –
so strong is their resolve.
Artembares the charioteer
and Masistres the archer,   30
noble Imaios and Pharandakes
and Sosthanes the horseman.
Then there were others, sent by great,
life-giving Nile; Sousiskanes,
Pegestagon the son of Aigyptos,
and sacred Memphis' ruler,
Arsames the great; Ariomardos,
governor of the ancient city Thebes;
and the marshdwellers, oarsmen –
terrible, innumerable.   40
Then a mass of graceful-living Lydians,
our sea-coast people
whom Mitragathes and noble Arkteus, kings,
and golden Sardis send abroad
with many chariots,
two- and three-poled,
fearful sight.

I. ELD   The men of sacred Tmolos threaten
they will throw the yoke of slavery on Greece –   50
Mardôn, Tharybis, anvils of the spear,
Mysians with javelins, and golden Babylon
which sends a serpent-tail of troops
from many lands, seamen
and archers, knowing they can draw a lethal bow.

I. ELD   A huge host carrying short swords
from all of Asia follows at
the fearful summons of the King.

I. ELD   The flower of Persia's men   60
has gone; the whole of Asia nurtured them,
and now it grieves in passionate desire.
Parents and wives count every day
and tremble as the time grows long.

ELD (AI)   Now the city-sacking army of the King
has crossed onto our neighbour's shore across the straits.
They bound a raft of boats across the Hellespont

with flax, and yoked a firmly bolted road   70
across the ocean's neck.

(A2)   Then the war-like lord of teeming Asia
drove his divine flock over their lands
two ways; his leaders both on land and sea
are faithful, rugged – and the god-like king,
descendant of the house of gold, trusts them.   80

(B1)   His eyes' dark gleam
is like a poison snake,
and as he speeds his Syrian chariot,
his myriads of men on land and sea,
he brings destruction by our archers
to the famous warriors of the spear.

(B2)   No one is great enough to stand
up to this mighty flow of men;
with mighty nets, no one is strong enough
to stop the great sea-wave.   90
The Persian army cannot be resisted,
and its courage is immense.

(B3)   But when a clever god deceives,
what mortal can escape?
Whose foot is swift enough;
what prince of athletes jumps so high?
Destruction fawns just like a friendly dog at first
and lures a man into her tightest nets;
a mortal cannot leap out and escape.   100

(C1)   The lot assigned us by the gods in ancient times
has won; it laid upon the Persians
war, the sack of citadels,
shock of the cavalry-charge, and razing cities to the
    ground.

(C2)   They also learned to look upon
the sacred, vast expanses of the deep,   110
foam-flecked by furious winds,
trusting in slender cables and in boats.

(D1)   That's why my grieving heart is terrified.
     'Cry for the Persian army!' The great citadel
     of Sousa is bereft of all its men; I hope it will not hear that
        sound,

(D2)   and that the Kissian city will not raise a
           matching   120
     cry, a crowd of women howling out these words,
     as tears fall on their linen robes –

(E1)   since all our cavalry and infantry
     have left us like a swarm of bees together with their King,
     crossing the yoke from land to land,   130
     across the bridge of boats.

(E2)   In longing for their men the marriage-beds are filled
           with tears
     by tender-grieving Persian girls – each loving, longing; she
     has sent away to war the brave spearman who shared her
        bed
     and now is left alone.

1. ELD   Come now, Persians, let us sit   140
     beside this ancient building
     and think deeply, wisely –
     for the need has come.
     How fares our King, Xerxes
     and all our nation named
     after the son of Danaë?
     Are bowmen winning,
     or have mighty troops
     of spearmen conquered us?

1. ELD   Look! A splendour such as gleams   150
     from eyes of gods; here is
     the mother of the king; my Queen. I fall in reverence.
     Now we must speak in words of greeting.

SCENE I

*Enter Queen left, on a carriage, in elaborate robes and orna-
ments, attended by Maidservants.*

1. ELDER   Oh Queen, greatest of all our lovely Persian
        women,
    greetings, mother of King Xerxes, widow of the King
        Dareios.
    You were the consort of the Persians' god, and mother of a
        god,
    unless the power who always helped our armies has deserted
        us.
QUEEN   That is why I've left my gilded palace,
    and the bed I once shared with Dareios.   160
    Anxious thoughts tear at my heart; now I will tell
    you what I think. My friends, I fear
    that our great wealth, raising a cloud of dust, may wreck
    all that prosperity Dareios won with a god's help.
    This is the double fear that lives, almost unutterable, in my
        heart;
    that wealth can't win respect if it's not backed by men,
    and poor men do not have as much of light and life as they
        deserve.
    Our wealth is still unharmed; my fear is for our eye –
    for me, the presence of a house's master is its eye.
    That's how I feel; so now, my faithful Persians,   170
    help me to understand my dreams;
    for all my faith in counsel rests in you.
1. ELD   Queen, know that you will never need
    to ask us twice to say or do whatever we can do.
    You call on us as your interpreters; we'll gladly help.
Q   I have been often visited by dreams
    since my son mobilized his troops
    and went to ravage Greece:
    but never yet have I seen anything as clear
    as this last night; I'll tell you now.   180
    It seemed two women in fine clothes,
    one costumed in the dress of Persians,
    one of Greeks, came into sight;

they were much taller than our women are today,
of flawless beauty, sisters from
a common stock. They had drawn lots; one lived
in Greece, the other Asia.
Then I seemed to see them turn
to enmity; my son saw this, and he
restrained and tamed them, put them in the yoke   190
beneath his chariot, and placed its straps
around their necks. One stood tall with pride,
and held her mouth submissive to the bit;
the other struggled, used her hands to break
the chariot straps, then wrenches off the bit
and bridle, smashes up the yoke.
My son fell down, and there his father stood,
Dareios, full of pity; when Xerxes saw him,
he tore his clothes.
That is what I saw last night.   200
When I got up, and dipped my hands into the water
of a fair, pure stream, I went with offerings
and stood before the altar to present a honey-cake
to gods who can avert such dreams, and need this ritual.
I saw an eagle fleeing to Apollo's hearth:
I stood still, paralysed by fear.
And then I saw a hawk fly at full speed
against the eagle, claw and tear
his head – while he just crouched
and let it happen. These are the fearful things I saw   210
and wanted you to hear. Know this; my son
if he succeeds will be most marvellous to all,
but if he fails . . . he renders no account to anyone,
and if he lives he's still the ruler of this land.

I. ELD   Queen mother, we don't want to make you too afraid
        by what we say
or give you undue courage. Go, turn to the gods,
and ask them to avert the bad things you have seen;
may good come true for you and for your son,
this city and its well-wishers. Then you must pour
libations to the earth and to the dead, and ask in soothing
        words   220
that your husband Dareios, whom you saw last night,
may send blessings up to the light for you and for your son,

and evils may be held below the earth, dark in the
   undergloom.
I prophesy by my own feelings, and advise in friendship; we
   believe
this dream means good will be fulfilled for you in every way.

Q   You are the first judge of my dream; you've spoken
solemnly in favour of my son and royal house.
May this good reading be fulfilled; I will do what you
have said both for the gods and for our friends beneath the
   earth,
as soon as I go back. But now I want to learn, my
   friends;   230
where in the world is Athens?

1. ELD   Far to the west, towards the setting of our lord the
   Sun.

Q   My son still wants to make Athens his prey?

1. ELD   Then all the rest of Greece will soon be subject to our
   King.

Q   Have they that many soldiers?

1. ELD   Yes, and they have done great harm to us.

Q   Do they have arrows of such piercing strength?

1. ELD   No; they use swords and heavy shields.   240

Q   What else? Do they have great wealth in their halls?

1. ELD   They have a spring of silver, treasure of their land.

Q   Who is the people's shepherd, telling them what they must
   do?

1. ELD   It's said they are the slaves and subjects of no man.

Q   How then could they resist invasion by a hostile power?

1. ELD   They did – when they destroyed Dareios' vast and
   splendid force.

Q   Your words are fearful for the mothers of the men who've
   gone.

1. ELD   I think you'll soon know everything with certainty;
   this man is running the way Persians do,
   and brings clear news to hear – for good or ill.

Enter Messenger, right.

MESSENGER   Oh cities of the whole of Asia,
   land of Persia, great storehouse of wealth,   250
   know at one stroke all our prosperity

has been destroyed: the flower of Persia's fallen; they're all
  gone.
I'm wretched; it is bad to be the first to bring bad news,
but still I must unfold our suffering completely.
Persians, our whole army is destroyed.

ELD (A1)   Terrible, terrible sufferings, new and
  cruel! Weep, Persians,
  as you hear this misery.

MESS Yes, weep – for everything is finished: 260
I did not think I'd see the light of my return.

ELD (A2)   Oh, far too long this life now seems
  to us old men, who've lasted long enough to hear
  this unexpected pain.

MESS I was there, I did not hear words from other men;
Persians, I can tell you all our sufferings.

ELD (B1)   Oh, in vain
  those many arrows all together
  went from Asia to destroy   270
  Hellas.

MESS The shores of Salamis, and all the sea nearby,
are full of corpses who met miserable deaths.

ELD (B2)   Oh, you say
  the bodies of our friends, sea-buffeted,
  plunged in the sea, are carried far and wide
  in their great flowing robes.

MESS Their bows gave them no help; the ships of Greece
attacked and tamed our whole armed force.

ELD (C1)   Lift up the cry of misery,   280
  ill-omened for our friends.
  The gods have wrecked us
  utterly: our army is destroyed.

MESS The worst name we can hear is Salamis,
and how I grieve, when I recall the power of Athens.

ELD (C2)   City hated by its enemies;
  you can remember how it made
  so many Persians lose
  their sons and husbands.

Q I have been silent long and wretched, stunned   290
by this disaster; it is so immense
that one could hardly speak or ask about such sufferings.
Still, we are human, and must learn to bear our pains

when gods send them. Speak, and unfold it all;
compose yourself, although you weep for what we're
   suffering.
Who has survived, and whom must we lament
among the leaders; who, among the men appointed
to command, has died and left his post?

MESS   Xerxes himself still lives and sees the light of day.

Q   Your words bring a great light into my house,   300
and day dawns white after the blackness of my night.

MESS   Artembares, the ruler of ten thousand horse,
is dashed against the jagged coast of Sileniai:
Dâdakes, Commander of a Thousand, gently fell
out of his ship, struck helpless by a spear;
and Tenagôn, great warrior, a true-born Baktrian,
beats on the surf-struck isle of Aias.
Lilaios and Arsames and Argêstes are dead:
beaten, they butt their heads against
the rock-hard land around the island of the doves.   310
Also a man who came from sources of the Nile in Egypt,
Pharnouchos, and three who fell out of one ship;
Arkteus, Adeues, and Pheresseues.
Matallas, the commander of ten thousand troops from
   Chrysa,
once had a golden, bushy beard; the bloom
upon his cheeks is now dipped in a blood-red sea.
Mâgos, Arabos, Artabes the Baktrian,
commander of three thousand dark-skinned cavalry,
found a new home in bare earth, and lie dead:
Amistris and Amphistreus, deft user of the battle-spear,   320
noble Ariomardos, who will give much grief
to Sardis; Seisames the Mysian,
and Tharybis, commander of two-fifty ships
– a man from Lyrna, he was beautiful;
now he lies dead, wretched, and far from glory.
That's what I have to tell about our leaders. We
have suffered many things, and I have told you very few of
   them.   330

Q   Alas, I hear the greatest depths of suffering,
shame for all Persians and shrill cries of grief.
Now tell me this, go back, explain:
was there so great a number of Greek ships

that they felt able to engage our army
in a fight, attacking us by sea?

MESS   As far as numbers go, be sure, the Persians
should have won; the whole Greek fleet,
taken together, only came up to three hundred
ships, including one small special group of ten.   340
Xerxes – and I am sure, I know the number well – led out
a thousand ships; two hundred, and an extra seven, were
marked out by extra speed. That is the count.
D'you think us short of numbers for this fight?
No. One of the daimones destroyed our army: there were
    loaded
scales, and fortune did not favour each side equally.
The gods have saved the goddess Pallas' city.

Q   So Athens was not sacked?

MESS   While men survive, they have their fortress still.

Q   Now tell us how the naval battle started. Who   350
began the combat – Greeks, or my own son,
proud, confident because he had so many ships?

MESS   My Queen, all of our suffering began from some
avenging spirit, or an angry god.
A Greek came from the camp of the Athenians
and told your son Xerxes
that once the shadow of dark night came on
the Greeks would not stay there, but they would leap
onto the rowing-benches and would try to save
their lives by separate, individual flight.   360
As soon as he heard this, not realizing the Greek
had played a trick or that the gods were jealous of him,
Xerxes told all his sea-commanders this:
when the sun's rays stopped burning up the earth,
and darkness took possession of his sacred place above our
    heads,
they should draw up a mass of ships in three long lines,
while a few others sailed around the isle
to block the exits, all the narrow channels of the sea.
If any Greeks escaped a savage fate,
finding some secret way out for their ships,   370
he told them his decree that they would lose their heads.
He said all this with confidence;
he did not know the future which the gods would bring.

They were both orderly and happy to obey: they saw
the evening meal was served; and then each man
fastened his oar against its peg.
Now, when the sun had set
and night came on, each master of the oar
went to the ships, and every lord of arms;
on each long ship the banks of oarsmen shout
    encouragement,   380
and they sail out to where each had been told;
all night the captains made the fleet
sail back and forward ceaselessly.
The night went on, and still the army of the Greeks
was not attempting to sail out in secret anywhere;
but when the dawn's white horses took
possession of the earth, clear, bright to see,
then first resoundingly a joyful sound came from the
    Greeks
singing their battle-hymn, and straight away
the echo came back from the rocky isle;   390
fear struck the hearts of every one of us,
mistaken in our plans. The Greeks
did not sing that inspiring song like men in flight,
but as they came courageously to war.
Their battle-trumpets' sound set the whole place aflame;
at once they pulled their oars together,
struck the sea responding to commands.
They came out fast; now we could see them all.
The right wing of the fleet came first
keeping formation, then the rest   400
advanced against us, and we heard in unison
this great war-cry: 'Oh sons of Greece, go on,
and free your country, free your wives and children
and the sacred places of our gods, and our
ancestral tombs; this battle is for everything!'
A clamour rose in Persian from our troops
to answer them, and we had no more time to waste.
At once a ship struck with its metal beak
against another; one Greek started the attack,
breaking the high poop off a Phoinikian   410
battleship, while others steered their boats against us too.
At first the stream of Persian forces

held its own; but once the mass of ships was forced
into a narrow channel, then they gave each other no more
   help,
and with their pointed metal beaks
they struck their own boats, breaking oars.
The Greeks saw this, and circled us,
struck savagely; our boats were overturned,
and now you could no longer see the water,
filled with shipwrecks and with slaughtered men.   420
Beaches and rocks were full of corpses too.
All the remaining Persian ships now fled,
rowing away in panic and disorder.
As if they were just netted fish, the Greeks
used broken oars and bits of wreck
to strike and cut our men; their moans
blended with shrieks, and filled the sea
until the night's black veil concealed the sight.
The number of our sufferings is such that even if
I spoke for ten days, I could not tell them all.   430
Know this: never in one day have
so many human beings died.

Q   Oh gods, how great a sea of suffering
has burst upon the Persians and the whole of Asia.

MESS   Now know I've hardly reached the middle of our
   sufferings:
so many more disasters came on them,
as to outweigh by double all I've told so far.

Q   What could have happened worse for us than this?
Tell us: what is this further tragedy which struck
the army, and tipped down the scales of suffering?   440

MESS   The very strongest of our Persian men,
the greatest souls, marked out by noble birth,
have died a shameful and appalling death.

Q   My friends, this new disaster makes me utterly
distraught. How do you say they died?

MESS   There is an island close in front of Salamis –
small, with no anchorage, a haunt
of Pan, the god who loves to dance upon the shore;
Xerxes sent them, so if some hostile troops   450
were shipwrecked and sought refuge there
they could kill Greeks when they were easy prey,

and save our friends and allies from the sea.
He read the future badly: when the god
gave battle-glory to the Greeks,
that very day they put on heavy armour,
leapt down from their ships, encircling
the whole island, so our men had no idea
where they could turn. The Greeks hurled many
stones at them, and from their bowstrings   460
arrows struck down many of our men.
Then finally they charged as one
and club, hack at the limbs of our poor men
until not one was left alive.
When Xerxes realized our depth of suffering, he cried
   aloud.
He had a throne with clear views of our troops,
on a high mound beside the beach;
he tore his clothes and uttered a shrill cry,
gave orders on the instant to the army,
rushed off in chaotic flight. All this we have   470
to grieve, as well as the disaster I told first.

Q   You hateful daimôn, how you have deceived
the Persians: vengeance, which my son had hoped to take
on glorious Athens, had a bitter end, and it was not enough
that Marathon had killed so many of us once before.
My son thought he could punish them for that,
and brought upon himself this huge amount of woes.
Now tell me of the ships which managed to escape:
where did you leave them? Do you know, can you say?

MESS   All the commanders of surviving ships fled hastily,   480
rushing downwind in a disordered rout,
while in Boiotia many more died
one by one, some tortured by the thirst for bright
spring water, others suffering
starvation. Gasping for breath,
survivors passed on into Phokis,
then through Doris and the gulf of Melia,
where Spercheios gives water graciously to the flat lands;
and after that the land of the Achaians,
then to cities of Thessaly, which took us in deprived
of food. There many of us died   490
from thirst and hunger; for we suffered both.

We went on to Magnetike and Makedon,
up to the crossing of the river Axios, and Lake
Bolbe with marshy reeds, and Mount Pangaios,
land of the Edonians. That night some god
aroused unseasonable winter weather, so the stream
of sacred Strymon froze right over; soldiers who before
that time believed the gods are nothing then began
to pray, prostrate before the earth and sky.
After the troops had called repeatedly   500
upon the gods, they went across the icy frozen stream.
And those of us who started out before the sun-god spread
his rays were saved: his bright and blazing orb
warmed and destroyed the middle of the way across.
They fell against each other, and the luckiest were those
in whom the breath of life was cut at once.
Then the remainder who survived
crossed Thrakia with difficulty and great suffering,
escaped, and have come – very few –   510
back to their native soil. So Persia's city must lament;
we've lost our youngest, dearest lives.
All this is true, but I have left out many more
disasters, which some god has hurled upon the Persians.

Exit Messenger, left.

Q   Terrible god, your foot has crushed
     the whole race of the Persians.
     Our army's been destroyed, and I am miserable.
     Night-vision, you were wholly plain;
     you showed me clearly all our sufferings.
     Elders, you read my dream too lightly.   520
     Still, I will do what you said:
     first pray to all the gods,
     then go and take some offerings
     to Earth and to the dead
     – a sacred cake out of my stores at home.
     I know it is too late for what is past:
     but for the future, I will pray for better times.
     In view of what has happened, you must now
     confer and work out good advice:
     and if my son arrives before I have come back,

console him, send him to the palace,   530
lest he bring new sufferings upon himself.

Exit Queen, followed by Maidservants, left.

CHOROS 2

1. ELDER   Oh Zeus our king, you have destroyed
    the army of the great and powerful
    Persians; you have plunged
    both Sousa and Agbatana
    into dark clouds of grief.
1. ELD   And many pitiable women
    with their tender hands
    tear their veils
    and share our sorrow,
    drench their breasts with tears.   540
1. ELD   Crying gently, Persian girls
    weep for the men they have just lost,
    see their soft and gentle marriage-bed,
    the joy of their voluptuous youth,
    and wail insatiably in their misery.

ELD (A1)   Asia is empty, and the whole
    land weeps.
    Xerxes took them – alas   550
    Xerxes lost them – alas
    Xerxes gave our ships
    every order wrong.
    Oh, why was Persia's undefeated archer-lord
    Dareios not our king,
    beloved by Sousa?

  (A2)   Marines and sailors;
    dark-faced, sail-winged
    ships took them – alas   560
    ships lost them – alas;
    ships charged and destroyed.
    And we have heard our king himself
    barely escaped the Greeks

through plains and bitter paths
of Thrakia.

(B1)   The others, left behind
          Alas!
          because they were the first to die
          Oh . . .
          around the beaches of Salamis   570
          Ah . . .
          still wander. Groan and bite, and shout
          a torment rending heaven
          Ah . . .
          draw out your long
          and horrid cries!

(B2)   Mangled by the cruel sea
          Alas!
          Eaten by the silent
          Oh . . .
          offspring of pure ocean depths
          Ah . . .
          The empty house grieves for the man it's lost,   580
          childless parents cry aloud for
          torment sent by heaven
          Ah . . .
          aged men and women know
          the measure of their pain.

(C1)   Through all of Asia soon
          the rule of Persia ends.
          They will not pay us tribute
          when our lords command;
          they will not fall to earth and
          worship; all our regal power
          has been destroyed.   590

(C2)   Tongues cannot be curbed;
          they can now say
          in freedom what they want;
          the yoke of power's broken.
          In the bloody, sea-girt soil

of Aias' island lies
what once was Persia.

SCENE 2

Enter Queen left, on foot and unadorned; bearing some liba-
tions, and accompanied by a Maidservant with others.

QUEEN   My friends, a person with experience
  knows that when waves of suffering fall upon   600
  a human being, he or she is terrified of everything,
  but when the daimôn flows in favour, then they think
  the winds of chance will always blow their way.
  Now everything fills me with fear:
  threatening visions sent by gods appear before my eyes,
  and in my ears alarming noises howl;
  such is the fear, caused by our sufferings, which terrifies my
    mind.
  That's why I've come back now, without my carriage
  and the costly ornaments I had before. I'm carrying
  libations to the father of my son to make him well disposed –
  all of the offerings that soothe the dead: 610
  white milk from sacred cows, easy to drink,
  and drops of gleaming honey made by bees,
  together with libations from a virgin stream,
  and this pure, unmixed drink grown in the wild,
  the brightly gleaming wine drawn from an ancient vine.
  Here too is fragrant fruit from golden olive
  trees, which live a fertile life clothed always in full leaves,
  and woven flowers, offspring of life-bearing earth.
  Now, friends, chant songs of good omen above
  these offerings to the dead, and summon up   620
  divine Dareios: I will send these offerings
  that earth absorbs down to the gods below.

CHOROS 3

1. ELDER   My lady, Queen, Elder of Persia,
  send offerings to underground,

and we will sing to ask
the escorts of the dead
for favour from below the earth.

1. ELD   Sacred gods and goddesses below –
Earth, Hermes, Plouton –
send his spirit up into the light: 630
if he knows of some cure for future sufferings,
no one but he could tell us.

ELD (A1)   Does the blessed, god-like king
hear me as I utter
wretched cries of grief?
I'll shout aloud
our anguish:
does he hear me down below?

(A2)   Earth, and other rulers of the dead,   640
approve, and let that noble spirit,
Persia's god born here at Sousa, come;
send to us such a man
as never yet before
was hidden under Persian land.

(B1)   He was beloved, beloved his tomb;
it hides a man whose ways we loved.
Hades, Hades, you can send him; free   650
the god-like King Darian.
Ah!

(B2)   He never killed our men
in a disastrous war:
we thought him like a god in wisdom;
such he was, when he guided our troops.
Ah!

(C1)   King, king from former times, come now,
appear upon the summit of your mound.   660
Lift your saffron royal slipper, show the peak
of your tiara;
come father and preserver, Dareios!

(c2)   You must hear your country's new
        misfortune; king of kings,
        appear! A death-mist's hovering around us:
        all the flower of our youth has perished;   670
        come father who did not harm us, Darian!

(c3)   Ah! Ah!
        When you died we mourned!
        My lord, my lord, why did this happen?
        Terrible disasters – and we've
        lost all our triple oar-banked
        ships, now ships no more!   680

SCENE 3

Enter Shade of Dareios, on the tomb.

DAREIOS   Most faithful of the faithful, men of my own age,
        Elders of Persia, what pain is the city suffering?
        The earth groans, struck and fretted by your sounds.
        I saw my Queen, and I was
        filled with fear; I took her offerings and came.
        Now you lament, standing beside my tomb,
        and call on me, shouting aloud with cries of grief
        that summon up the dead. It is not easy to ascend,
        especially because the gods below the earth
        are rather better at receiving than at letting go.   690
        But I was able to prevail on them,
        and I have come. Now hurry, so I may not stay too long:
        what new disaster has befallen you?
ELDERS (a1)   I am awestruck seeing you,
        I'm awestruck and cannot reply
        because I always reverenced you.
DAR   I came because your groans persuaded me,
        so do not make a rambling speech, but tell me quickly
        everything, and put aside your awe.
ELD (a2)   I am afraid to do your will,   700
        I am afraid to speak to you
        words that a friend won't want to hear.

DAR   Well, since this long-past fear stands in your way,
my noble lady, former consort of my royal marriage-bed,
do not wail and cry out, but speak out
clearly. We are human, and all human beings suffer:
mortals encounter many evils on both sea
and land, if they live a full life-span.

QUEEN   Your fate is very fortunate, surpassing other mortal
men:
you were most enviable, while you lived under the light of
Sun: 710
just like a god you made the Persians live in happiness;
and now I envy you because you died and did not see
this depth of suffering. Dareios, now hear all in brief.
To put it bluntly, Persia's finished, utterly.

DAR   How? Did blasts of plague, or civil war, afflict our city?

Q   No. At Athens we lost all our troops.

DAR   Tell me; which of my sons led them out there?

Q   War-like, impetuous Xerxes emptied our continent.

DAR   This foolish venture; was it land or sea?

Q   Both: there were two invading forces, on two fronts.   720

DAR   How did so large an army cross to Greece?

Q   He yoked the Hellespont and made a road across.

DAR   What? Xerxes closed the gap of mighty Bosporos?

Q   Yes – with some daimôn, I believe, as partner to his will.

DAR   A daimôn great enough to warp his mind.

Q   And we can see the fearful consequences of that deed.

DAR   What happened to them that has made you groan?

Q   The navy lost a sea-battle, and this destroyed the troops on
land.

DAR   They were all killed with spears?

Q   Yes; this whole city, Sousa, mourns its emptiness.   730

DAR   You've lost the army which protects and keeps you
safe.

Q   The Baktrians are totally destroyed; not one survives.

DAR   Misery! So he has lost our allies' finest youth.

Q   They say that Xerxes, desolate, with very few –

DAR   How, where? Will he survive?

Q   – came gladly to the bridge that yoked two continents in
one.

DAR   Did he get back to Asia? Is he safe so far?

Q   Yes; messengers are clear on that, and there is no dispute.

DAR Ah! Too swiftly have the oracles come true, and Zeus
  hurled down fulfilment of the prophecies upon my son. I'd
    hoped   740
  and prayed the gods would not fulfil them until after a long
    time:
  but when a man hastens along, the god joins in as well;
  and now it seems a well of sufferings is pouring out for all
    our family.
  My son, not understanding, in young folly brought them to
  accomplishment; he hoped to yoke the sacred Hellespont as
    if it were
  a slave, and bind its flowing stream, gods' holy Bosporos, in
    chains,
  trying to make the ocean dance his tune; he cast leg-irons
  over the stream, and made a mighty crossing for his mighty
    force.
  It was not wise, since he is human, to suppose that he could
    overcome
  all of the gods, especially Poseidon. Was this not mental
    disease   750
  that overcame my child? I'm terribly afraid that all
  the wealth I worked for may become
  prey to the first man who can come and take it.
Q Warlike Xerxes learned this folly listening
  to bad advisers. They said you had amassed
  great wealth by warfare for your sons, while he through
    cowardice
  fought all his battles in the palace, and did nothing to
    increase his royal
  wealth. Because he heard such words too often from those
    wicked men,
  he planned this expedition with his army into Greece.
DAR And so he has brought down catastrophe
  so great it will not ever be forgotten, which has emptied
    out   760
  this city and the plain of Sousa on a scale unparalleled
  since lord Zeus gave this privilege –
  that one man should rule all of Asia
  rich in flocks, and hold the sceptre and wield power.
  A Mede was first commander of our host,
  and then another Mede, a son of his, inherited this work;

for his mind always governed rasher impulses.
Third was Kyros, very fortunate;
his rule gave all his allies peace.
He gained the men of Lydia and Phrygia,   770
and he subdued all the Ionians;
not one god hated him, since he was wise.
The son of Kyros was the fourth to rule,
and fifth was Mardos, who disgraced his fatherland
and its ancestral throne. By trickery
noble Artaphrenes assassinated him
with trusted friends, who had this task.
The sixth was Maraphis; becoming seventh lay between
    Artaphrenes
and me – but good luck gave me my desire.
Then I made many wars, with many men at arms,   780
but never did I cast such great disaster on this place.
Xerxes, my son, is young still, and is bent on youthful
folly; he has totally forgotten my commands.
You are of my age, and know well
that all the former rulers of this land
could not be shown to have inflicted so much grief.

1. ELD   Now, lord Dareios, to what end
    do your words turn? How, given what has happened, can
    the Persian people find a better life?

DAR   Never send an expedition back to Greece,   790
    not even if the army of the Medes is greater still;
    their land itself becomes the ally of the Greeks.

1. ELD   What do you mean? How can it be their ally?

DAR   It starves too large an army till they're dead.

1. ELD   But we could send selected troops, fully equipped.

DAR   Not even those who've stayed in Greece
    will come back safe and sound.

1. ELD   What did you say? Will the whole Persian army not
    cross back across the Hellespont from Europe?

DAR   Few out of many, if the prophecies   800
    uttered by gods, that look towards what's happening now,
    are to be trusted; they do not come true in parts.
    And if that's so, Xerxes has left behind
    that chosen force deluded by his empty hopes.
    They're camping now where Asopos waters the plain
    with flowing streams Boiotian land loves to absorb;

and there it still remains for them to suffer terrible
disasters, payment for their violence and godless thoughts.
When they went into Greece, they did not scruple to defile
the statues of the gods, and set fire to their temples.   810
The altars are destroyed, and shrines of gods
uprooted, wrecked, torn from their pedestals.
They've acted stupidly, and in return
they suffer, and will suffer, and their spring
of sufferings has not run dry, but gushes fiercely out.
Great clots of gore from bleeding wounds will fill
Plataian soil, inflicted by the troops of Sparta:
silent piles of corpses will tell human eyes
for sixty years that we are mortal
and should not think thoughts too high.   820
Violence sowed its crop, and ears have grown
of sheer destruction, so the harvest is pure grief.
Now look at this, the consequence of Xerxes' act;
remember Athens and remember Greece. Persians must
     never
fail to trust the daimôn who is guiding them
and through desire for other wealth lose riches we already
     have.
Great Zeus chastises thoughts which are
too proud: he calls men to a heavy reckoning.
So when the king returns, entreat him
to be sensible; advise him in well-chosen words   830
to stop harming the gods with overbold and reckless
     deeds.
Now agèd, dearest mother of Xerxes,
go to the palace, take fine clothes,
and find and meet your son, since all
around his body pain caused by his sufferings
has left his splendid clothing torn to shreds.
Soften him with kind and gentle words;
I know that only if he hears your voice will he endure.
Now I am going back into the undergloom.
Farewell, my Elders; even when torments surround you,   840
give yourselves some pleasure every day,
since wealth is of no use at all once you are dead.

Exit Dareios behind the tomb.

1. ELD   I felt great pain as he told us about
        so many Persian sufferings now and yet to come.
Q   Oh god, how many fierce pains attack me,
    and this new misfortune bites my heart especially,
    hearing just how humiliating are
    the clothes my son now wears.
    I'll go, and get some fine clothes from my house
    and try to meet him; we must not   850
    abandon our dear ones when they are suffering.

Exeunt Queen and Maidservant, left.

CHOROS 4

ELDERS (A1)   We had a very good,
        well-governed way of life while agèd,
        all-sufficient King Dareios ruled
        our land: invincible, he did us no harm.

    (A2)   First evidence: our famous armies,
        lines of battle strong as masonry,   860
        and homecomings from war which led men back
        to happy households without wounds or sufferings –

    (B1)   and then: how many cities Dareios subdued,
        although he never crossed the Halys,
        never even left his hearth!
        – river-watered cities near Strymon's
        floodplain, the dwellings of the Thrakians: 870

    (B2)   cities on the mainland, by the lake, all
        fortified, knew him as king;
        and cities spread around Helle's great stream,
        and hollows of Propontis,
        and the mouth of Pontos,

    (C1)   seawashed islands lying near   880
        the headland of this continent –

Lesbos, Samos the olive island, Chios, Paros,
Naxos, Mykonos, and Andros joined
to its near neighbour Tenos.

(c2)   He ruled the islands further out –   890
Lemnos, Ikaria;
Rhodos, Knidos, and cities of Kypros –
Paphos, Soloi, and Salamis,
whose mother-city caused our sufferings.

(c3)   His wisdom ruled the prosperous
and populated towns
of Greek Ionia: 900
we had insuperable military strength
and many kinds of allies.
Now, beyond the shadow of a doubt,
the gods have changed all that:
we suffer in our wars, subdued
completely by the lashes of the sea.

FINALE

*Enter Xerxes right, on a tented carriage, in ragged clothes,
armed with an empty quiver.*

XERXES   Oh!
I am miserable, and there were no signs
to warn me of this wretched fate: 910
how savagely the daimôn has attacked
the Persians. What will happen to me?
All my strength is lost as I
confront the Elders of the city.
Zeus! If only I too was
among the men who've gone
and death concealed me.
1. ELDER   King, lament your noble army
and the glory of the Persian Empire
and the greatness of the men   920
the daimôn has cut down.

1. ELD   The Earth cries for her young
           whom Xerxes killed; he crammed
           Hades with Persians. Many of the chosen
           flower of this land of Persia,
           mighty archers, many thousand
           thousand men have perished.
           Cry for our marvellous defenders!
           King, the whole of Asia's
           fallen to its knees in misery.   930

XER (A1)   I am here, and it is me
           that you lament: I've caused disasters to
           my noble ancestors and native land.
ELD   I will greet your homecoming
           with cries of evil omen, evil-sounding shrieks
           like dirges of the Mariandynoi
           filled with my tears.   940

XER (A2)   Throw up a plaintive cry
           of frightful sound, for now the daimôn turns
           and veers back down upon me.
ELD   I will raise a heartfelt cry, to do
           full justice to the people's sufferings, the city's and
           the people's grief for sea-struck corpses;
           there will be many tears in my lament.

XER (B1)   The Greeks killed them,   950
           the sea-defending war-god gave the Greeks their strength,
           ravaged the seas of darkness and the fatal shore.
ELD   Cry out for grief and learn it all.
           Where are the many who were dear to us?
           Where is a man to stand beside you
           like Pharandakes,
           Sousas, Pelagon, or Agabatas,
           Dotamas, Psammis, or Sousiskanes   960
           who left Agbatana?

XER (B2)   I left them to their deaths:
           they fell from our ships, and they're swept around the
               beaches,
           dashed against the cruel shore of Salamis.

ELD   Oh, where did you leave Pharnouchos and
        the great Ariomardes?
        Where's King Seualkes,
        noble Lilaios,   970
        Memphis, Tharybis and Masistras,
        Artembares and Hystaichmas?
        I'm asking you.

XER (C1)   How can I tell you this?
        They saw the ancient, hateful
        city of Athena, and at one stroke
        breathed their miserable last upon her shore.
ELD   And what about the finest of all Persians,
        he who was your loyal Eye,
        who counted men by tens of thousands,   980
        Batanokos' favourite son?
        Did you leave behind
        Sesamos, son of Megabates,
        mighty Parthos, Oibares?
        Poor men!
        You've told us nothing good for noble Persians.

XER (C2)   Yes, you remind me of my longing
        for those great comrades,
        telling these cursed, hateful sufferings: 990
        my heart cries out aloud inside me.
ELD   Now we miss yet another man,
        Xanthos, commander of a thousand
        Mardians, and Arios, and Agchares,
        and Diaixis and Arsakes,
        lords of the horse,
        Agdadates and Lythimnes,
        and Tolmos, warrior insatiable;
        I am astonished that they do   1000
        not follow your tented chariot.

XER (D1)   They've gone the way of all the others.
ELD   Dead and nameless.
XER   Oh! Oh!
ELD   Oh! the gods

have given us an unforeseen
disaster, clear as Ruin's glance.

XER (D2)   We've been struck down from our prosperity
ELD   for all to see.
XER   New miseries, new miseries.   1010
ELD   We met the Greeks
at sea and lost:
the Persians are unfortunate in war

XER (E1)   – in every way: I'm stricken by the loss
of all my soldiers.
ELD   What has survived, great Ruin of the Persians?
XER   D'you see my rags?
ELD   I see, I see.
XER   – and this, for arrows . . .   1020
ELD   What d'you say is saved?
XER   . . . a quiver.
ELD   Not enough from all our riches.
XER   We have no defenders left.
ELD   The Greeks did not flee from our shafts.

XER (E2)   They're brave enough: and I have seen
disaster far beyond my fears.
ELD   You mean our mighty naval forces routed?
XER   Yes, I rent my garments at the sight.   1030
ELD   Oh . . . ! Oh . . . !
XER   Grief beyond that measure –
ELD   – double, triple grief –
XER   – painful, and joy to all who hate us.
ELD   All our strength has been cut down.
XER   I'm stripped of my attendants
ELD   all destroyed at sea.

XER (F1)   Weep, weep for this disaster, then go home.
ELD   Ah, ah, misery! Misery!
XER   Now raise a cry, responding to my cry;   1040
ELD   response of suffering to sufferings.
XER   Cry shrill together with me now:
ELD (+ XER)   Otototoi!

ELD   Heavy disaster:
        I grieve for it too.

XER (F2)   Beat, beat your heads and groan for me.
ELD   I weep in grief.
XER   Now raise a cry, responding to my cry.
ELD   My king, I've every reason to do this.
XER   Lift your voice; lament;   1050
ELD (+ XER)   Otototoi!
ELD   – and mingled with the groans
        black blows will fall.

XER (G1)   Beat your chests, and cry in Mysian mode.
ELD   Grief, grief.
XER   Tear at your white beards.
ELD   Clenched hands, clenched hands –
XER   Cry out shrill.
ELD   This too.

XER (G2)   Use your fingers, tear your clothes.   1060
ELD   Grief, grief.
XER   Tear your hair, pity our army.
ELD   Clenched hands, clenched hands.
XER   Wet your eyes.
ELD   This too.

XER (G3)   Now raise a cry, responding to my cry.
ELD   Ah! Ah!
XER   Go home in misery.
ELD   Oh! Oh!   1070
XER   Misery throughout the city.
ELD   Yes, yes.
XER   Lament with graceful steps.
ELD   Oh Persian earth, so hard to tread.
XER   Oh, they perished
ELD   in the battleships.
XER   Escort me to my home
ELD   with cries of grief.

Exit Xerxes escorted by the Elders, left.

SEVEN AGAINST THEBES

THE ACTORS AND THEIR ROLES

——————

Men, Old Men and Boys	Silent Faces
Eteokles	Actor 1
Scout	Actor 2
Unmarried women	Choros
Attendants	Silent Faces
Body of Polyneikes	Silent Face

Preset images of eight gods: Zeus, Hera, Poseidon, Apollo,
Athena, Ares, Aphrodite and Artemis.

SCENE I

Enter Men, Old Men and Boys of Thebes left, in ones and twos.

Enter Eteokles from the skene.

ETEOKLES   Citizens of Thebes, the man who guards our
    destiny
  must make the right decision, at the city's stern
  guiding the tiller, eyes not lulled to sleep.
  If we do well, the god is justly praised;
  but if – and may this never happen – some disaster falls,
  Eteokles would be the one the citizens abuse,
  in waves of angry music forged from jeers
  and groans. Zeus is the god who wards off such a fate;
  may he fulfil that role and save us all!

  But as for you, it is your duty now – even the boys   10
  not yet in youth's full bloom, and older men
  whose bodies are now growing rather fat –
  to show you care whatever way you can;
  rescue your city, save the altars of our gods,
  whom we must never fail to pay their due,
  and guard your children and the mother earth, our dearest
    nurse.
  For when you crept newborn over the bounteous soil
  she ministered to all your infant needs,
  nurtured you into citizens who carry shields
  so you can all be trusted now this need has come.   20

Up till today the god inclines our way;
so far the war has mostly gone
in favour of our long defence – thanks to the gods.
But now the prophet tells us – shepherd of omens,
using no fire, just listening and interpreting
with faultless skill prophetic cries of birds –
this master of such oracles
tells me the Achaians' greatest onslaught yet
against us was debated and decided on last night.

Swarm to the battlements and city gates,   30
speed off with all your armour;
fill the breastworks, guard the platforms
on the towers; at the entrance-gates
stand firm, be of good courage, do not fear too much
this mass of foreigners; the god will help us win.
I have sent scouts, observers out to spy upon the enemy;
I know they will not fail to come back soon.
When I have heard from them, I won't be caught by
    treachery.

Exeunt Men, Old Men and Boys in both directions.

Enter Scout, right.

SCOUT   Eteokles, most noble king of Thebes,
    I come to bring a true report out of the hostile camp;   40
    I can myself bear witness what they've done.

Seven fierce and eager captains of the troops
slaughtered a bull into a black-rimmed shield,
then dipped their hands into the dead beast's gore
and by Ares, Enyo and the goddess Terror who adores shed
    blood
they swore an oath either to raze this city to the ground
and plunder Kadmos' citadel by force of arms
or die, and mingle with their blood our native soil.
They crowned Adrastos' chariot with locks of hair,
mementos for their parents back at home.   50
Though tears ran down, they did not moan.
Their iron-hearted spirit, blazing with courageous zeal,

breathed out as if from lions glaring with the war-god's
   might.
The proof of this is not delayed by sloth;
I left them drawing lots, so each of them
could lead his troops against one gate.
Now you must quickly choose this city's greatest men
and station them at every city gate.
Nearer each moment all the Argive army's might
advances, raising clouds of dust; white foam pollutes   60
the plain, falling in droplets from their horses' flanks.
You must be like the skilful helmsman of a ship
and batten down our citadel before the war-god's blast
wrecks it completely. Their army is a land-wave, breaking
   now.

Seize on the first good moment to do this.
My eye will still remain a loyal scout by day;
from my clear speeches you will learn what they
are doing out beyond our wall, and so remain unharmed.

Exit Scout, right.

ET   Oh Zeus and Earth and city gods
   and mighty Curse and Fury of my father Oidipous   70
   do not root out and utterly destroy my city now
   and make it captive to the rest of Greece.
   The yoke of slavery must never take
   the liberty of Kadmos' city and its land;
   bring us your help. I know what I say's good for you and us;
   a city when it prospers pays great tribute to the gods.

Exit Eteokles, into the skene.

CHOROS I

Enter Unmarried Women of Thebes, left.

1. WOMAN   I shriek, I'm terrified.
1. W   Their army is let loose; they've left the camp;
     hundreds of horsemen stream in front.   80

1. W   I know; I've seen the dust rise in the air –
              a soundless message; but it's clear, and all too true.

1. W   The plains are echoing – the clash of armour
              fills my ears;
              it flies, it roars like water thundering down
              invincibly on mountain rocks.

1. W   Oh gods and goddesses ward off
              the danger that has come on us.

1. W   The cry of warriors leaps up
              over the wall;   90
              the whiteshield army, well equipped,
              is rushing on against our city.

1. W   Who will preserve us, which goddess or god
              will save us from them now?

1. W   Should I fall down before the altars
              of our native daimones?

1. W   Blessed gods, you sit on sacred thrones.
              Now we must clasp your images, so why
              do we delay? We're pitiful!

1. W   D'you hear? Is that a clang of shields, or is it not?   100
              When will there be a greater need than now
              to robe the images and garland them in prayer-
                  offerings?

1. W   I see the clattering of many spears.

1. W   What will you do? War-god, this is your land
              from ancient time; will you betray it?

1. W   God of the golden helmet, look, look on the city
              which you once held dear.

1. W (A1)   Gods who guard this city come, come all;
              look on this group of single women   110
              who entreat you now; save us from slavery.
              A wave of armoured men with slanting plumes
              foams round the city, blown against us by the blasts of
                  War.

1. W   Zeus, all-fulfilling Father, come what may
              save us from capture by our enemies.

1. W   The Argives have encircled Kadmos'   120
              city, and their battle-weapons terrify us.

1. W   The moaning bits in horses' jaws
              portend a massacre,

1. W   and seven noble leaders can be seen;
           armoured and bearing lances they stride on,
           chosen by lot, to stand against our seven gates.

1. W (A2)   Daughter of Zeus, lover of battle-power,
           save the city,   130
           Pallas Athena; and you, lord of the sea,
           horse-god with the powerful trident;
           free us from fear, please free us now.
1. W   War-god, destroyer, Kadmos' citadel is your own city;
           guard it well, show clearly that you care for us.
1. W   Goddess of love, you are the mother of our tribe; 140
           rescue your daughters, since
1. W   your bloodline gave us birth. We approach you now
           as suppliants, crying aloud.
1. W   Apollo, wolf-lord, now become a wolf yourself
           and hunt our enemies;
           daughter of Leto, bend your bow.

W (B1)   Ah ah ah ah!   150
           I hear the sound of chariots around the city.
           Oh Lady Hera,
           axle-boxes shriek, as overloaded axles turn.
           Beloved Artemis,
           the heavens are going mad, shaken by spears.
           What will our city suffer? What will happen?
           What end to this will the god bring?

   (B2)   Ah ah ah ah!
           Slingshot is coming at our battlements!
           Beloved Apollo,   160
           the din at the gates is a clash of bronze-bound shields.
           You are the son of Zeus, who steers
           the battle to its sacred end.
           Lady Athena, blessed guardian of Thebes, protect
           the seven-gated citadel.

   (C1)   Hail, all-powerful divinities!
           Hail, all-fulfilling gods and goddesses
           who guard the towers of this land;
           do not betray this spear-tortured city

to a foreign enemy.   170
Listen, you must listen to us single women
as we stretch our hands in prayer.

(C2)   Hail, dear gods and goddesses!
Come, embrace the city, save it, show
how much you love your city
and enjoy our public offerings;
enjoy them – and preserve us now.
This city's ceremonies give you sacrifices –   180
show me that you remember them!

SCENE 2

Enter Eteokles from the skene.

ETEOKLES   I'm asking you, insufferable creatures;
is this the best that you can do to save the city,
give an army courage under siege,
to fall before the images of all the city's gods,
wail, howl – and earn the hatred of the self-controlled?

Neither in time of trouble nor in peace and happinesss
do I like living with the female sex.
If woman wins, her boldness is unbearable,
and when she's scared she brings disaster on her home and
    city-state.   190
Now, for example – running terrified around the city you've
    inspired
a dreadful cowardice among the citizens;
the men who hammer at our gates are greatly helped,
while we're besieged from inside by ourselves.
And that is what you get for sharing house with women.

Now, if anyone should disregard what I command –
men, women, anybody in between –
my vote will be cast on them; death
by public stoning and without escape.
This siege is man's work; woman must not meddle in   200

outside affairs. She'll do no harm indoors.
D'you hear, or don't you? Am I speaking to the deaf?

WOMEN (A1)   Dearest son of Oidipous, I heard
the terrifying sound of chariots, chariots
when wheels turned and the axles shrieked,
and horses' mouths cried out around the fire-forged bits
that steer them into battle.

ET   Well? Does a sailor, if he flees up to the prow
abandoning the rudder, find a means of safety
when the ship is buffeted by ocean waves?   210

W (A2)   See, this is where I ran – towards the ancient
images
of daimones; I put faith in gods when I began to hear
the deadly roar of stones raining upon our gates.
Then I made ready in my fear to pray the blessed ones
might hold their strength over our city.

ET   You prayed the walls will keep their spears from you.
By all the gods, I know that that will happen! But it's said
the gods depart a city when it's sacked.

W (B1)   Never while I still live may this gathering
of gods abandon us, and may I never see   220
this city filled
with foreigners, devoured
by enemy soldiers' fire.

ET   Then don't lose common sense when calling on the
gods.
Obedience is mother, so the proverbs say,
of Fine Achievement which will save us all.

W (B2)   She is – but still a god has greater strength;
and often in a time of trouble, when a dreadful cloud
of misery hangs over all our eyes,
he sets right things we cannot do ourselves.

ET   This is the job of men – to render sacrificial offerings   230
up to the gods before they test opponents' strength;
you must be silent and remain inside the house.

W (C1)   Thanks to the gods our city is untamed;
our battlements protect us from the horde of enemies;
what just resentment could despise this prayer?

ET   I do not mind your paying tribute to the gods –
but so you do not weaken all our citizens,
be calm, and do not show excessive fear.

w (c2)   I heard the flying sounds of clattering and human
   shouts
  and in a dreadful fright here to the highest citadel, 240
  seat of our gods, I came.

ET Now, if you hear of fighters dead or wounded,
  don't be eager to lament and groan;
  This is what Ares feeds on, slaughtered men.

1. w Listen! I can hear the horses neighing.

ET Listen – but do not hear too much.

1. w The city is surrounded and the earth groans loud.

ET It is enough if I plan what we have to do.

1. w I'm terrified; the clattering stones are louder at the gates.

ET Shut up! Don't talk about this all around our city! 250

1. w Gods of the city, do not make me be a slave.

ET You will make slaves of you and me and all of us.

1. w All-powerful Zeus, turn your thunderbolt against our
  enemies.

ET Oh Zeus, why did you give us women?

1. w Women suffer – so do men, after their city's sacked.

ET Ill-omened words, when you are touching images of gods?

1. w I'm sorry; terror has turned my tongue to cowardice.

ET If only you would give me what I ask – a simple thing. 260

1. w Tell me as fast as possible, and I will know.

ET Silence, unhappy woman – do not undermine your fighting
  men.

1. w I will be silent; with the rest I'll tolerate my destiny.

ET I will accept these words in place of what you said before.
  Also, you must leave the images
  and make a better prayer – for all the gods to be our allies
   now.
  First listen to my prayers, and then
  raise up the sacred song, good-omened sounds,
  the proper custom of all Greeks; cry out with sacrificial joy,
  a source of courage for your relatives, an end to fear of
   war. 270

  So now I promise all the gods of Thebes
  – the plain-dwellers, the guardians of the market-place,
  the springs of Dirke and Hismenos' stream –
  if all goes well for us and Thebes is saved,
  we'll make our flocks' blood flow upon the altars of the gods

and set up trophies for the conquest of our enemies;
the spoils of war, won by the spear, inside your sacred halls.
Make prayers like these; do not lament,
or utter wild and useless groans;   280
it will not make a difference to your destiny.

Meanwhile I will position at our seven gates
six men – together with myself as seventh –
against that lordly manner of our enemies,
before the Scout comes back with hurried and swift-flowing
    words
and burns us with the urgency of need.

Exit Eteokles, left.

CHOROS 2

WOMEN (A1)   I'll try; but terror keeps my heart
        awake, and fear
        kindles my terror   290
        of the army all around us, as a timid dove
        is terrified by snakes which could attack and kill
        her nestling chicks.
        They're coming now
        against our walls –
        yes, all their army; what will be my fate?
        We're totally surrounded, and
        they're shooting jagged rocks.   300
        Gods, Zeus' children,
        you must save
        Kadmos' people and our city, Thebes.

(A2)   Where will you go and find
        a plain on earth more fertile, if you let
        them take this deep-soiled land
        and Dirke's water, the most nourishing
        of all the rivers poured out by the ocean-god   310
        Poseidon and by Tethys' children?
        That is why, dear city-gods, you must
        throw panic down into our enemies

outside the city walls;
destroy their strength,
send Madness on them; they will
throw away their armour, and increase
the glory of our citizens.
Become the saviours of this city;
you will live here pleasantly
because of our shrill prayers.   320

(B1)   It would be wretched if this ancient land
were hurled to Hades, captured by the spear,
enslaved, in powdery cinders,
sacked by the Argives (would the gods
allow such outrage?);
women taken prisoner, led away,
Ah!, Ah! – both young and old
dragged by the hair like horses, and
their clothing ripped around them; emptied out,
the city cries in anguish   330
as its people is destroyed.
I fear this savage fate.

(B2)   It is terrible for newly nurtured girls unripe
to leave their homes, before
the lawful rites – a hateful path.
I say the dead are better off.
And often when a city is subdued
Ah!, Ah! – people are dragged away   340
and killed; fires are set, and smoke
pollutes the city everywhere.
Maddened, the god of War blows out his rage,
tamer of people, defiling holiness.

(C1)   Terrible noises inside the city, and a net of enemies
around its towers; man kills man
with spear-thrusts.
Bloody bleatings cry
from newly nurtured babies
at the breast.   350
Rapes, and brotherhoods of pillage;
looters encounter looters,

empty-handed men
call out for partners in plunder,
eager for a more than equal share.
We can tell what happens next.

(C2)   All kind of fruits fall to the earth; the house is hurt
as it receives bitter new housekeepers.
Everywhere mixed up   360
the produce of the Earth
is poured away
in streams of waste.
New slave-girls have fresh misery;
they'll suffer in the spear-won bed
of some successful man –
their only hope is that the conquering enemy
will make them reach the climax of the night,
the moment when they'll pour out all their grief.

SCENE 3

1. WOMAN   Here is the army scout, my friends;
I think he comes with news – see how   370
he moves his feet in haste to bring the message!

Enter Scout, right.

1. W   And look, here is the king himself, the son of Oidipous,
just at the fitting time to hear the messenger;
he too comes here in haste and eagerness.

*Enter Eteokles left, in full hoplite armour except for his
greaves.*

SCOUT   I know, and I can tell you all about our enemies
and who has drawn the lot for each of Thebes' gates.
Tydeus already thunders on towards the Proitid gate,
but he is checked – the prophet will not let him cross
Hismenos' stream; their sacrifice has not been good.
Tydeus is raging mad, and in his battle-lust   380
he cries aloud like snakes that hiss in noonday sun,

and hurls humiliation on their prophet, Oikleus' son,
saying he is a coward, fawns on death and war.

As he calls out, he shakes three giant plumes
that overshade his helmet – and below his shield
bronze bells ring out to strike the enemy with fear.
Upon the shield he bears this arrogant device
engraved; the sky at night, blazing with stars,
and in the middle, standing out, a clear full moon,
eye of the night – greatest, most eminent of stars.   390

Such is the joy, or madness, in his overboastful shield;
he shouts aloud beside the river bank, in love with war,
like horses breathing down the bridle, chafing as they wait
in anguish for the trumpet-cry to start the fight.

Whom will you place against him? Who will stand pledged
    firm,
when we unbar and open Proitos' gate?
ETEOKLES   I would not ever fear a man for ornaments,
nor do the signs marked on a shield have power to harm;
a plume and bell do not have bite without a spear.
As for that night you say is blazoned on his shield,   400
sparkling with all the stars of heaven,
stupidity so great might have prophetic power.
If he dies, night descends upon his eyes;
then rightfully and properly this overboastful sign
would live up to the omen of its name;
the owner would be truly prophet of his arrogance.

Against this Tydeus I will place to stand
before these gates the trusty son of Astakos;
a man of very noble birth, who honours Modesty,
and hates all words that go too far.   410
His roots go right back to the warriors Ares let live,
the Sown Men (truly he is a son of native soil!);
Melanippos. Ares will judge the outcome with his dice.
His parents' Justice sends him out today
to keep the enemy away from this, his motherland.
W (A1)   If only the gods grant
    my champion wins, the one

who justly fights for his city. I tremble, and I do not want
to see the bloody deaths   420
of men who fight for us.

SC   Yes, may the gods grant he will win;
now, Kapaneus has drawn the Elektran gates by lot.
This is another giant, greater still than he who came
before; his boast exceeds the power of mortal thought.
He says that he will sack our city whether god
wants it or not; not even Zeus' angry strife
hurled to the ground will halt his course.
Those lightning-flashes and god's thunderbolts   430
he likens to the midday heat.
His shield-device, a naked man who carries fire;
he holds a lamp which blazes out between his hands
and says in golden letters 'I will sack this town'.
Against a man like that send . . . who will stand?
Who can stay firm and fearless, facing such a boast?

ET   This also is a boast in which there's gain for us;
the tongue becomes a sure accuser
when men think such vain and futile thoughts.
Kapaneus threatens, and he is prepared to act;   440
but he has stripped his speech; he nakedly offends the gods.
His exultation's futile; mortal man, he sends a shout on high
to heaven, words which swell like waves and spatter Zeus.
I'm certain that his fire-bearer will bring on him
the thunderbolt of Zeus as he deserves – and it is nothing like
the midday heat sent by the Sun.
He talks too readily; against him I have set a man
of blazing courage – Polyphontes, full of strength,
a firm-pledged guardian who has goodwill
from Artemis protector and the other gods.   450
Name me another man, allotted to another gate.

W   (A2)   He boasts great deeds against our city – may he die
checked by the thunderbolt,
before he leaps into my house and drives me
from my chaste retreat
with thrusting spear.

SC   I'll tell you: Eteoklos is third, and the third lot
leapt from the brazen helmet up and out
for his troop to attack us at the Neis gate.   460
His horses snort into their nosebands, as

he wheels them round in eagerness to fall against our gates.
Pipes on the muzzles whistle an outlandish mode
filled by the beasts' proud nostrils full of breath.
The decoration on his shield is marvellous;
a hoplite trooper climbs a ladder's rungs
determined he will sack the towers of his enemy,
and cries aloud in written syllables
that even Ares could not cast him down.
This man too needs a warrior pledged firm   470
to keep from us the yoke of slavery.

ET   He is already sent, his boast is in his hands –
Megareus, son of Kreon, sprung from the Sown Men.
He will not run away in terror from the gates
scared by the noisy snorting of some frenzied horses;
either by death he'll repay this his motherland,
or he will bring two men back and a city on a shield
to ornament his father's house with spoils of war.

Give me another's boast; I want to hear it all.   480
W (BI)   I pray that he will prosper – Oh! –
the champion fighting for my home, and they will not.
They speak such haughty words
against the city in their madness; so may Zeus
see them in anger and exact revenge.

SC   There is another man, the fourth; he has the gates near by
Athena's temple, and he stands before them with a shout –
Hippomedon; a man of huge and fearful shape.
He whirled a mighty threshing-floor – I mean the circle of his
    shield –
and made me tremble; no denying that.   490
The metalworker was not poor
who wrought the symbol on that shield;
Typhon, breathing from his fiery mouth
a smoky flame, a dappled brother to pure fire.
Surrounding him, enfolded coils of snakes
are fastened to the edging of the concave, hollow shield.
The man cries out aloud, filled with the god of War,
in full-pitched bakchic frenzy; terror's in his glance.

We must guard well against this monster's armed attack;
now Terror stands in person boasting at our gates.   500

ET   Well, first Athena is a neighbour to our gates;
     her place is right beside the city, and she hates all violence;
     she'll shield her children from this deadly snake.
     And then Hyperbios, the trusty son of Oinops,
     was chosen, stands against him man to man. He wants
     to learn his fate in this crisis – bring fortune what it may;
     in form, and spirit, and in bearing arms
     you could not fault him. Hermes was right to yoke this
         pair.
     Our man will stand in enmity against their man,
     and they will bring together on their shields two hostile   510
     gods. For he has Typhon breathing fire;
     Hyperbios has Zeus the father on his shield,
     standing in majesty to hurl a dart of flame.
     And nobody, I think, has yet seen Zeus done down.
     Such is the way the gods have taken sides;
     we have the winning god with us and they the losing
         one,
     since in a battle Zeus will surely beat Typhon.
     Hyperbios has Zeus upon his shield,
     and Zeus will be the Saviour, as the words there say.   520

W (B2)   I believe that he, who placed
         upon his shield the enemy of Zeus,
         the body of an anti-god from Hades –
         image hateful both to mortals and
         the long-lived gods –
         will break his head in front of Thebes' gates.

SC   So may it be. Now I tell you about the fifth,
     the man set at the fifth, our Northern gate,
     right by the tomb of Amphion the son of Zeus.
     He swears this by the spear he holds (and worships
     more than god, and trusts even more dearly than his
         eyes);   530
     that he will sack the citadel of Thebes by force.
     Such is his boast – the war-god's son, child of a mother
     from the mountains; fair of face, a boy but yet a man.
     The sideburns just begin to show beside his cheeks,
     he's reaching manhood, thick hair growing fast.
     He stands against us with a savage mind
     and gorgon eye, with no resemblance to his maiden
         name.

He threatens at our gates, and does not come without a
    boast;
this city's shame is what he bears upon his bronze-bound
shield, the round protection for his body; yes,   540
the Sphinx that eats men raw is fastened on
with rivets, clear-embossed for all to see.
He carries underneath her, living, one of us – a man of
    Thebes;
most of our missiles will impact upon our own.

He has not come to do small business in his trade
of war – no, he will make his long road here worthwhile;
Parthenopaios, all the way from Arkady – and what a man!
Argos once welcomed him, and he repays his keep
with threats of terror, which I pray god won't fulfil.
ET Yes – may the gods give them exactly what they would
        inflict,   550
these very boasts which are so impious;
then they would suffer in complete oblivion.

There is one also for this warrior from Arkady;
a man who never boasts, a hand that sees what must be
    done,
Aktor, brother to him I spoke of last.
He will not let a tongue bereft of deeds
flowing outside our gates nurture harm,
nor will he let the bite of that most loathsome Sphinx
get in from out there; she will blame her bearer, when   560
she's beaten bitterly beneath our city walls.
With the gods' help, what I say will be true.
W (CI)   These words reach into us,
        our hair stands straight on end
        hearing the awful boasts of these
        appalling men; I pray
        the gods will make them perish in our land.
SC Sixth now I'd tell you of a very prudent man,
a prophet of the greatest bravery, Amphiaraos.
He's taken up position at the Homolian gates,   570
and speaks with much contempt about the strength of
    Tydeus –
murderer, city-destroyer, man

who taught the Argives this insanity;
Fury's herald, manservant of Fear,
Adrastos' counsellor in this madness.

He tosses high another name –
that of your brother, sown in the same womb,
and twice dwells on the strife that it implies
and calls upon him, saying this:
'Is it a deed of greatness, favoured by the gods,   580
and fair to hear of and to tell posterity,
to storm your native city and its local
gods, by throwing in an army brought from other states?
What legal claim can dry the stream of mother earth?
When sacked by eager spear of yours, how can
your native land become your ally once again?
Myself, I will enrich this land –
a prophet buried under hostile soil.
Let's fight; I trust my fate will not lack fame.'
Such were the words the prophet spoke, untroubled   590
as he held his shield. There was no sign upon its circle; he
does not just want to seem, but actually to be the best –
a man who ploughs deep furrows through his mind,
and reaps the best ideas and thoughts.

Against him I advise you send opponents who are wise
as well as strong; a man of such great piety is terrible.
ET   Oh, I lament the bird-omen that brings
a man of justice in with foes so impious.
In all affairs there's nothing worse than company
that's bad, a crop you cannot harvest.   600
Suppose a pious man embarks upon a boat
with hotly reckless sailors bent on wickedness,
he perishes together with those men the gods spit out.
Sometimes a man of justice finds himself with citizens
who hate all strangers and forget the gods;
then he unfairly suffers, captured in the net
and struck by god's whip-hand together with the rest.
Just so this seer, son of Oikleos,
a sober, just, an excellent and pious man,   610
a mighty prophet, joins with these unholy,
bold-tongued men against his will;

they have now stretched this journey to a place beyond
    return,
and with the will of Zeus he too will be dragged there.
I don't think he will even come against the gates;
not that he lacks the spirit or is faint of heart,
but just because he knows that he must meet his end in
    war,
if Loxias' prophecies bear any fruit.

Still, we will place against him someone mighty –
    Lasthenes,   620
a gate-defender hostile to all foreigners.
He has an old man's strength of mind, a young man's
    muscles, and
his eye is swift; his hand's not slow
to strike with spear the flesh left unprotected by the shield.
It is the god's gift, if good fortune comes to men.

W (C2)   Gods, hear our just prayers, and
        fulfil them so the city flourishes,
        and turn the sufferings of spear-wounds
        onto our invaders; may Zeus strike
        with deadly thunderbolts outside our walls.   630

SC   Well, now the seventh at the seventh gate
    I'll tell you – he is your own brother, and upon
    our city he is praying for a catastrophic fate;
    he'll mount the walls and be proclaimed as king
    and sing a frenzied victory-song,
    then meet with you in combat; killing you he'll die,
    or if you live he'll drive the man who drove him out
    to exile, paying you back just the same.
    That's what he shouts, and to the gods who gave us birth
    he calls, praying the guardians of his fatherland   640
    to be completely his, give aid to Polyneikes' strength.

    He holds a new-made, perfect circle shield,
    and on it there's a double image fixed –
    a warrior displayed in beaten gold
    led by a woman, modestly;
    she claims she's Justice – that is what the writing
    says: 'I'll bring this man back home, and he will have
    the city of his fathers and his house to roam again.'

So there – that's all their clever tricks;   649
don't ever blame this messenger for what he tells;
you are the helmsman, you must steer our native land.

Exit Scout, left.

ET   Oh maddened, greatly hated by the gods,
Oh utterly lamented race of Oidipous!
Oh me, for now my father's curses are fulfilled.

Still, I must not cry out aloud or weep;
that might give birth to even greater suffering.

Now, for this man so rightly named, the lord of strifes,
we will soon see how his device turns out,
if all the golden letters sculpted on his shield   660
will bring him back, this madman babbling stupid words.
If Zeus' pure and virgin daughter Justice ever was with him
in any of his deeds or thoughts, perhaps this could have been.
But neither when he left the darkness of his mother's womb
nor when he was a child or beardless youth,
nor when the hairs of manhood joined together from his
    cheeks
did Justice look upon him and approve.
So when he's injuring his native land
I do not think she'll stand beside him now.
Indeed in justice she would not deserve her name   670
of Justice, if she went with such a man of reckless, daring
    mind.

That is what I believe; against him I will stand
myself; could any other man more justly serve?
Ruler and ruler, brother and brother, we will join
as enemy and enemy. Let someone quickly bring
my greaves, to shield me from the spears and arrow-flights.
1. W   Dearest of men, son of Oidipous, do not become
like in your nature to that man so badly named.
It is enough that men of Thebes should come
to grips with Argives – such blood can be purified;   680
but when two kindred die slain by each other's hands,
the stain of blood will never age.

ET   If a god brings evil, men must bear it
      without shame; that is the only glory after we are dead.
      You'll never speak the praise of bad and shameful deeds.
W   (A1)   What is this, child?
      Do not let blind desire for combat fill your soul and carry
            you
      away; banish this dreadful love before it starts.
ET   The god urges this on – so let us go,
      swept by the wind, bound for the river Kokytos;   690
      Apollo hates the whole of Laios' race.
W   (A2)   Too much this monstrous, biting need arouses
            you
      to pluck the bitter fruit of killing when
      the bloodshed is abhorrent to both gods and men.
ET   Yes – now the hostile Curse of my dear father sits
      against my dry and tearless eyes
      and tells of glory first – and then of death.
W   (B1)   But don't you stir it on! You won't be called
      a coward if you've done no wrong; the black-cloaked Fury
      will depart from here, when at the hearths the gods   700
      receive due sacrifice.
ET   The gods, it seems, already care no more for me;
      so will they take my offerings when I am going to die?
      Why then do I still fawn on death?
W   (B2)   Stay, while it stands right by you! Later
      the god might change
      and come with gentler breath;
      now he is raging still.
ET   Yes – Oidipous' curse has made him boil with rage,
      and all too true the phantoms that I saw in dreams,   710
      dividing up our fathers' property.
W   Obey a woman, though you don't love to.
ET   Say only something practical; and quickly too.
W   You must not go out to the seventh gate.
ET   I'm sharpened; you will not blunt me with speech.
W   The god rewards even ignoble victory.
ET   No fighting man should ever love such words.
W   Then do you want to harvest your own brother's blood?
ET   When gods inflict it, you cannot escape from harm.

Exit Eteokles, right.

CHOROS 3

WOMEN (A1)   I shudder at the house-destroying   720
        god unlike the other gods,
        prophet of evils, always true
        – the father's Fury
        fulfilling the angry curses
        of Oidipous in his madness;
        this child-destroying Strife now spurs it on.

   (A2)   A foreigner sets out the lots,
        a visitor from Skythia,
        a bitter arbitrator for their goods.
        His name is Iron; savage-hearted, he's   730
        dividing up the earth for them
        to have when dead, without a share
        in these great plains.

   (B1)   Kindred now kill each other,
        strike each other down. The dust of earth
        drinks their black slaughtered blood.
        Who could free them from pollution,   740
        purify our soil? Oh, new torments now
        mix in this house
        with ancient evils.

   (B2)   Yes, I mean a crime from long ago
        soon punished, but still lasting
        to the sons of sons. Laios defied
        Apollo, who said thrice
        at Delphi, at the navel of the earth
        in oracles that he must die
        without offspring to keep the city safe.

   (C1)   Thoughtless desire for children conquered him,   750
        and he created his own fate,
        the father-killer Oidipous,
        who sowed inside his mother's sacred field
        where he had grown

a bloody root; destructive madness
brought them to the marriage bed.

(C2)   A sea of evils brings the wave;
it falls, and then it lifts
like talons, foams   760
even around the city's prow.
This citadel is just
a tiny barrier.
I fear that with its kings
the city may be tamed.

(D1)   When curses uttered long ago
come to fruition, bitter is the settlement;
such deadly things never depart.
When human happiness
is overweighted, then the ship   770
will sink, and all is lost.

(D2)   What man was so admired
by all our city gods
and in the market-place
as Oidipous
when he threw out
the murderous Sphinx?

(E1)   When he was sane again,
but swept along by grief
about his horrifying marriage,   780
in his crazed heart he could not bear
the dreadful things his hand had done
that once had killed his father.
Now he lost all reason;

(E2)   on the children of his wretched
union he let loose in anger
bitter curses – that some day
they would divide
their property
with iron hands. And now I fear   790
the Fury's running to fulfil that curse.

SCENE 4

Enter Scout, right.

SCOUT   Take courage, daughters of our noble women;
  you are free! The city has escaped the yoke of slavery;
  those fierce men's boasts have tumbled down.
  In calm seas and in all the battering
  of waves the city shipped no water.
  Walls protected us, the gates were saved
  by pledged defenders fighting man to man.
  And mostly things are well, at six gates. Lord Apollo seized
  the seventh, dread captain of sevens, and he
  brought down upon the heads of Oidipous' sons   800
  the ill-advised deed of Laios long ago.
1. WOMAN   What is this new, worse burden on the city?
SC   The men are dead; they perished at each other's hands.
1. W   Who? What d'you say? In fear I do not understand.
SC   Be calm and listen; Oidipous' sons –
1. W   Oh misery. I see what's coming.
SC   Not to mince words, they're slain.
1. W   They're lying out there? Tell this heavy fate.   810
SC   In flows of kindred blood their hands destroyed
  each other; for they shared the savage daimôn of this house,
  and he has surely finished off this miserable family.
  So there – occasion for both joy and tears;
  a city faring well – but the leaders, the two
  generals split up their inheritance
  with steel from Skythia.
  They'll have the land they need to make their graves;
  their father's prayer swept them to miserable deaths.   819

Exit Scout left.

FINALE

WOMEN   Oh Zeus our king, and daimones of
  this city, who protect the towers
  of Kadmos and the citizens;

shall I rejoice and cry out
for the good fortune which has freed our city,
or lament the poor, unfortunate
and childless warlords
who died according to their names,
the truly noble and the lord of strifes,   830
driven by unholy madness?

(A1)   Oh black and all-fulfilling
curse of this race, curse of Oidipous.
A ghastly grief falls on me and my heart.
I make a song for their tomb
in frenzied lamentation for
their deaths
by such a bloody fate;
ill-omened is the harmony
of their duet for spears.

(A2)   It all worked out, was not denied,   840
the father's curse, his wish;
and Laios' thoughtless deed has had its consequence.
The city grieves,
and prophecy is never blunted.
Much-lamented men, you did
this crazy deed; these miserable
sufferings have come, not just in words.

Enter Attendants with the corpses of Eteokles and Polyneikes.

(A3)   Now we can see the proof; his words are visible.
I see a double evil, double cause for grief –
self-killed, a double death, the crowning agony.   850
What can I say but 'torture at the very hearth of
        home'?
Dear friends, row down the wind of sighs,
striking around your heads the splash of oars to
        speed
them on their way, music that always crosses Acheron,
sending the black-sailed sacred ship to land
upon the shore the god of Healing never sees,
the dark place where we all must go.   860

1. W (B1)   Misguided ones, you did not listen   875
               to your friends; disaster did not weary you,
               wretched men who sacked
               your father's house with violent spear.

W   Yes, wretched – and you found a wretched death
         sharing your house.   880

1. W (B2)   Yes, you destroyed your house,
               and reaped disaster for the kingship. Now
               you have been reconciled with iron.

W   The sovereign Fury of your father Oidipous
         made his curses all too true.

1. W (C1)   Struck down from the left,
               struck down through the ribs,
               born of the same mother.   890
               Oh, the daimôn's
               curses causing death on death.

W   That blow pierced through
         the household as it pierced their bodies.
         Their silent fury
         and their father's curse
         met in one fate.

1. W (C2)   The mourning spreads right through the city; 900
               towers weep, and plains
               that loved them dearly. Thebes is still here
               – for which they fought,
               for which they died a cruel death.

W   Sharp-hearted, they split up their goods
         so each got equal shares.
         We are their friends. We blame
         the god of war, their referee;
         he is not dear to us.   910

1. W (D1)   Iron-struck, that's how they are;
               and iron-struck there wait for them
               – so you might say –
               spade-shares in their ancestral grave.
1. W   The ritual lament for slaughter sounds,
           sends them to burial.
           It feels the pain itself; its cry is

terrible and horrible, and draws
tears from my heart, which shrivels up as I   920
weep for these two dead kings.

1. w (D2)   We can say about these two poor men
that they did many things – to their own people
and the lines of foreign troops they brought,
many destroyed in combat.
1. w   Their mother was unfortunate
beyond all women
who have borne children;
she made her son
her husband, bore these two
who've died like this,   930
killing each other with hands
from the same seed.

1. w (E1)   From the same seed – completely destroyed,
parting as enemies
in maddened strife,
as their dispute came to its end.
1. w   Their hatred is over; in the earth
their lives are mingled in the flow
of gore, and they are truly now one blood.   940
Bitter the solver of strife, the Black Sea
stranger forged from fire,
the sharpened Iron; bitter the war-god,
evil divider of spoils – he made
their father's curse come true.

1. w (E2)   Poor men, they have their lot,
because of suffering imposed by Zeus;
under their bodies will lie
the bottomless wealth of the earth.   950
1. w   You crowned your house
with many flowers of misery.
Finally the Curses cried
the victory-song over a family
completely routed;
Blind Destruction's victory-monument is fixed

before the gates where they were stricken, and
the daimôn, now he's conquered both of them,
has ceased his rage.   960

Now the lament is tossed rapidly between individuals.

1. W (E3)   You struck and were struck
1. W   You killed and died
1. W   killed with a spear
1. W   died with a spear
1. W   terrible deed
1. W   terrible fate
1. W   you lie there
1. W   you killed
1. W   groan
1. W   weep!

1. W (F1)   Oh!
1. W   Oh!
1. W   Mind maddened by misery
1. W   heart weeping
1. W   poor man
1. W   wretched man   970
1. W   your brother killed you
1. W   you killed your brother.
1. W   two terrible deeds
1. W   two terrible sights
1. W   such awful suffering
1. W   brother fallen on brother.
W   Terrible fate with hideous gifts,
          powerful shade of Oidipous,
          black Fury, truly your strength is great.

1. W (F2)   Oh!
1. W   Oh!
1. W   horrible to see
1. W   what he brought back to me from exile
1. W   he didn't come back home; he killed   980
1. W   so when he came he lost his life.
1. W   Yes, lost it
1. W   killed his brother

1. w   pitiful deed
1. w   horrible sight
1. w   horrible kindred pain
1. w   triple suffering.
w   Terrible fate with hideous gifts,
          powerful shade of Oidipous,
          black Fury, truly your strength is great.

1. w (F3)   You know her power; you felt it
1. w   you learnt it when he did   990
1. w   when you came back to the city
1. w   and you raised your spear against him.
1. w   Wretched family
1. w   wretched fate
1. w   Oh torment
1. w   Oh disaster
1. w   for the house
1. w   and the land
1. w   Oh for your sufferings, my king
1. w   Oh for your sufferings, exiled lord
1. w   Oh most unfortunate in all you did.   1000
1. w   Oh possessed by madness
1. w   Oh, where shall we bury them?
1. w   Oh – where they will have most honour.
1. w   Oh, the pain, to lie beside their father.

*Exeunt left Attendants with the corpses of Eteokles and Poly-
neikes, followed by the Women of Thebes.*

SUPPLIANTS

THE ACTORS AND THEIR ROLES

The Suppliants, daughters of Danaos   Choros

Danaos   Actor 2

Pelasgos, King of Argos   Actor 1

Herald   Actor 2

Argive Soldiers   Silent Faces, later
Supplementary Choros

Aigyptian Soldiers   Silent Faces

Preset an altar BC, surrounded by statues and emblems of the twelve gods, placed to left and right of it along the rear perimeter of the orchêstra.

CHOROS I

Enter the Suppliants right, carrying suppliant wands.

1. SUPPLIANT   Zeus god of suppliants look down with
        favour
    on this group of women who've sailed here
    from fine-sanded foremouths of
    Nile. We left a land
    sacred to Zeus, the pastures next to Syria,
    not through expulsion for blood-crime,
    condemned by public vote,
    but by our own choice fleeing men
    because we will not tolerate an impious
    marriage with Aigyptos' sons.   10
    Danaos our father planned this revolt;
    he played our game this way, and claimed
    it as the best of several ills –
    to fly without restraint across the waves
    and land in Argos, our ancestral home,
    descendants of the gadfly-driven
    cow through touch and breath of life
    from Zeus.

1. S   So is there any other land which we could
    rather hope will favour us,   20
    arriving only with the weapons of a suppliant –
    branches of olive wreathed in wool?

Oh native daimones of Argos;
gods most high, and lords
of heavy vengeance in the earth, who own
this city, land, and crystal waters,
and Zeus – third, Saviour, guardian of the homes
of pious men – receive this group of female
    suppliants
with reverent, favourable winds. As for the violent
    swarm   30
of men, Aigyptos' sons,
before they set their feet from their fast boat
upon this marshy land, send them
into the sea! And there,
struck by a storm, by thunder, lightning,
wind and rain and savage seas,
may they be killed before they come
into our beds to which they have no right,
stealing their uncle's children,
against our will.

S (A1)   I call upon the calf of Zeus   40
from far beyond the sea to succour us;
the offspring of my ancestor, the cow
who grazed on flowers, by breath and touch of Zeus;
the due time was completed perfectly when she
gave birth and named her child Epaphos – 'laying on of
    hands'.

  (A2)   Him I have chosen now as here,
among the meadows where his mother once   50
fed on the grass, I call to mind her sufferings
and show proofs now which will surprise
the people here;
all will be known when I unfold my tale.

  (B1)   If anyone is near who knows the song
of birds and listens to my cries,
he'll think he hears the voice   60
of the unhappy wife of Tereus – Metis,
hawk-chased nightingale

(B2)   who, driven near green rivers, grieves
          for places where she lived,
          and sings the story of her son's
          death, how he was destroyed
          by kindred murder, at her hands,
          in terrifying mother-fury.

(C1)   So I indulge my grief here
          in Greek pastures, and I rend   70
          my soft and sunbrowned cheek
          and heart not used to misery.
          I feed upon the flowers of sorrow,
          fearing there may not be a guardian for
          these friendless exiles from
          the Misty Land.

(C2)   Ancestor gods, you see what's just – now hear me
          well;
          if you do not, against my fate,   80
          let them fulfil their manhood in the wedding-rites,
          but truly hate their violence,
          then I could have a marriage which is right.
          Even for weary refugees from war
          an altar where the gods are reverenced
          grants protection.

(D1)   May Zeus make sure all this comes true.   92
          What he desires is hard
          to hunt down, for the paths
          inside his understanding stretch
          through thick and shady woods
          and they seem infinite.   95

(D2)   It falls out safe, not on its back,   91
          if some deed's been
          perfected by the nod of Zeus;
          its flame shines everywhere   88
          with black misfortune for
          poor human kind.

(E1)   He hurls men down to be destroyed   96
from their high battlements of hope,
though he needs no armed force,
since gods do all things easily.   100
He sits upon his sacred throne
and he fulfils his thought
from there in ways we cannot know.

(E2)   So he should look down on this violence –
how pursuing us has given new life to
the stock of Belos. It has grown
new shoots – demented hearts,
goaded by mad desire which cannot
be escaped, deluded into paths   110
of self-destruction.

(F1)   I tell these pitiable, shrill and heavy
sufferings with cries
(Ah, Ah!)
conspicuous among songs of lament;
while still alive I sing for my own funeral.
        I call upon the hills of Argos –
        you can understand my foreign speech;
        I tear and tear and rend my fine-spun   120
        linen veil.

(F2)   But when life's going well, and death is far
away, the gods may intervene.
(Oh, Oh!)
I hate uncertainty!
Where will this wave drive us?
        I call upon the hills of Argos –
        you can understand my foreign speech;   130
        I tear and tear and rend my fine-spun
        linen veil.

(G1)   The oar-blade, and the flax-bound
timber which wards off the foam,
brought me upon the wind
without a storm, and I am grateful.
Zeus, father who sees all,

grant us in time
a favourable outcome.   140
    We are the offspring of a great
    and holy mother; gods, grant we escape
    unmarried, unsubdued
    from beds of men.

(G2)   May the pure daughter of the greatest god
look willingly on me as I need her.
Her solemn face provides security;
may she use all her strength
to save us from pursuit.
She is a virgin; so are we.   150
    We are the offspring of a great
    and holy mother; gods, grant we escape
    unmarried, unsubdued
    from beds of men.

(H1)   If not, then we –
a black and sunburnt race –
will go and supplicate
the god below the earth
(he gladly welcomes everyone);
Hades, the Zeus among the dead.
We'll hang ourselves, if the Olympians   160
don't help.
    Oh Zeus, Io –
    the anger of the gods found her.
    I know about the fury of a wife that won
    the battle up above. First the fierce wind,
    and then the storm.

(H2)   Could Zeus not be assailed
by just reproaches, if
he does not pay respect to Epaphos,   170
the offspring of the cow
and his own son –
if his eyes turn away
from our appeal?
Hear from on high; we call on you!
    Oh Zeus, Io –

the anger of the gods found her.
I know about the fury of a wife that won
the battle up above. First the fierce wind,
and then the storm.

SCENE I

Enter Danaos, left.

DANAOS   Children, we need to think; and you have come with
      one who can –
   this trusty old man, your sea-captain and father.
   Now we're on land; I've thought ahead, and I advise
   you to remember and take care of what I say.
   I see some dust, an army's silent messenger;   180
   the wheel-hubs sound as axles make them move –
   and I can see a mass of men with shields and spears,
   with horses and curved chariots.
   It's probable the rulers of this land
   have heard from messengers about us,
   and are coming here to see.
   So – whether they are friendly, or this force
   was sent against us sharpened to a savage rage –
   it's better every way, my daughters, if
   you take up refuge on this mound shared by the gods.
   An altar's better than a citadel – a shield that can't be
      broken.   190
   So come now, take the white-crowned wands
   of supplication, ornaments for Zeus the god of reverence,
   hold them solemnly in your left hands
   and with these strangers you must talk as suppliants
      should;
   show reverence and need, pour sorrows out
   and make it plain that you are exiles but have not shed
      blood.
   Your voice must have no hint of boldness,
   nothing wild; your faces must look sensible
   and in your eyes there must be calm.
   Do not become too forward in your speech,   200
   nor drag it out (these Greeks find that especially

offensive); and defer. You are
a foreigner in need of refuge, and
the weaker party should not speak emboldened words.

1. S   Father, you've spoken thoughtfully
to daughters who can think; may Zeus the father
see I won't forget your careful words.

DAN   Yes, may he look on us with gracious eyes.
Don't wait; command the means to make him so.

1. S   Yes, I think we should sit near you.
Oh Zeus, look down and pity us,
do not let us be utterly destroyed.

DAN   If he so wishes, this will come out well.   211
So now call on this eagle, Zeus' sacred bird.

1. S   We call upon the sunlight now to rescue us.

DAN   And on Apollo, pure god once exiled from heaven.

1. S   He knows this fate, and he will pity us.

DAN   Yes, may he pity us and stand beside us in support.

1. S   Which other gods should we call on?

DAN   I see a trident here, the emblem of the sea-god.

1. S   Yes, he brought us here; may he receive us now.

DAN   This other one is Hermes, as the Greeks portray him. 220

1. S   May he bring us good news, that we are free.

DAN   Now worship at the altar common to these kings
and queens, and sit inside this sacred place like doves
swarming in fear for refuge from those hawks,
the kindred who are enemies, defilers of the family.
How can bird eat bird, and claim purity?
How can a bridegroom take a girl against her will
from an unwilling father, and be undefiled? Not even when
   he's dead,
in Hades, could he flee the charge of outrage;
there, it's said, another Zeus surveys   230
our wrongdoings among the dead, and makes the final
   judgment.
Consider, and reply in some such way,
so your needs may win out in this affair.

Enter King Pelasgos left, with Argive Soldiers.

PELASGOS   What kind of group is this – not clothed like
   Greeks

but in fine linen clothes and headbands; an exotic garb!
What should I call you? This is not what Argive women
wear; you don't come from anywhere in Greece.
You reached this land unharmed, without the help
of heralds, or ambassadors or guides;
how did you dare to come? That is most marvellous.   240
At least beside you, following the custom for newcomers,
I see wands at the common altar of the gods; in this
alone I might imagine you are Greek.
As for the rest, I could make many further guesses now,
if there were not a person here to tell me with her voice.

I. S   You are quite right about our clothes.
Do I address in you a private citizen,
a warden with a sacred staff, or leader of the city?

PEL   You can reply and speak with confidence to me.
I am the son of Palaichthon, sprung from the Earth –   250
Pelasgos, ruler of this land;
those who cultivate its crops
are rightly called Pelasgoi, after me.
I rule the entire region through which Strymon's pure
and holy waters flow, on the side nearer to the setting sun;
I mark out as my boundaries the land of the Perrhaiboi,
    and
the country on the other side of Pindos, near Paionia,
and mountains round Dodona; there the border is cut
    short
by waters of the sea. I rule out to those marks.

The plain where we are now is called the Apian land   260
from long ago, after a man of healing.
A prophet-healer once came here from Naupaktos –
Apis, the son of lord Apollo, and he cleared
this land from man-devouring monsters, which
the Earth, polluted by the blood of ancient murders,
had let loose; hostile snakes, grim residents.
Apis cut herbs to cure the Argives, freed this land
from plague, and took no fee; he found
an everlasting memory in Argive prayers.   270
Now you have all this evidence from me, and you
should tell me who you boast to be; speak out – though in
this city we do not prefer long speech.

1. S   Our word is clear and simple; we tell you
we're Argive, and descended from the cow
whose son was royal. This is true, and I will prove it now.

PEL   Strangers, your words cannot be true;
how can you be from Argos?
You seem much more like Libyans
and not at all like natives of this place.   280
The Nile could have engendered such a race;
and I am told that Indian nomads' girls
ride round on camels fast as horses –
neighbours of the Aithiopians.
There are Amazones – who have no men, and feast on meat;
if you were armed with arrows, I'd have thought that you
were similar to them. You'd better teach me, so I can know
    more,
how you could be of Argive race and seed.   290

1. S   They say that in this land of Argos once
Io was Hera's priestess and her temple-guardian.

PEL   Indeed she was; such is the universal tale.

1. S   There is a story that Zeus slept with her.

PEL   Yes; Hera did not know of their affair.

1. S   You're right so far; let us go on.

PEL   What end came of this conflict between king and queen?

1. S   The Argive goddess turned the girl into a cow.

PEL   Did Zeus still meet with her now she had graceful
horns?   300

1. S   They say he did, shaped like a bull to mate with cows.

PEL   What did the powerful wife of Zeus do then?

1. S   She put upon the cow a guard who can see everything.

PEL   What do you mean? Who was this magic cowherd for a
single cow?

1. S   Argos, son of the Earth, whom Hermes killed.

PEL   What else did she devise to hurt this miserable cow?

1. S   She sent a cattle-driver who had wings.

PEL   You mean a fly to sting her, drive her on and on.

1. S   In Egypt it is known as the gadfly.

PEL   What you have told me sticks together with my story
here.   310

1. S   She went as far as Kanobos and Memphis.

PEL   He drove her that far from this land?

1. S   Yes, and Zeus' healing touch made her a mother.

PEL   Who do you claim was the cow's calf by Zeus?

I. S   Epaphos, named for the moment when Zeus seized Io.

PEL   [And who was Epaphos' child?]

I. S   Libye, who reaps a harvest greater than all other lands.

PEL   Can you tell me of any child of hers?

I. S   Belos, who had two children – one of them my father
       here.

PEL   Now let me know his wise and splendid name.   320

I. S   He is Danaos; his brother has fifty sons.

PEL   Do not begrudge me further speech; disclose his name.

I. S   Aigyptos. Now you know my family descent,
       you should receive us into your protection as Argives.

PEL   I think you share our land from long
       ago; but how did you gain courage to depart
       your native country? What misfortune fell on you?

I. S   Lord Pelasgos, human torments come in many colours;
       trouble's feathers never shine the same.
       Whoever would have thought that we,   330
       your former kindred, would land far away in Argos,
       roused to flight by hatred of the marriage-bed?

PEL   What do you ask me in the name of these
       assembled gods, with new-cut wool-bound olive branches?

I. S   Not to let me become the slave of Aigyptos' sons.

PEL   Is it because you hate them, or is such a marriage
       impious?

I. S   What woman would reject a man she loves?

PEL   [Men have some right to take the woman whom they
       want.

I. S   How do you think we could agree with that?]

PEL   Even a loveless marriage can give greater power –

I. S   but it is easy to abandon women in their misery.

PEL   How can I treat you with due reverence?   340

I. S   Do not give us back to Aigyptos' sons.

PEL   You ask a heavy thing – to start new war.

I. S   Justice protects her allies –

PEL   only if she has always shared in the affair.

I. S   This altar with its garlands heads the ship of state;
       respect it now.

PEL   I tremble as I see the gods' seats shaded by your
       wands,
       and Zeus' anger weighs down on the side of suppliants.

s (A1)   Son of Palaichthon, listen to me;
               grant your favour, king of Argos.
               See me, the suppliant chased into exile
               like a calf, wolf-hunted up to   350
               craggy rocks where she – trusting
               that refuge – bleats out loud
               to tell the herdsman of her plight.

PEL   I see a company of suppliants before
      our gods, shaded by new-cut boughs.
      Here are some strangers who are citizens. May their affair
      bring no disaster; may these unexpected new events
      not lead my city into strife it does not need.

s (A2)   Yes; may the Right of suppliants, daughter of Zeus,
               make sure our flight brings no disaster.   360
               Old in wisdom, you must learn
               from one who's younger;
               if you respect a suppliant, you will not
               be poor; the gods receive
               a good man's offerings.

PEL   You do not sit as suppliants beside
      my hearth alone; if pollution falls on all
      the city, it should be the people's task to find a cure.
      I would not make a pledge to you before,
      but only when I've taken counsel with the citizens.

s (B1)   You are the city, you are the people.   370
               A lord subjected to no scrutiny,
               you rule the altar of this country's central hearth,
               with just one vote – your own assent;
               and sitting with one sceptre on one throne
               you decide everything; now ward away pollution.

PEL   Pollution – may it fall upon my enemies.
      I cannot help you now without some harm,
      nor is it sensible to disregard your prayers.
      I'm at a loss; fear grips my heart
      whether I act, or don't, and take my chance.   380

s (B2)   Look up and see the watcher from above,
               the guardian of suffering humans who
               take refuge and do not receive
               the justice they deserve. Zeus is the god
               of suppliants; his anger stays, and cannot be
               assuaged by tears.

PEL   Suppose under our city's laws Aigyptos' sons
        say they as next of kin own you;
        who'd want to make a counter-claim?
        You'd have to plead that your own country's laws   390
        give them no legal right to you.
S   (C1)   I never will be subject to the hands
        and power of men! I would fly off
        up to the stars to flee
        this hateful marriage.
        Take Justice as your ally, make the choice
        the gods revere.
PEL   The judgment is not easy; do not make me be the
        judge.
     I've told you once before, I would not act in this
     without the people, even though I rule; may they never say,
     if some disaster falls on us, 'Paying respect   400
     to strangers you destroyed your native land.'
S   (C2)   Zeus, guardian of kinship, watches us both;
        he can incline each way, and he assigns
        an unjust fate to wicked men, a righteous one to those
        who stay within the law; if they are weighed
        on equal terms, how could you suffer afterwards
        for doing what is just?
PEL   I need deep thought to save myself,
        plunge like a diver down into the depths
        sharp-sighted, sober, so that this affair
        brings no destruction on my city,   410
        and goes well for me; let battle-strife
        not seize our lands and goods! If we
        give you, established in this holy place, to them,
        we'll make the all-destroying god of Vengeance come –
        a heavy burden on the house; and he will not
        free traitors even down in Hades' realm.
        Do I not need some thought to save myself?

(CHOROS 2)

SUPPLIANTS (A1)   Yes, think – and then become a just
        and right protector; you must not
        betray the girl who's fled,   420

driven out far away
by impious pursuers;

(A2)   you must not see me
dragged out from this holy place.   430
You are all-powerful in Argos – recognize
the violence of those men, and fear
the anger of the gods.

(B1)   You could not suffer seeing me, a suppliant,
hauled by my finely woven headband
like a horse, unjustly, from the statues,
violent hands grasping my clothes.

(B2)   Know that, whatever choice you make,
it will remain for your house
and your children; they must pay the dues in full.
Consider this. Zeus makes the just cause win.

PELASGOS   Indeed, I have considered – and my thoughts have
        run aground.
I have to undertake a mighty war with gods
or men. My ship is ready – firmly bolted,   440
held on shore by cables; but it cannot sail
to any port without some suffering,
if we set off with lethal goods on board.
When a house is plundered, lost possessions may
in time find some replacement, thanks
to Zeus the god of ownership:
when the tongue shoots wrongly, other words
can heal the wound made by the word;
but kindred bloodshed must not happen;
sacrifice and offerings – many, to many gods, –   450
must first occur in an attempt to ward off pain.
So now I stand aside from this dispute.
I'd rather be a man of ignorance than schooled
in hardships. May this turn out well – though I think it
        won't!
I. S   Now hear the end of all these solemn words.
PEL   I'm listening, so tell me; it will not escape.
I. S   I'm wearing bands which hold my clothing tight.

PEL   Such as a woman usually wears.

I. S   And they suggest an excellent device.

PEL   Tell me; what do you wish to say?   460

I. S   If you don't give us some firm pledge –

PEL   What will you do with your waistbands?

I. S   These images will gain new ornaments.

PEL   You speak in riddles; tell me clearly what you mean.

I. S   We'll hang ourselves at once from them.

PEL   I hear a word that strikes my heart.

I. S   Good – now I've made you understand.

PEL   So this affair is hard to wrestle with.

The mass of troubles comes against me in full flood;
unfathomable seas of evil which cannot be crossed   470
– that's where I am, without a harbour.
If I do not give you your just deserts
you've threatened a pollution which I cannot overshoot;
but then, if I stand up against your kinsmen, the Aigyptioi,
and fight before our city walls,
how could the reckoning not be a bitter one,
if men's blood stains the earth for women's sake?
Still, I must bow before the wrath of Zeus
the god of suppliants, the greatest power that human beings
    fear.
Now you, Danaos, father of these girls,   480
must take these wands up in your arms at once,
and on the other altars of our country's gods
place them at once, so all the citizens can see the evidence
that you have come for refuge, and no idle rumours circulate
against us; people often like to blame their leaders.
They'll see these symbols of your cry for help,
and might then hate the violence of those men;
the people would be more inclined to favour you,
since most give their goodwill to underdogs.

DANAOS   Of many things we value this the most,   490
to find in need a champion who shows reverence.
Now – send attendants with me, who can give advice about
local conditions, so I can find
the altars and the temples of the city gods,
and I may walk in safety round
the town; we do not look the same as you.
Aigyptians don't resemble Argives;

do not let my confidence turn into fear –
for even friends have been killed by mistake.
PEL   The foreigner is right – so go, my men.   500
Lead him to altars and the temples of our city gods;
but do not speak too much with those you meet, as you convey
this suppliant to sit before our gods.

*Exeunt Danaos and some Argive Soldiers left, with some of the
suppliant wands.*

1. S   You've spoken to my father; he goes to his place.
But I – how should I act? What confidence can you give me?
PEL   First leave your olive branches there – the symbol of your
suffering.
1. S   I leave them here, handmaiden to your words.

The Suppliants begin to come out into the orchêstra.

PEL   Now move towards this sacred grove.
1. S   But how could that be safe for me?
PEL   We will not give you up as prey to birds.   510
1. S   – or to the hatred of those hostile snakes?
PEL   You have sacred protection; do not speak ill-omened
words.
1. S   It is no wonder I'm depressed; I'm scared.
PEL   The helpless always show immoderate fear.
1. S   Then give me confidence by words – and deeds.
PEL   Your father will not leave you here for long.
I'll go and gather up the people of this land,
so I can have their full assembly on our side,
and I will teach your father what he needs to say.
So wait here, and implore the gods   520
with prayers for all that you desire;
I'll go, and do what I have said; I hope Persuasion
will be with me and Good Fortune, the accomplisher.

Exit Pelasgos left, followed by the remaining Argive Soldiers.

CHOROS 3

SUPPLIANTS (A1)   King of kings, most blessed
    of the blessed ones, most perfect
    of all perfect powers, Zeus god of riches;
    hear us, and shield your daughters from
    male violence which you truly hate;
    hurl their black-thwarted, evil ship
    into the sea's depths!   530

  (A2)   Look what is on the female side
    – our race's origin, as told in
    ancient legend; since you loved that woman, now
    you should renew your promises of kindness.
    Healer of Io, remember us; we boast
    we are of Zeus' race,
    descended from an Argive.

  (B1)   I have come back upon an ancient path,
    my mother's flower-browsings under guard –
    the cow-pasture from which Io,   540
    forced by the gadfly to move on,
    fled maddened
    through the haunts of many men.
    Then she, in terrible distress,
    swam right across the storm-tossed channel,
    and she marked a boundary for Asia
    – Bosporos, the cow-crossing.

  (B2)   She rushes on through Asia,
    right across the Trojan sheepland,
    passes by the city of the Mysian
    Teuthras, the vales of Lydia,   550
    mountains of Kilikia,
    flies across the land
    of the Pamphylians – ever-flowing rivers,
    deep, rich soil; then Aphrodite's
    fertile corn-land.

  (C1)   A new track carries her to Egypt, stung
    by her winged herdsman

– fruitful grove sacred to Zeus,
land nourished by snow,
through which there flows   560
the clear pure water of the Nile –
maddened by her unworthy punishment,
agonizing gadfly-bites;
the goddess Hera's mainad.

(C2)   The people living there,
shaking in bile-green terror
at the fearful sight,
saw that distressing animal
– part woman, partly cow –
and were amazed.   570
Who cured her then,
Io who'd suffered much and wandered
bitten by the gadfly?

(D1)   The god who rules for ever
made her stop,
with painless violence
and by his breath; he made
her cry away her shame
in grief and tears.
Then she conceived and bore a perfect child   580
who was in truth the son of Zeus,

(D2)   and had a long and happy life;
because of that all Egypt shouts aloud
these are the true descendants of
the life-giver, lord Zeus.
Who else could have stopped sufferings
which Hera had imposed?
This is the work of Zeus; if you say we
are Epaphos' children you will hit the mark.

(E1)   Which of the gods could I   590
more justly call?
Our forefather, who made us with his hand,
the king, the long-wise maker of our race,
contriver of all things, god of fair winds.

(E2)   He speeds ahead unchecked;
          no one has greater power.
          He does not worship from below some other force
          which sits on high. He can do deeds as fast as words;
          which of these things has not been brought by Zeus' will?

SCENE 2

Enter Danaos, left.

DANAOS   Take courage, children; we have done well with the
          people here;   600
          the citizens have voted with their full authority.
1. SUPPLIANT   Greetings, my father: you bring me news dear
          to my heart;
          please tell us what the outcome is, which way
          the sovereign hands of the majority were raised.
DAN   The Argives never wavered, and
          their choice made my old heart grow young again.
          The air was bristling with their hands
          as they unanimously voted this decree;
          that we should be free settlers living here
          immune from seizure of our persons or our property.   610
          Then no one – whether citizen or foreigner – may take us off
          as slaves; if we're attacked by force,
          a citizen of Argos who does not help us
          will lose his civic rights, expelled by public vote.
          Such was the speech about us which the king
          used to persuade them – warning of the mighty power
          of Zeus the god of suppliants, which would grow
          through time; we are – he said – Argives as well as
          foreign suppliants, so double the pollution would appear
          in front of Argos – evils nourished to beyond a cure.   620
          When they heard this, the people voted
          with their hands, unprompted, that it should be so.
          Pelasgos' citizens accepted what he said, swayed by
          his speech; and Zeus confirmed the outcome.

Exit Danaos, right.

CHOROS 4

1. SUPPLIANT   Come, let us pronounce a prayer for good
        to fall upon the Argives, in return for good.
        Zeus god of suppliants guide what we sing to them
        after our journey, so we win their favour.

S (A1)   Gods, children of Zeus,   630
        listen as I pour out
        invocations for my native land;
        never may the city of the Argives
        be destroyed by fire –
        the song unfit for dance, the wanton
        cries of Ares, god of war,
        who reaps a crop of human lives
        in fields others have sown
            – because they pitied us,
            and voted kindly,   640
            helped the suppliants of Zeus,
            this pitiable flock.

   (A2)   They did not vote
        on the male side,
        disparaging a woman's argument,
        because they looked at Zeus'
        avenging guardian –
        a bitter enemy
        no house can stand
        when it befouls the rooftop;   650
        heavy burden.
            They showed respect for us,
            the kindred suppliants of Zeus,
            and they will please the gods
            because their altars will be pure.

   (B1)   So let a prayer
        fly from our mouths
        to do them honour.
        Never may plague
        empty this city of its men;   660

may citizens not strike each other down
and shed their blood on Argos' plains;
> Ares the butcher,
> lover of the love-goddess,
> must not pick out the flower of youth
> and cut their finest down.

(B2)   Let the hearths blaze up,
tended with care
by worthy elders;
this is how the city will   670
be governed well – if all revere
great Zeus, the lord of strangers, highest god,
who by his ancient laws makes straight their destiny.
> We pray that they beget
> new leaders for the future.
> Artemis must guard
> the labour-pangs of women here.

(C1)   May no havoc rend
this city into pieces,
decimate their men,   680
arming Ares,
god bereft of music,
father of tears,
creating civil war.
> Let swarms of wretched illnesses
> settle away from them,
> and may the wolf-god not destroy
> the younger men.

(C2)   May Zeus fulfil
the harvest, bringing perfect fruits
in every season;   690
may he give them flocks
that multiply, and may they thrive
in everything the gods can give.
> Thanksgiving songs
> must be well omened –
> voice and lyre entwined
> in purity.

(D1)   The people rule the city,
         wise in counsel;
         they must keep their power intact!   700
         May they not injure strangers,
         but grant them fair settlement
         before the god of war is armed.

(D2)   Like their fathers, they must always pay
         the gods who own this land their dues,
         with laurel-branches and with oxen.
         The third command
         that mighty Justice has inscribed
         is reverence for parents.

SCENE 3

Enter Danaos, right.

DANAOS   These prayers are wise; I welcome them.   710
         Now do not be afraid, as I tell you
         some unexpected news.
         Here, from the look-out at the place of refuge,
         I can see the ship; it's very clear;
         the sail-braids, and the side-screens, and
         the prow, with eyes that see the course ahead,
         all too obedient to orders from the tiller at the stern.
         The men upon it have black limbs
         conspicuous in contrast to white clothes;   720
         and other ships, and their auxiliary troops,
         stand out clear, while the flagship furls
         her sails, and beating oars bring her to land.
         So you must quietly and calmly face
         what's happening – and don't forget these gods;
         I will return with helpers to defend your cause.
         Perhaps a herald or an embassy might come
         wanting to seize the prize and take you off –
         but that won't happen; do not be afraid of them.
         It would be better, if I'm slow in getting help,   730
         not ever to forget the strength this place can give.

Take courage; when the right day comes,
those who do not respect the gods will pay the penalty.

1. SUPPLIANT   Father, I am afraid, since swift-winged ships
      have come,
and there is no time now before our enemies are here.

S (A1)   I'm paralysed by fear, and do not know
      whether my flight will help me;
      Father, I am beside myself with fright.

DAN   Children, the Argive vote is binding;
be brave; I'm certain they will fight for you.   740

1. S   The ravening sons of Aigyptos are horrible
and they love battle, as you know.

S (A2)   They've sailed here in dark blue-eyed
      wooden ships with haste spurred on by rage,
      and with a huge black army.

DAN   They will encounter men, with arms
well toughened in the midday sun.

1. S   Just do not leave me here alone!
A woman on her own is helpless; we can't fight.

S (B1)   They're deadly, and deceitful, and   750
      impious; they're like crows, and do not pay
      regard to sacred altars.

DAN   That would work out quite well for us –
if they are hated by the gods as well as you.

1. S   They will not fear this trident, or the other symbols
of the gods, enough to keep their hands off us.

S (B2)   They're very arrogant, with godless strength –
      as ravenous as shameless dogs;
      they do not listen to the gods.

DAN   The saying is the wolf is stronger than the dog;   760
papyrus fruit will not beat sheaves of corn.

1. S   It also has a temper like reckless, impious beasts,
whose mastery we must avoid.

DAN   Putting a naval force to sea is not done easily,
nor is their anchoring; captains of ships
lack confidence when bringing cables from the stern
secure to land, riding at anchor, and especially
when they are landing on a shore without a port,
when sun sinks into night; the night
gives birth in a wise steersman to great agonies of care.   770
They cannot even disembark their troops

efficiently, until they have the courage to attack.
So you, despite your terror, must make sure
not to neglect the gods. I will return
when I have brought you help. The city will not fault
an old man's message; in both mind and voice I'm young.

Exit Danaos, left.

CHOROS 5

SUPPLIANTS (A1)   Oh sacred earth, land of the cow,
        what will we suffer? Where in Argos
        can we flee; is there a hiding place?
        Can I become black smoke
        up in the clouds near Zeus,   780
        and fly away invisible and wingless,
        like the dust that vanishes
        to nothing – and then die?

    (A2)   There is no more escape!
        My heart is quivering, black with fear.
        The ship my father saw has caught me, and
        I'm terrified. I'd rather meet my fate
        hung in a plaited noose, before a man
        I hate touches my flesh;   790
        sooner may Hades be our lord after our deaths!

    (B1)   Where could I find a resting place up in the
            sky,
        near which the snow turns into clouds of mist?
        Or else a slippery crag too steep for goats,
        too high to see – a vulture's rock,
        of solitary thought, which could bear witness
        to my fall into the depths before I'm forced
        into a marriage which will pierce my heart.

    (B2)   Then I would not object if I became   800
        a prey to dogs and birds;
        the dead are free
        from miseries that make the living weep.

Let death come quick, before I'm forced
to marry and have sex.
How can I cleave a path which sets
me free from marriage?

(CI)   Shriek out a great song –
prayers to heaven, to gods and goddesses –
but how will they be answered?   810
Father, look upon me with your gaze
of freedom and deliverance, and justly see
their violence with hostile eyes;
show the reverence due your suppliants,
all-powerful Zeus, lord of the Earth.

(C2)   The sons of Aigyptos, unbearable,
are hunting me, the fugitive,
with all the violence of the male
and lustful shouts; they mean   820
to take us all by force.
Yours is the scale of justice;
what is fulfilled for human kind
without your help?

SCENE 4

Enter Herald right, with Aigyptian Soldiers.

SUPPLIANTS   Ah . . . !
He's here to seize us
from the ship, now on the land;
you'll die before you do it.
HERALD   Come down at once
with us to the ship.
I. S   Now I shriek out
a miserable cry.
I know my fate;
I see this will mean trouble   830
for the man who protects me.
Ah . . . !

Flee to safety.
He revels in his savage heart
unbearable on land or sea.
Lord of this land, bring help!
HER   Go, go down to our ship
as quick as you can.
(*pause*)
Well then!
Tearing, tearing, branding;
pools of blood,   840
severed heads.
Go, go you bitches, down to our ship.

S (A1)   If only somewhere on
the ever-flowing salty sea
you could be dead
together with your vicious masters
and your boat.
HER   I'll get you on the ship
covered in blood.
Shut up, and cut your losses;
Stop this screaming;
suppress these desires   850
that make you sick;
your cries are useless.
Leave the altar, go towards the boat.
This city of the pious pays
you no respect.

S (A2)   I hope you never see again
the cattle-feeding river
which augments and swells
the blood of living creatures
to a rich and splendid life.
HER   I am a warrior, of power
and noble birth.   860
You will soon go onto the ship,
on the ship if you want to or don't;
for might is right, and you have lost.
Go then, you wretched nuisances –
helpless, delinquent, sexy girls.

s (b1)   Aiai!
        Die without hope of rescue, forced
        to wander on the sacred paths
        of ever-flowing sea,
        blown on Sarpedon's sandy spit   870
        by winds from Syria.
HER   I tell you now, go to our ship as fast
      as possible; let none of you be slow.
      Dragging will not show any reverence to your long
          hair.

s (b2)   Aiai!
        Outrage! Goddess of love, be merciful;
        Herald, you revel in your arrogance.
        May the great destroyer, Destiny,
        wreck you and utterly confound   880
        your reckless violence.
HER   Shriek, howl, call on the gods;
      you will not leap out from Aigyptos' ship.

s (c1)   Father, protection by your altar
        has destroyed me; now he leads me to the sea
        just like a spider, step by step; a black, black dream.
        Aaah!
        Mother Earth, Oh Mother Earth, I fear   890
        his violence; turn it away.
        Oh Father, son of Earth, Oh Zeus!
HER   I do not fear these gods.
      They did not nurture me, and I won't grow old here.

s (c2)   He's raging close to me – this double-footed
        snake; and like a viper now he stares at me.
        The beast is near,
        and I am petrified.
        Aaah!
        Mother Earth, Oh Mother Earth, I fear   900
        his violence; turn it away.
        Oh Father, son of Earth, Oh Zeus!
HER   If you do not give in and go now to the ships,
      the rending of your woven gowns will not be merciful.

The Herald and his soldiers now begin to seize the Suppliants.

S (D1)   Chiefs, leaders of the city, I am overpowered.
HER   It looks as if I'll have to drag you by the hair,
  since you have failed to listen carefully to what I say.   910

S (D2)   We are destroyed; lord of this land, we're suffering
      unspeakably.
HER   You will soon have a multitude of lords –
  Aigyptos' sons; be sure, you won't complain you're left in
  anarchy.

Enter Pelasgos and Argive Soldiers, left.

PELASGOS   You, what are you doing? What are you thinking
      of, that you
  pay such great disrespect to this, the land of the Pelasgians?
  Do you suppose you've reached a city with no men?
  For one from overseas, you act too freely in the face of
      Greeks;
  your mind has guided you awry, and you have erred in many
      ways.
HER   What error have I made? How have I strayed from
      justice?
PEL   You do not seem to know how strangers should behave.
HER   How? I have found possessions which were lost – and
      take them back.
PEL   Did you give notice to the relevant authorities in Argos?
HER   The greatest of authorities; Hermes, the searcher.   920
PEL   You told the gods, but show them no respect.
HER   I worship all the gods who live beside the Nile.
PEL   And ours are nothing – so I hear from you.
HER   I'll take these girls unless I'm robbed of them.
PEL   You'll suffer, if you touch them – not for very long.
HER   I hear you; you are not at all friendly to strangers.
PEL   I don't respect a stranger who steals from the gods.
HER   I'll go and tell the sons of Aigyptos all this.
PEL   That's not a thought which worries me.
HER   Then – so I know, and can tell openly   930
  (for it's a herald's job to relay everything
  quite clearly) – I'm going back without this group of women,

their own cousins; how and by whom was I deprived of
   them?
The god of war won't arbitrate by calling
witnesses, nor will our quarrel be resolved
by paying silver; many men must fall
before the end, and kick away their lives.

PEL   Why should I speak my name? You'll learn it
in good time – you and your fellow-travellers.
As for these women; if persuaded by some reverent
   words,   940
willing and friendly, you could take them back.
It is the people's will, expressed in a unanimous
decree of Argos, never to let go by force
this company of women; and a nail is driven clear
right through, so it will stay fixed.
What I say is not written down on wooden
tablets, or sealed up in folds of papyrus,
but you have heard clear words, all uttered by
a tongue that has free speech. Get out of sight – right now.

HER   Know this will make new wars for you;   950
may victory and power go to the men!

PEL   You will find the people here
are real men; they don't drink beer.

Exeunt Herald and Aigyptian Soldiers, right.

I offer you an escort of goodwill;
take courage, go into our city; it's well fortified,
barred up by mighty bastions.
Inside are many homes owned by the people; also,
I myself am not exactly poorly housed.
You could share well-appointed rooms
with other people; or, if you prefer,   960
you could live on your own, in your own ways.
You have the choice to do what's best,
and to your liking; choose! I myself am your protector;
so is every citizen whose hand fulfilled
this vote. Why wait for any greater power than ours?

CHOROS 6

1. SUPPLIANT   For your good deeds may you grow rich
                with goodness, divine king of the Pelasgians!
                Please send our father Danaos to us
                full of courageous zeal; he's wise, and he   970
                advises us. He should be
                first to think
                where we should make our home.
                Even if a city's friendly, people tend
                to gossip about foreigners; but still,
                may the best happen!

Exit Pelasgos with Argive Soldiers, left.

1. S   Let us go with good fortune, and may
              the people meet us free from all
              hostility. . . .

SCENE 5

Enter Danaos, escorted by Argive Soldiers, left.

DANAOS   Children, we must give thanks to all the Argives: 980
          sacrifice to them, and pour libations as if they were gods,
          since they have been steadfast and saved us.
          I told them what was happening; and they were well
              disposed
          towards you as their kin, but very bitter at the cousins.
          They have given me this bodyguard,
          so I might have a privilege and mark of their esteem
          – and not die unexpectedly killed by a spear,
          and be a burden on this land for evermore,
          nor be abducted by the sons of Aigyptos.
          We have had such great good fortune, we
          must thank them from the bottom of our hearts.   990

          Now, carve these new thoughts in your minds
          to add to all your father's other wisdom, since

it takes some time to test and trust the worth of foreigners.
Everyone keeps a hostile tongue ready for use
on new settlers, and it is easy to express distaste.
So I now ask you not to bring disgrace on me,
since you are young and turn men's heads.
The tender, ripened fruits cannot be guarded perfectly;
they are devoured by beast and man; what else?
The love-goddess makes proclamation to   1000
all winged birds, and animals that walk the earth,
to pluck the fruits of love, and softens up
the unripe fruit to drive them mad; so everyone
who comes near to the beauty of a shapely girl
shoots out an arrow of enchantment, overcome by his desire.
We must not suffer anything from which
we struggled to escape, and travelled far over the sea;
do nothing which will shame us, and might make my enemies
rejoice. We have a choice of lodgings, since
Pelasgos offers one, the citizens another   1010
place to live, and both are free from rent; no problem there.
Only, you must remember what your father's said;
value your chastity far more than life itself.

1. s The gods on high will make us prosper in all else;
as for my 'ripeness', father, lay your fears to rest.
Unless the gods have some new plan,
my mind will not be turned back from its present course.

FINALE

1. SUPPLIANT (A1)   Now go to the city,
    glorify its blessed gods –
    the city lords, and those who live   1020
    around the ancient stream Erasinos.
    Attendants, hear our song;
    we will now praise this city, Argos,
    and no longer reverence
    the Nile in any of our words,

1. s (A2)   only rivers which pour out
    their gentle draught throughout this land
    full of fertility, and propitiate

this earth with their smooth waters.
Holy Artemis, look down on us   1030
with pity. We must not be forced
to marry; may such weddings
lead to death.

1. ARGIVE SOLDIER (B1)   To honour Kypris – that
    command
is wise; for she, with Hera, is the next in power to Zeus,
and she, deceitful god of love,
is honoured; all her deeds have sacred power.
Her loving children help her; sexual
Longing, and that magical
Persuasion to which nothing is denied.   1040
Aphrodite has a share in Harmony
and love-cries, and the touch of flesh on flesh.

1. ARG (B2)   For the fugitives from love's hot breath I
    fear
both sufferings and bloody wars;
why did the cousins sail
so fast in their pursuit?
When something's destined, it will happen:
Zeus' mighty, endless will
cannot be crossed;
like other women in the past,   1050
perhaps you will be married too.

1. S (C1)   Great Zeus, do not let me
be married to Aigyptos' sons.
1. ARG   It might be best.
1. S   You will not make me change.
1. ARG   You do not know the future.

1. S (C2)   How could I see into the mind
of Zeus? It is unfathomable.
1. ARG   Utter moderate prayers.
1. S   What should I choose?   1060
1. ARG   Not to ask too much from the gods.

s (D1)   May Zeus the lord withhold
              from us a marriage to
              an enemy, a man I hate,
              since he freed Io from her torments,
              checking her with healing hand,
              and brought her to a gentle life.

   (D2)   And may he give the victory to
              the women! I will be content to have
              the better share of evils – at the most two-thirds;   1070
              let Justice follow my just cause, according to
              my prayers for freedom and
              whatever means the god contrives.

Exeunt Suppliants, Danaos and Argive Soldiers, left.

FRAGMENTS

PART ONE: TRAGIC DRAMAS

1 Archer-Maidens

A drama about the fate of Aktaion. The 'Archer-Maidens' were a choros of nymphs, attendants of Artemis in her role as goddess of hunting. The context of this quotation is not clear in the source.

> In maidens who are pure, and do not know
> the marriage-bed, the eyes' darts fall to earth in reverence;
> but I don't ever fail to mark the burning gaze
> of a young woman who has tasted men:
> my sense is keen enough to know such things.

2 and 3 Bone Gatherers

A drama based on the closing phases of the story told by Homer in the Odyssey. *Both fragments come from Odysseus' speech about the dead suitors.*

2

ODYSSEUS   Here lies Eurymedon, who also wounded me
> beyond all justice with his violence;
> his target always was my head,
> and with his arm bent he made many throws;
> his hand was young and he aimed true.

3

> There is the man who once made them all laugh;
> he hurled at me an evil-smelling chamber pot.
> It did not miss, but crashed around my head,

was broken into shards, and breathed
a smell upon me very different from a perfume-jar.

4 *Children of Herakles*

A description of Herakles' tenth labour, fetching the cattle of
Geryon. The golden bowl was lent to him by Helios, the sun-
god; see fragment 7.

> . . . when he left there
> he crossed the ocean in a golden bowl, and drove
> the straight-horned cattle from the farthest part of earth,
> slew the foul herdsmen and their triple-bodied master
> Geryon – who wielded three spears in his three right hands,
> put forward three shields in his lefts, and shook three helmet-
>   crests;
> when he advanced, he was as strong as Ares.

5 and 6 *Danaides*

The third drama of the Suppliants *trilogy.*

5
DANAOS (?)   And then the clear light of the sunrise comes,
while I, singing the morning song with boys and girls,
awake the bridegrooms who are well disposed to us.

6
APHRODITE   . . . The sacred Heaven yearns to penetrate the
    Earth,
and Earth itself is yearning for the wedding too;
desire makes showers of love fall down from Heaven,
impregnate the Earth; then she gives birth
to food for flocks and to Demeter's gifts for all
mankind. The moisture of this marriage makes the trees
grow perfect fruits. Of all these things I am the cause.

7 *Daughters of Helios*

> . . . There
> in the west, your father's

bowl, made by Hephaistos,
on which he speeds across
the mighty, swelling stream which girdles Earth,
fleeing the dark of holy Night
black-horsed.

8 Edonians

This drama told how Dionysos and his exotic worshippers arrived among the Edonians. King Lykourgos opposed and expelled the god, who drove him mad; he killed his son. Dionysos then made the land barren until the Edonians put Lykourgos to death.

EDONIANS   ... practising the sacred rites of Kotyto ...
one, holding in his hands the pipe
turned by the lathe,
fingers the notes and fills the air
with melodies arousing frenzy.
Another with brass cymbals makes a clash
[. . . .]
... the plucked string cries aloud;
and bull-voicèd mimics
from the darkness bellow fearfully,
while the drum's echo rolls like thunderclaps
from far beneath the earth, profoundly terrifying.

9 Karians

This drama was also known by the alternative title Europa.

EUROPA   ... and in a fruitful meadow I gave loving welcome
to the bull.
Such was the trick which Zeus devised
to steal me from my agèd father effortlessly, standing still.
What then? I tell you my whole story in few words.
I had sex with a god, and passed from virgin radiance
to womanhood, united with the god who fathered all my
sons.
Three times I struggled, suffered all a woman's agonies;

that noble father's seed could not reproach the field he
   sowed,
that it did not bear fruit. My firstborn was
the greatest of my offspring,   10
Minos . . . .
. . . Rhadamanthos, my immortal son.
But life does not hold him within my eyes'
bright gleam, and absent relatives give no delight.
Third was the one who makes my mind storm-tossed with
   fear,
Sarpedon, lest the war-god's spear has struck him down.
There is a story that the flowers of the whole of Greece
have come, a company supreme in war-like strength,
and boast that they will sack the Trojan citadel by force.
That makes me fear lest, raging with his spear,   20
he may both do and suffer an unconquerable harm.
My hope is slender, and I stand upon the very edge;
I may be dashed against a reef and lose all that I have.

10, 11 and 12 Myrmidones

*Neither of the first two fragments is certainly assigned to this
drama; both, however, would fit well into Aischylos' Iliad-based
trilogy* Myrmidones, Nereides, Phrygians.

10
Perhaps from towards the opening of the drama?

Zeus' glory takes the first place in my prayers;
I come here as his suppliant, that this day's sun
may see us change our sufferings for lucky days,
and the commanders of the whole of Greece,
who join with Menelaos to exact
from Paris son of Priam vengeance for the savage rape
of Helen, may solve in friendliness their bitter argument.

11
Achilleus rejecting appeals to return to battle.

ACHILLEUS   They'll stone my body! But do not expect
   that torturing Achilleus, hurling rocks

will help the Greeks in Trojan land.
No; then the Trojans could just sit and win
the victory without a spear; and you would die
more easily; this heals all sorrows of mankind.
In fear of the Achaians shall I rush to take the spear
into a hand that's furious with rage at our bad leader?
If my comrades say just I, one man,
by being absent from the battle caused so great a rout,   10
then am I not myself all you Achaians need?
Respect does not stop me from saying this;
for who could say that chieftains and commanders such as
     these
are better born than I?
... one man has shaken, scattered you
... across young shoulders ....

12
Speaker unknown; the subject is the death of Patroklos.

This is the famous story which the Libyans tell;
an eagle, when a bow-shot arrow pierced it, said
– seeing this feathered thing which caused his death –
'so not by any other hands, but by our own
plumage we die'.

13–17 Niobe

13
*A speech to the choros, possibly by Niobe's old Nurse, during
the famous scene ridiculed by Aristophanes (Frogs 911f.) in
which Niobe long remained silent, grieving over the tombs of
her children.*

NURSE?   There's nothing else for her to do but weep
     because her father Tantalos gave her away,
     and beached her in a marriage which was no safe haven.
     Blasts of every kind of misery attack this house,
     and you yourselves can see the outcome of that marriage.
     Three days now she's been sitting at this tomb
     half-dead, and pouring out her grief, mourning

the wretchedness her children's beauty caused.
Brought to ruin, humankind is nothing but a shadow.
Tantalos the great will soon come here;   10
his purpose then will be to take her home.
What was Zeus' grievance against Amphion
that he has ruthlessly destroyed the family from root to
    branch?
Since you bear us no ill will, I will tell
you that a god first grows a fault in men,
when he is minded to destroy a household utterly.
Despite that, we are mortal, and a man should never boast
about the happiness the gods have given him.
Those who do very well in life never expect
that they may trip, and spill the plenty that they hold.   20
She was exultant in her beauty, and . . .

14 and 15
Two fragments from a speech by Tantalos.

14
TANTALOS   I sow a field it would take you twelve days to cross,
    the land of Berekynthia, where Adrasteia's seat and Ida's
    mountain lie, filled with the sound of lowing cows and
        bleating sheep,
    and the whole plain beats loud with sound . . . .

15
    My day of destiny, which stayed above in heaven, now
    falls to the earth and says these words to me;
    'learn not to pay excessive reverence to human cares'.

16
Speaker unknown.
    Alone among the gods Death has no love for gifts;
    neither by sacrifice nor by libation can you bend his will.
    He has no altar, and no hymns of praise; from him alone
    of all the daimones Persuasion stands aloof.

17
NIOBE   . . . the kinsmen of the gods,
    men near'to Zeus, who own the sacred place high up

on Ida, with the altar of their father Zeus in clear blue skies,
and in their veins the blood of gods still flows.

18 Oreithyia

BOREAS   ... and check the oven's leaping flame;
for if I see some soot above the hearth,
weaving a single wreath of flowing flame,
I'll fire the roof and turn it into ash.
Still, I have not yet roared my noble song.

19 Philoktetes

Death the healer, don't reject me – come!
For you alone release us from incurable disease,
and no pain takes a hold once we are dead.

20 Phrygians

Hermes consoles Priam for the death of Hektor.

HERMES   It doesn't matter if you want to do
good to the dead, or harm them;
they do not feel joy or grief.
The gods' displeasure is more powerful than them,
and Justice will fulfil the anger of the dead.

21 and 22 Summoners of Dead Souls

The subject of this drama was the scene in Odyssey 11, *when
Odysseus summons up souls from the underworld, to learn his
future from Teiresias.*

21
(Choros to Odysseus)
Come now, stranger; let it stand
in grassy sanctuary beside the dreadful lake;
cut through the offering's
neck and throat,
and send its blood as drink

for dead men down
into the gloomy depths beside the reeds.
Call on primaeval Earth,
and Hermes of the underworld, the escort of the dead,
and beg Plouton to send a swarm
of riverlets night-wandering from their great source,
of which this dreadful water is a branch
that flows polluted back
to streams of Styx.

22
(Teiresias to Odysseus)
 A heron, flying up above,
 will strike you with the dung dumped from its guts;
 a spine from this sea-nurtured beast
 will rot your aged, balding head.

23 *Wool-Carders*

*A drama from Aischylos' trilogy about the coming of Dionysos
to Thebes; the climax was the tearing to pieces of Pentheus by
mainads on Mt Kithairon. Hera disguised herself as a priestess,
and persuaded Semele, the mother of Dionysos, to ask Zeus to
appear before her fully armed with his thunderbolt. He did so,
and Semele was destroyed.*

 *The first fifteen lines are very fragmentary, but plainly form
part of a song by the Choros in praise of Semele, and the
prosperity which Zeus has given her, including (8–12);*

 May jealous people stay away
 and all unseemly rumours. We pray
 Semele's good fortune may remain
 on a straight course through everything.

After four more fragmentary lines, Hera enters in disguise.

HERA   I collect offerings for nymphs who speak the truth, the
    noble goddesses,
 life-giving children of the Argive river Inachos.
 They witness everything that human beings do;
 banquets and feasts, and the sweet songs of marriage rites,

and they initiate young women newly married, new to sex.
[fragments of two lines]
Pure modesty is far the best adornment for a bride,
and families achieve a harvest-full of children, if
the nymphs visit in kindness, and with honey in their hearts;
but they can be both harsh and hateful. . . .

24 Women of Aitna

*The drama which Aischylos composed for Hieron on his first
visit to Sicily in 476, to celebrate the foundation of the new city
of Aitna. Zeus impregnated a nymph called Thaleia or Aitna; in
fear of Hera's anger she prayed that the earth might open and
swallow her alive. When she was about to give birth to twin
boys, the earth opened again and she came back. Different
(unknown) speakers alternate with line.*

1. ANON   What name should mortals call them now?
1. ANON   Zeus told us we must call them sacred 'Palikoi'.
1. ANON   And shall this name stay with them? Is it rightly
          theirs?
1. ANON   Yes, for they will come back from darkness to the
          light of day.

PART TWO:
FRAGMENTS FROM UNKNOWN TRAGEDIES

25

I know the Aithiopians well; and I can praise
their land, where seven-channelled Nile
rolls his refreshing tide fed by the wind-born rain;
the fire-eyed sun shines down on earth
and melts the mountain snow; and all of fertile
Aigyptos, filled with the sacred flood,
sprouts up Demeter's grain that gives us life.

26

A man does not die, even if he's wounded many times
upon his breast, unless his life's end has caught up with him;
but no one, just by sitting home beside his hearth,
will any more escape from his appointed day of death.

27

They who are named the seven daughters of Atlas
cried out against their father's greatest task –
supporting all the heavens, where they have the forms
of phantoms of the night – the wingless Doves, the Pleiades.

28

A female choros.
    Zeus, god of guests and hosts, look now upon
    a house that welcomed strangers but has been destroyed.
    Do the gods give any benefit

to men of justice?
So I do not spare my hand,
but tear my hair
and beat my head, and miserably
wail about your fate.

29

Probably from the same drama as 28.
    ... not to sow wickedness –
then there's peace among mankind.
I praise this goddess; she gives blessings to
a city resting in a life of peace and calm,
and if its lovely houses are admired she makes
them richer than the neighbours who have envied them
– and does not let it grow. They eagerly desire
some land for ploughing, and the war-trumpet
sounds here no more; no garrisons ...

30

A choral lyric cites Aias *as an example.*
    I will dissolve in tears ...
    who ...
    sufferings ... might receive ...
    ....

(A1)   He was the lord of a land girded by the sea,
    protector of the city;
    strong lords of the people,
    leaders, commanders
    all destroyed him when
    he hoped to win the armour.   10

(A2)   The generals colluded with Odysseus,
    gave unbalanced judgment
    ... guide them ...
    heart shrouded in blackness.

(B1)   Just as the noble son
    of Telamon took his own life ....

31

Herakles' self-immolation, after his wife Deianeira unknowingly gives him a poisoned robe. The narrative is clearly retrospective, perhaps being told after his apotheosis.

HERAKLES   ... Then you could see a place destined by nature
      for a pyre
   up on the leafy mountainside of Oita.
   These children of mine by different mothers
   carried me there aloft with trees for fuel,
   flesh swollen and skin peeling from the poison's strength.

32

Thetis narrates how she was deceived by Apollo, who guided Paris to slay the otherwise unconquerable Achilleus by striking him in the heel, his only vulnerable place.

THETIS   He told me several times how happy I would be,
   with children who would live long and know no disease,
   then summed this up by saying my fortune was blest by gods,
   and sung a song of triumph which gave me much happiness.
   And I believed that Phoibos was a god who never lied;
   but he who sang this song himself, and came to celebrate
   my wedding day – he was the murderer
   of my own son.

PART THREE: FRAGMENTS OF SATYR-DRAMAS

33 Fishermen

(Silenos, Diktys)

SIL   Do you see . . . ?

DIK   Yes, I see. . . .

SIL   What should I look for?

DIK   In case somewhere, in the sea . . .

SIL   Not a sign; the water's calm.

DIK   Now look inside those hiding-places in the rocks.

SIL   All right, I'm looking.
    (pause)
    Ah! What's this? A monster from the sea –
    a whale? a shark? a seal?
    My lord Poseidon, Zeus god of the sea, what   (10)
    a gift you've sent us from the depths!

DIK   What sea-gift is concealed there in your net?
    It's covered up in seaweed. Is it some
    warm-blooded creature? Has the Old Man of the Islands
    sent us something in a chest? It's very
    heavy; we're not getting anywhere.
    Hey! Hey! Come here! All of you – farmers, ditch-diggers,
    herdsmen, shepherds, anyone who is around,
    men of the coast, sea-workers.   (20)

He leaves to find them; but the choros of satyrs reappears instead. In the next fragment, the chest has been opened, revealing Danaë and the infant Perseus.

SIL   . . . I ask the gods to be my witnesses,
    and hear what I now say in front of everyone.

Whatever you do, please don't run away from us;
it's not too late for you to understand, and recognize me as
a very kindly rescuer who will help you.
Look how your son fawns on me, just as if I was   770
his dear old Gran, and speaks so gently to me.
Won't he still be like this as time goes on?

DANAE   Rivers of Argos, gods of my native land,
and Zeus, who brings me to this end of all my sufferings,
will you give me to such wild beasts
to be defiled and raped by them
and be their prisoner, suffering dreadful tortures?
Anyway, I'm going to escape. I'll tie a noose,
and cut myself a desperate remedy against
abuse, so nobody can put me back to sea again –   780
neither a randy animal nor my own father!
                         No, I am afraid.
Great Zeus, send me some help – if you are willing;
you're responsible for our big problem,
but I'm the one who's paid in full for it.
I've called on you to set this right. That's all.

SATYRS   Sweetly he smiles as he looks at me,
the little baby, as he sees
the red and shiny, bald old crown. . . .

*– Of Silenos' head. Fragments of up to ten lines follow, including
(presumably when Perseus reacts to the sight of the satyrs'
phalloses as they dance) 'this little boy really loves pricks' [795].
When the text resumes, Silenos has taken up the song.*

SILENOS   . . . if I am not delighted when I look at you.
To hell with Diktys, if he wants   800
to cheat me out of such a prize.
(to Perseus)
Come here, my little one.
(He makes clucking noises.)
Do not be frightened. Why are you upset?
Let's join my sons, and very soon,
dear boy, you'll come to my
protecting arms (l do like you),
and you'll enjoy the martens, fawns
and baby porcupines,

| | and you can be the third in bed | 810 |

and you can be the third in bed 810
with Mummy and your brand-new Dad
(that's me!). I'll give you lots of fun,
and healthy food, so when
you have grown strong – your Dad is not
so hot at running after fawns these days –
you'll catch wild animals without a spear
and give them to your Mum to cook
the way her husband's family enjoys –
for you must earn your keep.   820

I SAT   Come on then, off we go, my friends,
to hurry on this wedding; Time
is ripe, and silently consents.
I see the bride's right here;
she really wants to gorge herself
upon our love.
That's no surprise; for a long time she pined,
a lonely widow in her boat
swept by the foam. But now she sees   830
us in our youthful strength, she's happy,
she's in ecstasy; such is the husband who,
lit by the torches of the love-goddess herself, . . .

34 Glaukos the Fisherman

HERDSMAN   . . . foolish . . .
. . . whirlwind . . .
. . . few . . .
. . . know that . . .
and I still trust clear evidence from my own eyes.
I was not bleary-eyed or looking carelessly
when I saw this appalling thing.
Know I'm a countryman, a local here,
always roaming the land which faces Chalkis;
I take my cattle for a place to graze
up from their cow-shed to Messapion, the treeless peak.
From there I saw this miracle; when I came to
Euboia's bend, near to the headland of
Kenean Zeus, right by wretched Lichas' tomb, . . .
. . . four-horsed chariot . . .

35 *Ambassadors to the Isthmian Games*

(Hephaistos and Satyrs)

HEPHAISTOS   ... when they see images not made by human
   skill.
   Whatever you do now, all this is holy work.

Exit Hephaistos into the skene.

1 SAT   I'm very grateful to you; you've been kind.
   Now everyone must listen, silently. . . .
   Look, and decide whether you think
   this image could be more like me,
   wrought by the craftsman; it does everything
   but talk!
1 SAT   Do you see there?
1 SAT   D'you see? Come here,   10
   come!
1 SAT   I bring this offering as an ornament to the god,
   this beautifully painted votive effigy.
1 SAT   It would disturb my mother; I am sure
   that if she saw it
   she would run off screaming,
   thinking it was me, her son –
   it's so like me.
1 SAT   So now, look at the sea-god's house, the earthshaker,
   and everyone hang up this silent,
   clear announcement of his handsome face,   20
   a traveller-stopper; he would halt all strangers on the
      path
   with terrifying looks.
   Hail to you, King Poseidon, our protector.

Enter Dionysos, right.

DIONYSOS   I knew I'd find you here, my friends!
   I cannot tell you that 'I couldn't find you on the way'.
   The path itself has left some traces,
   ... then I saw your friends ...
   ... and that told me and led me clear to you.

[one line illegible]
And now I see your penises are short and bent like mouse-
   tails!
You've obviously exercised quite hard   30
in training for the Isthmian games: you've not been slack.
Well, if you'd gone along with the old saying, I
would rather have expected you to practise dancing; but
you're playing Isthmian competitors – a new hobby;
great muscles, but you're wasting all my cash!
[one line illegible]
So don't you think it's fair if I
am furious? To hell with all of you!

*Fifteen lines almost unintelligible; from the few legible words it
is clear that Dionysos continued to reproach the satyrs, and they
tried to defend themselves. Then eight lines totally missing, and
two unintelligible.*

DIONYSOS   ... covered with a shield.
  You sow this tale around. You lie,
  and fib, and turn your anger onto me,
  and say that I know nothing about forging iron;
  I'm just effeminate, and don't belong among the men!
  And now you have these other, brand new tools,
  most hateful of all weapons, in your hands.   70
  And you abuse me and my dancing, even though
  I've brought together all the people of this land,
  while everyone who can, both young and old,
  has come to join my double dancing rows.
  But you are playing Isthmian competitors, and crowned with
    wreaths
  of pine you do not pay due honour to my ivy leaves.
  For that you will weep real tears, not stung from you by
    smoke.
  Hey, look; I see your favourite is coming here.
SILENOS   I will not ever leave
  this temple; why do you   80
  keep threatening me?
  I'm going to my new home
  in Poseidon's Isthmian house,
  and you must give these gifts to others.

Enter Hephaistos from the skene.

HEPHAISTOS   You love all novelties,
   so I have brought you these new toys
   fresh from the adze and anvil.
   Here is your first plaything.
1. SAT   It's not mine; give it to one of my friends.
HEPH   Do not refuse; think of the evil omen, my good
   friend.   90
1. SAT   How d'you enjoy it? What's it for?
HEPH   For your new job, it is ideal.
1. SAT   If you join us, what will you do for me?
HEPH   Help you to win the games; what better gift?
1. SAT   Come, friend, tell me how we can enter.

36 *Prometheus the Fire-Kindler*

SATYRS   . . . your gracious kindness set me dancing.
   Throw your shining cloak down by
   the never-wearied gleam of fire.
   A Naiad, when I've told her this, will chase
   me many times beside the blazing hearth.
      I'm sure the nymphs
      Will join in dances honouring
      Prometheus' gift!

Beautiful, I hope, will be their song
   to celebrate the giver, telling how   10
   Prometheus hastened to mankind
   and gave them means to live.
   So they will dance, and hope will come for freedom
   from the storms of winter. . . .
      I'm sure the nymphs
      will join in dances honouring
      Prometheus' gift!

PART FOUR:
FRAGMENT FROM AN UNKNOWN SATYR-DRAMA

37
(Justice. Satyrs.)

[Fragments of four lines.]

JUSTICE   ... he sits upon his father's throne; he overcame
    Kronos with Justice. His father started their dispute,
    so he can boast he paid him back with Justice.
    That's why Zeus shows me high regard
    – because he got his recompense for injury with help from
      me.
    I sit in honour near the throne of Zeus,   10
    and he himself sends me to those he likes –
    Zeus, who has sent me in goodwill to this land here.
    You'll see if what I say is vain.
1. SAT   How then shall we address you and be right?
JUST   I'm Justice, much revered in Heaven.
1. SAT   What privileges, please tell me, can you create?
JUST   I give the just rewards for their just life.
1. SAT   ... this law to mortal men?
JUST   – and I make reckless men grow sober hearts.
1. SAT   By using spells of Persuasion, or by brute force?   20
JUST   I note their wrongdoings upon a tablet kept by Zeus.
1. SAT   And when do you unfold this list of crimes?
JUST   When the appointed day for them reaches its perfect
    form.
1. SAT   Surely the people should receive you eagerly?
JUST   They would gain much, if they received me with
    goodwill.

[two lines unintelligible]
. . . no city, group or individual,
since such good fortune is her harvest from the gods.
I'll give you proof which makes this clear to see.   30
Hera made love to Zeus, gave birth and raised
a violent son, a god who swiftly gets enraged,
impossible to rule, and lacking all respect.
He shot at travellers with lethal arrows;
with no respect for life, he hacked with hooked spears,
    ruthlessly,
rejoiced and laughed at evil deeds. . . .

PROMETHEUS BOUND

by an unknown author
(possibly Euphorion)
traditionally ascribed to Aischylos

THE ACTORS AND THEIR ROLES

Power	Actor 2
Violence	Silent Face
Prometheus	Actor 1
Hephaistos	Actor 3
Daughters of Okeanos	Choros
Okeanos	Actor 2 or 3
Io	Actor 3
Hermes	Actor 2

Preset a rock BC.

SCENE I (A)

Enter Power and Violence right, leading Prometheus and accompanied by Hephaistos with chains, shackles, a spike and a hammer.

POWER We have come now to the very ends of Earth,
the plain of Skythia, a desert uninhabited by man.
Hephaistos, you must now obey the orders which
the Father laid on you, to yoke this criminal
against these jagged, rocky cliffs
with adamantine chains, fetters invincible.
He stole your flower, the gleam of all-creating fire,
to give to mortal men. For that outrageous act
he must be punished by the gods,
so he may learn to love the rule   10
of Zeus, and stop his favours to mankind.
HEPHAISTOS Power and Violence, you've finished all
that Zeus commanded; you have nothing left to do.
I am not brave enough to bind a kinsman and a god
by force to this storm-lashed ravine.
Still, I must find the bravery to do this deed;
it's dangerous to disregard the Father's word.

Over-ambitious son of Themis who is wise,
against your will and mine I nail you fast
in brazen bonds beyond escape to this deserted place   20
where you will never see a human face
or voice, but burnt by the bright glare of sun
you'll lose the fair bloom of your skin; you will be very glad
when Night's star-spangled cloak conceals the light

and then again, when Sun disperses morning frost.
So you will always be distressed by pain
of present suffering; your saviour has not yet been born.
That is the harvest from your favours to mankind;
you are a god, but did not cower before the anger of the
    gods.
You have bestowed great gifts on men, beyond all justice,   30
so you stand on guard against this joyless rock
erect and sleepless; never will you bend your knees.
You'll utter many cries and groans – quite uselessly:
for Zeus' mind is very hard to change,
and every ruler's prickly when he's new to power.

POW   Well then! Why d'you delay, and weep for him in vain?
Why don't you hate the god most hated by the gods,
the traitor who gave your great privilege to mortal men?

HEPH   I am his kinsman and his friend; that has some power.

POW   True, but how could you ignore   40
the Father's words? Do you not fear that more?

HEPH   You're always ruthless, totally unmerciful.

POW   Feeling sorry for him won't cure anything – so don't
expend your energy on things which cannot help.

HEPH   I truly hate my skill in craftsmanship.

POW   Why do you hate it? Frankly speaking, there's no way
your craftsmanship has caused the present problems.

HEPH   I still wish this was someone else's task.

POW   All things are wearisome, except controlling all the gods;
the only one who's free is Zeus himself.   50

HEPH   These chains tell me you're right; I have no more to
    say.

POW   Get on then, throw them all around him,
so the Father doesn't see you slacking off!

HEPH   Look: the bridle is right here at hand.

POW   Cast it around his arms with all your strength;
strike with your mighty hammer, nail him to the rock.

Hephaistos begins to fasten Prometheus to the rock.

HEPH   My work is getting on; there's no delay.

POW   Strike harder still, squeeze tight, with no slack
    anywhere;
he's very clever, and can make impossible escapes.

HEPH   This arm is fastened so he cannot get away.   60
POW   Well then, secure the other, so he'll learn,
  this sophist, he is stupider than Zeus.
  Now cast the bands around his ribs.
HEPH   I have to do this; do not order me so much.
POW   I'll give you orders, and I'll hound you on.
HEPH   This one alone could find fault with my work.
POW   Now nail the stubborn jaw of this great spike
  of adamant right through his chest with all your strength.
HEPH   My good Prometheus, how I weep for all your
    sufferings.
POW   You are still hesitating? You lament for one who is
  Zeus' enemy. Watch out, or one day you'll be crying for
    yourself.

Hephaistos drives in the spike.

HEPH   You see a sight revolting to the eyes.
POW   I see him getting just what he deserves.   70
  Get down below, fasten his legs by force.
HEPH   It's done. This work did not take long.
POW   Now fasten the clamped shackles on
  with all your strength; our overseer is severe.
HEPH   Your speech is just as ugly as your face.
POW   You can be soft, but do not criticize
  me for my strength of will and rugged temperament.   80
HEPH   The shackles are around his legs; let's go.
POW   There, now; annoy us, take the privileges of
  the gods and give them to a creature of a moment. How
    d'you think
  that mortal men could bail you out of this?
  The gods were very wrong to call you by a name which
    means
  Forethought; you need a person who can think
  for you, how you can wriggle out of these well-crafted
    bonds.

Exeunt Hephaistos, Power and Violence, right.

SCENE I (B)

PROMETHEUS   Oh heavenly sky, and swift-winged winds,
   and springs of rivers, countless laughing
   ocean waves, and mother Earth,   90
   and Sun, all-seeing globe, I call on you:
   you see what I, a god, now suffer at the hands of other gods.
        Look how I'm worn down
        by torments, and will suffer for
        a full ten thousand years;
        such is the shameful bondage which
        the new lord of the blessed ones has found
        for me. I cannot stand my present
        or my future sufferings; where is the limit
        set for all these torments?   100
   Wait. What am I saying? I know all
   the future quite precisely, and no unexpected pain
   can come on me. I must bear the fate
   laid down for me as best I can, and recognize
   Necessity is strong, invincible.
   I cannot speak, I cannot hold my tongue
   about my situation: I am yoked to this
   Necessity because I gave our privilege to mortal men.
   Inside a fennel stalk I hid
   the stolen fount of fire, which teaches   110
   every kind of skill, and solves their many problems.
   That is the dreadful crime for which I pay
   nailed here, enchained, under the sky.
        Ah! Ah!
        What sound, what smell wings down on me?
        Divine, or human, or whatever's in between,
        who's come here to the end of Earth
        to watch my sufferings; what do they want?
        You see me here a prisoner, a luckless god,
        the enemy of Zeus, the one who's hated now   120
        by all the other gods who live
        inside his halls, because I had
        too much compassion for mankind.

Enter the Daughters of Okeanos, left.

Oh! Oh! The rustling wings
of birds? The air is whistling
with gentle fluttering of wings.
I'm terrified of everything that comes.

CHOROS 1

DAUGHTERS OF OKEANOS (A1)   Don't be afraid: this is a
    group of friends
  who came in eager rivalry
  of wings, winning our father's leave   130
  with difficulty.
  Swift winds have brought me here;
  the sound of hammering pierced to
  the inside of our cave, and struck from me
  my virgin reticence.
  Barefoot, I rushed here in my winged chariot.
PROMETHEUS   Oh! Oh!
  Offspring of fertile Tethys,
  daughters of Okeanos, who whirls
  around the whole of Earth
  with never-tiring stream, look! See!   140
  I'm pinned in chains upon the rocks
  above this chasm; I endure
  guard duty none would envy.
D (A2)   I see, Prometheus: and in fear
  a mist of tears falls on
  my eyes, as I see you
  wasting away upon this rock
  humiliated by these adamantine bonds.
  Olympos has a new god
  at the wheel, and Zeus rules by   150
  new made-up laws against all Right;
  the mighty powers of old are gone.
PROM   If only he had sent me underground,
  even below where Hades takes the dead,
  to endless Tartaros, fixed in unbreakable
  bondage, so no one, god or man,
  could triumph over me.

I'm just a play-thing for the wind, and in my misery
I suffer, giving joy to those who hate me.

D (B1)   What god could be so cruel   160
as to see joy in this?
Who would not sympathize with what
you're suffering, except for Zeus? He's set
his mind unbendingly to anger, and he's conquering
the race of Ouranos; nor will he stop
until he's sated, unless someone comes
with force or sleight of hand
to overthrow his rule.

PROM   I tell you that this president
of the immortals will have need of me,
humiliated though I am by powerful fetters;
I can show him how he'll be stripped   170
of both his sceptre and his throne.
He won't charm me by singing honeyed songs
of sweet Persuasion, nor will I be cowed
by empty threats and warn him, till
he frees me from these savage chains,
and compensates me for humiliation.

D (B2)   You are too bold, and unrelenting
even in your bitter pain;
your words are far too free.   180
A piercing fear disturbs me,
and I'm scared;
how will we ever see
you safely landed after all
these troubles? Kronos' son's
inflexible in manner and in heart.

PROM   I know he's savage, and a law
unto himself; but still, I think,
he will be soft one day,
when my plan's smashed him;
he will smooth his boundless anger out   190
and come to friendly terms –
both he and I full willing.

SCENE 2 (A)

1. DAUGHTER   Unfold the story, and reveal it to us;
    what's the charge on which Zeus seized you, and
    humiliates you so outrageously and bitterly?
    Teach us, unless to speak might harm you.
PROMETHEUS   There's bitter pain for me in speaking out,
    and pain in silence; I'm unfortunate in every way.
    When first the gods began their rage,
    and civil war broke out and grew,   200
    with some determined to drive Kronos from the throne
    so Zeus could reign (indeed!), while on the other side
    the rest were eager he should never be the ruler of the gods,
    I wanted to give good advice to all
    the Titanes, children of Heaven and Earth –
    but could not. They despised my clever plans
    because in their inflexible self-confidence they thought
    that they could win quite easily by sheer brute force.
    Then more than once my mother Themis – Right –   210
    who's Earth as well (one form, but many names)
    told me the way future events would be fulfilled;
    that neither strength nor violence would give
    the victory, but those superior in trickery would win.
    I told them clearly all of this, but they
    thought it not worth a moment's glance.
    Of my alternatives, it seemed the best
    to bring my mother and join up
    with Zeus' party, willingly and by consent;
    thus through my plans the dark, deep pit of Tartaros
    now holds the ancient god Kronos   220
    and all his allies. That's the help
    the ruler of the gods received from me,
    and paid me back for it in this outrageous way.
    For one-man rule always has this disease;
    the tyrant never trusts his friends.

    And now I'll tell you clearly what you asked –
    the reason why he treats me so outrageously.
    As soon as he sat down upon
    his father's throne, he gave out different privileges to

the various gods, and shared the power   230
between them; he took no account at all
of wretched, miserable mankind. No; he decided that
he would annihilate their race, and then create another
     one.
No one did anything against this plan, except for me –
but I dared to; I freed mankind
from being totally destroyed, and sent to Hades' halls.
That's why I'm bent by many torments, terrible
to suffer, pitiable to see.
I never thought that just for pitying mankind
I'd suffer this myself; now I am cruelly   240
brought into line, a shameful sight for Zeus.
1. D   Iron-hearted, carved from stone,
Prometheus, would be anyone who did not sympathize
with what you suffer. I never thought I'd see
this torture; now I have, my whole heart is in pain.
PROM   Yes, I am pitiable to see for all my friends.
1. D   Did you do more?
PROM   Yes, I stopped mortals from foreknowing death.
1. D   What cure could you have found for that disease?
PROM   I sowed blind hopes in them.   250
1. D   That is a great help which you gave mankind.
PROM   I gave them fire as well.
1. D   Do creatures of a moment now have blazing fire?
PROM   From it they will learn many skills.
1. D   So that's the reason why lord Zeus –
PROM   humiliates me, and will persecute me now in every
     way.
1. D   Is no end fixed for all your suffering?
PROM   None other, than when it seems good to him.
1. D   When will that be? What hope? Do you not see
that you've done wrong? How you've done wrong, it
     would   260
hurt me to say and you to hear. Let us leave that,
and find some way to free you from your suffering.
PROM   It's easy, if you've kept your foot
well out of trouble, to advise and chide
those who are suffering; I know all this.
I did this wrong on purpose; I will not deny,
in helping mortals I made trouble for myself.

And yet, I never thought of such a punishment –
wasted away bound to these rocks high in the air,
stuck in this empty place where no one lives.   270
Come now; do not bewail the torments I am suffering now.
Descend to earth, and hear about the future which
is creeping up on me, so you may learn it all, right to the end.
Obey me, please, and share the misery
of one who's suffering now, since pain wanders around
and seats itself first on one person, then upon another.

D   You have called out to us, Prometheus, and we're willing.
        Now with gentle feet
        I'll leave my speedy chariot
        and sacred Air, flight-place of birds   280
        and will approach this rocky land;
        I want to hear all of
        your troubles.

SCENE 2 (B)

Enter Okeanos left, on the mechane.

OKEANOS   I have reached the end
        of the long road to you,
        Prometheus, steering this swift-winged bird
        by power of mind, without a bridle.
        I sympathize, you know, with your misfortune;
        kinship, I think, compels me to,
        and anyway, there's no one   290
        I should give
        a greater part of me than you.
        You'll learn that this is true; it's not
        in me to speak fine, empty words; so come, tell me
        what I must do to help you;
        you will never say you have
        a better friend than me, Okeanos!

PROMETHEUS   Hey! What's this? You too have come
    to look upon my suffering. How did you dare to leave
    the stream that bears your name, and naturally formed   300
    rock caves, to come here to the land
    which nurtures iron? Did you come to see

my fate, and share my anger?
So, behold this sight – the friend of Zeus,
the one who helped him gain his throne,
the torments which he's bent me to.

OK   I see, Prometheus, and I want to give
the very best advice to you, for all your subtlety.
Know who you are, and change your ways
to new; the ruler of the gods is new.   310
If you throw out words harsh and sharp
as these, perhaps – although he sits far up above –
Zeus might hear you; and then your present host
of tortures would just look like toys.
My suffering friend, give up your present attitude,
and seek release from all these pains.
Perhaps I seem old fashioned, saying this;
but really, Prometheus, this is what you get
for such excessive arrogance of tongue.
You aren't yet humble; you don't yield,   320
and now you want to add more to your present sufferings.
If you will let me guide you,
you won't kick against sharp spikes, because
our monarch is severe, and subject to no scrutiny.
I'm going now, and I will try to see
if I can free you from these chains;
be quiet, do not let your tongue get loose.
Or don't you know for certain – since you are so very wise –
that empty words bring punishment?

PROM   I envy you for being free of blame,   330
since you have dared to share in everything with me;
but let things be, do not exert yourself.
You never could persuade him; he is obstinate,
and even coming here might hurt you.

OK   You are much better at advising others
than yourself. I know from what you do, not what you say.
Do not oppose me when I'm set on going;
I tell you, I tell you that Zeus will grant
this gift to me – release for you from all this suffering.

PROM   I praise you, and will never cease to praise   340
you for enthusiasm; but
do not disturb yourself, for you will work for me
in vain, quite uselessly – if you really want to.

Better, be quiet, keep out of the way;
myself, simply because I'm down, I do not want
to hurt as many others as I can.
Certainly not; I'm pained by what has happened to
my brother Atlas, who is stuck in the far west
supporting on his shoulders pillars of the Heaven
and Earth – a burden hard to bear.   350
I saw, and pitied, one, a son of Earth,
inhabitant of caves in Kilikia,
fearsome, hundred-headed monster tamed by force;
Typhos the impetuous. He challenged the gods,
hissing out fear from terrifying jaws,
and from his eyes there flashed a gorgon glare;
he thought to overthrow the rule of Zeus by force.
Zeus hurled on him his never-sleeping dart,
descending thunderbolt breathing out flame,
which struck him from excessive   360
boasts; it pierced him to the very core,
his strength was thundered and burnt out of him.
And now his useless body lies spread out
near to a narrow strait of sea, crushed down
beneath the very roots of Aitna.
Sitting upon his crown, Hephaistos
forges iron; from there one day will burst
rivers of fire to bite with savage jaws
the lovely plains of Sicily that's fair of fruit.
Such is the rage which Typhos will boil out,   370
with red-hot darts of fiery spray no one can touch,
although he has been burnt to cinders by the thunderbolt of
    Zeus.
You are no fool, you don't need me
to teach you; save yourself as best you can.
I'll drain my fate down to the dregs, until
Zeus' mind is no more weighed down by his rage.
OK Do you not recognize, Prometheus, that
    for a diseased temperament words are the cure?
PROM Yes – only if the heart is softened when the time is
    right;
    you can't impose a cure when it's still swollen hard. 380
OK What fault d'you see in eagerness
    and courage? Teach me now.

PROM   Excessive work and empty-headed silliness.
OK   Allow me, please, to suffer from this malady,
   since it is best for wise men to seem fools.
PROM   That would appear to be my problem.
OK   It's clear; your words send me back home.
PROM   Yes; pitying me could lead you to be hated.
OK   By the new holder of the seat of supreme power?
PROM   Take care you never vex his heart.   390
OK   Your own misfortune teaches that.
PROM   Get on your way, go home, preserve your present
   sense.
OK   I was just going anyway, before you said these words;
   my four-legged bird now flaps his wings upon
   the flat pathways of Air; he will be glad to bend
   his knee once more in stables back at home.

Exit Okeanos on the mechane, *left.*

CHOROS 2

DAUGHTERS (A1)   I grieve for you, Prometheus, and
   your terrible misfortune; from my gentle
   eyes pours out a flood of tears;
   streaming, it soaks my cheeks.   400
   Zeus rules without restraint
   by new laws of his own; he holds a spear
   of arrogance against the gods
   who ruled before.

(A2)   The whole land has cried out
in misery, laments the breaking of
your great and ancient, honoured power   410
and your brothers'; the men who rule
in sacred Asia's settled home –
they too are troubled by
your sufferings, and they cry out;

(B1)   so do the girls who live in Kolchis,
battle-fearless Amazons,
and Skythians, who have the furthest

territories of the earth, around
Maiotis lake,

(B2)   and war-like flower of Araby,   420
         men who rule a city
         close by Kaukasos,
         an all-consuming army clashing
         with their sharply pointed spears.

(C1)   I've only ever seen
         one other god subdued
         by torments such as these –
         the powerful strength of Atlas,
         who supports both Earth and Heaven
         on his back.   430

(C2)   Prometheus, even Earth itself laments your
              fortunes,
         and the breaking wave of ocean
         cries aloud in sympathy. The depths lament;
         black Hades, recess in the Earth, roars down below
         in answer; streams of sacred rivers all
         lament your pitiable torment.

SCENE 3

PROMETHEUS   Please do not think I am so self-indulgent I
    have nothing more to say; no, I am eaten up at heart
    by painful thoughts, because I'm so maltreated.
    Who else but me assigned to these
    new gods all their new powers?   440
    I will not speak of that; I would be telling you
    what you already know. Now listen to how mortals
    used to suffer, how I found them full of foolishness
    and made them capable of thought; intelligent.
    I'll say this, not because I blame mankind,
    but showing how much kindness lay in what I gave.
    At first they saw – but saw in vain;
    hearing, they did not hear, but like the shapes
    in dreams their whole life long they were confused

and acted randomly; they did not know how to   450
construct warm houses out of bricks or wood.
They lived in holes like ants, who scurry round
– in sunless depths of caves.
They had no way of telling when
the winter, or the flowering spring, or summer
harvest started; they did everything
in total ignorance, until I showed to them
the rising of the stars and when they set – both hard to tell.
Then mathematics, most pre-eminent of all the skills,
I found for them – and writing, which preserves   460
all kinds of information, and is mother to the Arts;
I was the first to help them yoke wild beasts,
so they were subject to the bit and saddle, and
could take the greatest burdens over
for mankind. I also led beneath the chariot
horses that love the reins, a play-thing for rich men;
and no one else but me showed them the use
of ships, sail-winged, and striking at the sea with oars.
These were the things I found out – wretched me –
for human beings; but I do not have a clever trick   470
to free me from my present sufferings.

1. DAUGHTER   You've suffered shamefully; you're wandering,
     deprived
   of all your natural cleverness; you're in despair, like a
   bad doctor who is sick; you do not have a means
   to find the drugs to cure yourself.

PROM   You will be even more amazed when you
   hear all the crafts and methods I devised for them.
   The greatest – if someone fell ill,
   there was no cure, eaten, or drunk,
   or rubbed upon the skin; through lack   480
   of drugs they shrivelled up, until
   I showed them how to mix up healing remedies
   with which they could avoid disease.
   Then I established all the many kinds of prophecy;
   I was the first to judge future realities
   from dreams, and I interpreted for them chance words
   which were too hard to read, and signs found travelling,
   and carefully distinguished for them how the birds of prey
   fly in the sky – which ones are naturally favourable,

which of evil omen; and their habitats,   490
their hatred or affection for
each other, how they sit together;
and the smoothness of the entrails, what colour
bile would give some pleasure to the gods,
also the mottled symmetry of liver-lobes.
I wrapped the thigh-bones and the long chine up in fat
and burnt them: so I set mankind upon the path
to this most precious skill. I made the signs from fire
all clearly visible; before that, humans were all blind to them.
That's that; and then the riches hidden deep   500
beneath the earth – all helpful to mankind –
bronze, iron, gold and silver, who
could boast that he found them before me?
No one, of course, who does not want to babble nonsense.
Learn everything in one short word;
all mortal skills and crafts come from Prometheus.

I. D   Do not help humans more than they deserve,
and give yourself no thought when you are suffering; myself,
I'm confident that you will yet be freed
from bondage, and you'll be as powerful as Zeus.   510

PROM   No part of destiny has been appointed yet
to fulfil these things in that way; I cannot escape these bonds
until I have been bent by countless torments, endless pains.
Skill is far weaker than Necessity.

I. D   Who is the helmsman of Necessity?

PROM   The three goddesses who apportion lots, and the
   avenging Furies.

I. D   Is Zeus really less strong than them?

PROM   If something's been ordained, he can't escape.

I. D   And what has been ordained for Zeus, apart from
   everlasting power?

PROM   You'll never learn that; do not even ask.   520

I. D   Is this some solemn secret you are keeping to yourself?

PROM   Think about something else! In no way is it time
for this to be revealed; it must be hidden
carefully. For only if I keep it secret will I have
a chance to free myself from shameful chains and sufferings.

CHOROS 3

DAUGHTERS (A1)   Never may Zeus, the lord of all,
wrestle with all his strength against my will.
Let me not fail to go towards the gods
with holy offerings of cattle sacrificed   530
beside my father's ocean stream,
nor give offence in what I say.
No; let this hold for me and never melt away –

(A2)   it is a pleasant thing
to live long and with confidence,
feeding the spirit with bright cheerfulness;
but now I'm terrified as I see you   540
crushed by a thousand torments.
You did not fear Zeus; you
gave humans far too much, Prometheus.

(B1)   How, my friend, how could your favour be
returned? Where can you find some help?
Mortals can give you none! Did you not see
the helpless feebleness, like dreams, which has
confined them in their blindness? Never will   550
the plans of humans go beyond the order set by Zeus.

(B2)   I learnt this when I saw your
suffering, Prometheus;
now very different songs spring to my lips
from those I sang around your wedding bath and bed
rejoicing for your marriage, when you won Hesione
my sister as your wife to share your bed.   560

SCENE 4

Enter Io, a young woman with the horns of a cow, left.

10   Where am I? Who are you? Whom do I see
bound to the rocks,
exposed? What did you do

to suffer this? Tell me
where I have wandered in my misery.

Ah! Ah! Oh! Oh!
A sting pricks me again –
keep it away!
I see the herdsman with ten thousand eyes!
He's moving with his terrifying eye –
not even death has kept it underground;   570
he's coming from the underworld to hunt me down,
and drives me hungry down the sandy shore.

(A1)   The shepherd's pipe
sounds in my ear, keeps me awake.
Oh god, where have my distant wanderings brought me?
What did I ever do, lord Zeus,
to make you yoke me to these sufferings?
Ah! Ah!
Why d'you torment me till I'm mad   580
with terror, driven by the gadfly's bite?
Burn me to death or bury me, or let sea-monsters
eat me!
Don't begrudge me this,
my lord; my wanderings have been too much,
they've stripped me naked, and I do not know
how I can flee from misery.
D'you hear the voice of the poor girl with horns?

PROMETHEUS   How could I not hear you, gadfly-driven girl,
daughter of Inachos? You set the heart of Zeus alight   590
with sexual passion; hated by Hera, you're now stripped
and forced to run beyond your strength.

10 (A2)   How can you speak my father's name?
Tell me, poor me; who are you?
You are suffering, and so am I; but you tell me the truth,
and know the agony the gods have put on me,
which withers me away with maddening stabs of pain.
Ah! Ah!
Humiliated, leaping high,
I'm driven furiously on, tamed by   600
the angry will of Hera. Is any other

creature so tormented?
No. Tell me what there still must be
for me to suffer. Is there any end or cure
for my disease? If you know this, show me.
Speak to the poor girl who wanders in misery.

PROM   I'll tell you everything you want to know,
not weaving it in riddles, but in simple speech   610
such as is right when speaking to a friend;
you see the one who gave fire to mankind, Prometheus.

IO   You did great good to all humanity;
oh poor Prometheus, for what reason are you suffering?

PROM   I've only just stopped pouring out my agony.

IO   So you won't give this gift to me?

PROM   Ask what you like. I'll tell you anything you want to
know.

IO   Show me who yoked you onto this ravine.

PROM   The plan was Zeus'; Hephaistos did the work.

IO   And for what crime is this the punishment?   620

PROM   It is enough if I just tell you what I've said.

IO   But still, show me the end of all my wanderings,
and tell me how much longer I must suffer them.

PROM   It's better for you not to know than to know that.

IO   Please do not keep from me what I am to endure.

PROM   I don't begrudge you any of this gift.

IO   Why then d'you hesitate to tell me all?

PROM   I won't refuse, but I don't want to drive you mad.

IO   Do not concern yourself; it's what I want.

PROM   If you're so keen, then I must speak; now listen.   630

I. D   No! Not yet! Give me some pleasure too.
First we must learn the story of this girl's
disease. Let her tell us about her great misfortune,
then she can find out all her future trials from you.

PROM   Io, I think it is your task to do this favour to the
nymphs –
especially since they're your father's sisters;
it's worthwhile to cry out aloud, lamenting your
misfortune, when you're going to wring
a tear from your spectators.

IO   I do not see how I can disobey,   640
so you will have a clear account of all
you ask; but still, I weep even to talk about

the storm of troubles sent by gods, and the destruction
of my shape, and how it suddenly afflicted me.
Visions kept coming every night
into my bedroom, and spoke to me
in gentle words: 'Most blessed of young women,
why d'you remain a virgin for so long, when you can make
a splendid match? Zeus is inflamed by darts
of his desire for you, and wants to make love   650
to you now; girl, do not kick away advances made
by Zeus, but go out into Lerne's
grassy meadow, to your father's herds and flocks,
so Zeus' eye may be relieved of its desire.'
I was affected every time I went to sleep by dreams like that –
and how I suffered! – till at last I dared
to tell my father all about these nightly dreams;
he sent to Delphi, and many other messengers set off
    towards
Dodona to inquire, so he might learn what he
should do or say to satisfy the gods.   660
They came back bringing riddling oracles,
in language which was meaningless.
At last a clear pronouncement came to Inachos
telling him absolutely and commanding him
to thrust me out of home and native land
to wander freely to the very ends of Earth.
And if he didn't, Zeus' fiery thunderbolt
would come and utterly destroy our family.
Apollo's oracle persuaded him;
he drove me out, expelled me from my house   670
against his will and mine; the bridle-bit of Zeus
compelled him forcibly.
At once my face and sanity were terribly
distorted; wearing the horns you see now I was stung
by the sharp gadfly teeth, and maddened, leaping
I ran off towards Kerchne's good stream
and Lerne's spring; the earthborn cowherd
with a vicious temper, Argos, followed me and used
his many eyes to oversee my every step.
Then suddenly an unexpected fate   680
deprived him of his life; but still the frequent gadfly bites
whipped me and drove me on from land to land.

You've heard what happened; if you know what still remains
for me to suffer, tell me. Do not pity me
and comfort me with lies; for I believe false words
to be the most shameful disease of all.

(CHOROS 4)

DAUGHTERS   Oh! Oh! Keep away from me!
   I never thought that such
   unheard of words would reach my ears –
   that sufferings, disfigurement, and terror   690
   so unwatchable, unbearable
   would lash my soul with double-pointed goad.
   Oh human destiny,
   I shudder when I look at Io's fate.

PROMETHEUS   You're full of fear and lamentation far too
   soon;
   hold back until you've heard her future!
I. D   Tell us and teach us; when you're sick, it's comforting
to know the future course of your disease.
PROM   You had your earlier request from me with very
   little   700
   trouble, since you wanted to find out from her
about her troubles, telling you herself.
Now hear what future torments this young girl
must suffer at the hands of Hera;
daughter of Inachos, put in your heart
my words, so you may learn your journey's end.
First, you must turn from here towards the risings of
the sun, and cross fields never ploughed;
and you will come to Skythian nomads, who live off
the ground in woven wicker huts on wagons,   710
armed with far-shooting arrows.
Do not go near them, but pass through their land
keeping your feet near the sea-sounding shore.
On your left hand live Chalybes,
workers in iron, whom you must guard against,
for they are savage, not approachable by foreigners.
Then you will come to the Hybristes, violent like its name.

Don't cross the river – that's almost impossible –
until you go right up to Kaukasos itself, the highest
of all mountains, where the river pours its strength   720
out from the brow; when you have crossed
peaks which reach to the stars, you must go on
into the South, where you will find the Amazons,
an army of man-haters, who will one day live
in Themiskyra round the Thermodon, where the rough jaw
of Salmydessos juts into the sea; it gives
a hostile welcome to all sailors – stepmother of ships!
The Amazons will show you on your way, and very gladly
    too.
Next you will reach the Isthmos of Crimea, narrow gateway
to the lake; you must be brave, and leave the Isthmos,
    cross   730
the straits of Lake Maiotis.
For all the rest of time, mortals will tell great tales
about your crossing, and the place will then be called
Bosporos after you. So leaving European land, you'll go
into the continent of Asia. Don't you think
the tyrant of the gods is equal in his violence
to everyone? The god imposed these wanderings
upon this mortal just because he wanted sex with her.
Dear girl, you ran into a bitter suitor for
your hand in marriage; you must realize what I've just
    said   740
is not even the prelude to your sufferings.
IO   Oh no! Oh no! Ah!
PROM   You're crying out and groaning; what will you
    do when you learn of all your future sufferings?
I. D   There's something worse than this?
PROM   A wintry sea of endless torments.
IO   Why do I want to live? Why don't I straight away
    hurl myself from this rugged rock,
    plunge headlong to the ground and find relief from all
    my torments? Better to just die at once   750
    than suffer terribly for all your life.
PROM   I think you would have trouble putting up with my
    complaints,
    since I am fated never to be dead;
    for that, indeed, would give relief from what I suffer;

as things are, there's no end prescribed for me
until Zeus falls from his tyrannic throne.
IO   Then it is possible for Zeus to fall from power?
PROM   I think that you would gladly see that happen.
IO   Of course, since he has caused my sufferings.
PROM   Well then, rejoice; it's going to happen.   760
IO   Who'll take the tyrant's sceptre?
PROM   Zeus himself, with his own stupid plans.
IO   In what way? Tell me, if it won't hurt you.
PROM   He makes a marriage which will do him harm.
IO   With goddess or with woman? If you can, please say.
PROM   Why do you ask? I cannot tell you that.
IO   Will his own consort then depose him?
PROM   Her son is fated to be mightier than his sire.
IO   Has he then no escape from that?
PROM   None except me – when I am freed from bonds.   770
IO   But who will free you, and defy the will of Zeus?
PROM   It's fated he will be one of your offspring.
IO   A son of mine will free you from these sufferings?
PROM   Your offspring in the thirteenth generation.
IO   It is now hard for me to understand this oracle.
PROM   Do not demand to know about your labours.
IO   Please don't first promise me and then refuse.
PROM   I'll give you either one of two stories.
IO   Which? Show them, let me choose.
PROM   I will; now I will either tell you all about   780
your future sufferings, or who will free me.
I . D   Give one of them to her, and please give me
the other as a favour; do not sleight me.
First show this poor girl where she has to wander,
then tell me about your rescuer; that's what I want.
PROM   Well, since you're eager, I will not refuse
to tell you all you ask.
First, Io, I will tell you your long wanderings;
write all this in the tablets of your memory.
When you have crossed the stream dividing the two
     continents,   790
go on towards the fiery settings of the sun,
beside the noisy sea, until you come
to Gorgon-plains of Kisthene, where
Phorkeus' daughters live, aged virgins –

three, with swan-white hair, who share a single eye
and have one tooth; on them the sun does not cast beams
nor does the moon by night see them.
Nearby are their three sisters, winged,
the snake-fleeced Gorgones who hate mankind,
whom nobody can see and still survive.   800
That's what their stronghold's like;
and now I tell you of another awful sight.
Watch out for Zeus' unbarking, sharp-mouthed dog,
the griffin, and the one-eyed Arimaspians,
a tribe of horsemen, who live round
the streams of Plouton, river rich in flowing gold.
Do not go near them; you will reach a distant land,
where all the men are black, because they live beside
the sources of the sun, near Aithiopia's river.
Go down beside its banks until you come   810
to the Great Cataract, where sacred Nile's pure water flows
down from the Mountains of Papyros.
It will take you on your way down to
the Delta, where at last it's fated you, Io, and your
descendants will found your long-lasting, distant home.
If anything I've said is hard to understand,
repeat your question so you know it clearly;
I have more time to spend here than I'd like.
I. D   If any more remains or was left out
that you must tell her of her painful journey,   820
speak; but if you've told her everything, then please
give us the favour which we asked; I'm sure you've not
      forgotten it.
PROM   She has already now heard everything,
but so you know you are not listening to nonsense, I
will tell you all her sufferings before she reached this place,
and so give proof that what I say is true.
I'll leave out the great mass of words,
and just describe the last phase of your wanderings.
You came to flatlands of Molossia
and the high ridges of Dodona, where   830
there are an oracle and throne of the Thesprotian Zeus,
and that sheer miracle, the speaking oaks
which told you clearly, not in riddles, that
it was your destiny to be the famous bride

of Zeus – does this appeal to you?
From there, the gadfly drove you on a path
beside the sea, until you reached the mighty gulf of Rhea,
where you turned, and ran your storm-tossed path inland.
Now learn the truth; in future time that sea
will bear your name – Ionian Gulf –   840
so all men will remember you once passed by there.
This is a sign to you about my intuition;
I can see more than there is openly revealed.
Now I will teach the rest to all of you,
returning to the track of what I said just now.
There is a city, Kanobos, the last on earth,
right by the mouth and Delta of the Nile;
that's where at last Zeus will restore your senses,
simply by touching you with hand you will not fear.
In memory of how he was conceived, your dark-skinned
     son   850
by Zeus will be called Epaphos, 'created by the healing
     hand',
and he will harvest all the basin of the Nile.

Five generations later, fifty female offspring of your line
will come back here to Argos, not because
they want to, but in flight from kindred marriage to
their cousins; they – the hawks,
following close behind those frightened doves –
will go there hunting for a marriage it is wrong to seek;
the god will not allow them to possess their bodies.
Then the land of Argos will be drenched in blood   860
when murderous women kill them fiercely at the dead of
     night.
Each bride will take her husband's life,
plunging a sharpened sword into their throats.
May Aphrodite go among my enemies like that!
Desire will warm one of the girls, and she
will save her partner. Her resolve
will lose its sharpness; she will choose
to be called coward rather than a bloodstained murderess,
and she will found the royal line of Argos.
It would need many words to teach you clearly   870
all that follows. One of her descendants,

a brave man, famous for archery, will free
me from these torments. That's the prophecy my ancient
mother gave to me, the Titaness Themis;
to tell you how and why, would need a lengthy speech
from me to say; and you would gain nothing by learning it.

10   Ah! Ah!
        Spasms, and madness striking at my wits
        burn me again, and the gadfly
        bites me with fiery spearhead;   880
        in terror my heart kicks my ribs,
        my eyes spin round.
        I'm carried off my course
        by the fierce blasts of madness, lose control
        over my tongue, and muddied words strike uselessly
        against the hateful waves of my destruction.

Exit Io, right.

CHOROS 5

DAUGHTERS (A1)   Wise, very wise was he
        who weighed this thought
        and told it with his tongue.
        To wed in your own class is far the best;   890
        you must not yearn to marry
        men inflated by their wealth,
        or raised on high by noble birth
        if you work with your hands.

    (A2)   Never, never may you see
        – oh mighty goddesses of Destiny –
        me going as a mistress to the bed of Zeus,
        and may I never marry any of the gods;
        I'm scared when I see Io, virgin
        who rejects her mate, burnt up
        by wandering, the torment sent by Hera.   900

    (A3)   To me, marriage of equals brings
        no fear. I do not dread it; only, may the eyes

of greater ones, invincible, not look on me.
That is a fight which can't be won,
against a force beyond all counterforce.
I do not know what I would then become;
I do not see how I could flee
from Zeus' plan.

SCENE 5

PROMETHEUS   I tell you this; for all the boldness of his mind,
   Zeus will be humbled. Such is the act of sex which he
   now seeks to consummate, which will soon cast him
   from tyrant throne to his extinction; then the curse   910
   of father Kronos will be utterly fulfilled,
   the curse he uttered falling from his ancient throne.
   Zeus' troubles are so great, no other god
   could show him clearly his escape except for me;
   I know both when and how. So let him sit up there
   with confidence, and shake his lightning-bolt;
   it will not stop him falling down,
   wrestled to earth dishonourably, unbearably.
   Such is the combatant he now prepares   920
   himself against himself, a prodigy who's very hard to beat.
   He'll find a fire more powerful than lightning,
   and stronger noises which will overcome the thunderbolt,
   and even shatter the sea's blight,
   Poseidon's three-pronged spear.
   Dashed on this rock of sorrow, Zeus will learn
   how very different ruling is from slavery.

I. DAUGHTER   You're telling just your empty hopes.

PROM   It's what will be fulfilled – and also what I want.

I. D   So someone's really coming who will conquer Zeus?   930

PROM   And his torments will be much harder on the neck than
   mine.

I. D   How can you not be scared to hurl out words like
   these?

PROM   What could I fear? I am immortal.

I. D   He could make your torments even worse than this.

PROM   Well, let him do it! I'm prepared for everything.

I. D   Those who pay due respect to Nemesis are wise.

PROM   Worship, beseech, and flatter whoever's in power;
        to me, Zeus is much less than nothing.
        He can act, and he can hold the sway for this short length of
            time
        whatever way he wills; he won't rule very long among the
            gods.   940

        But wait! Here is the errand-boy of Zeus,
        this menial servant of the latest tyrant;
        I am sure he's come to bring some piece of news.

                            FINALE

Enter Hermes, right.

HERMES   Hey, you – the clever one, so sharp you've cut
            yourself,
        who angered all the gods by giving mortal men
        their privileges; you, the thief of fire!
        The Father bids you speak about this marriage which
        you boast of, which will force his fall from power;
        and this, mind you, without a riddling speech;
        speak out, tell all the truth, and do not make me   950
        come here once again, Prometheus. You can see –
        Zeus is not softened by defiance.
PROMETHEUS   A solemn speech, and really full
        of thought – most fitting for the lackey of the gods.
        You're new, you rule a brave new world, and think
        your lovely palace free from grief; but I have seen
        two tyrants fall already from that throne.
        And now I see the third to hold the crown
        will do the same – both shamefully and quickly. Do I seem
        to be a little scared, and cringing to the latest gods?   960
        I couldn't be much further from it! As for you –
        just hurry back along the path by which you came;
        you will learn nothing that you ask of me.
HERM   Outrageous boasts like these
        brought you to anchor in these torments.
PROM   Know clearly; I would not exchange
        my own misfortune for your slavery.

HERM   Well, I'm sure it's better to be this rock's slave
    than Zeus the Father's trusted messenger.
PROM   Get out of here, you piece of scum!
    That's how insulters should be paid insult in turn.   970
HERM   You seem to revel in your situation.
PROM   You call this revelling? I'd like to see my enemies
    revel like this! Among them, I count you.
HERM   Am I in any way responsible for this?
PROM   Quite simply, I hate all the gods;
    I helped them, and they have no right to wrong me.
HERM   I think you're mad – quite sick.
PROM   I would gladly be sick, if it is sickness to hate
    enemies.
HERM   You'd be insufferable, if you were free and strong.
PROM   Alas!
HERM   . . . A word Zeus does not recognize.   980
PROM   As Time grows old, it teaches everything.
HERM   But you have not yet learnt good sense.
PROM   You're right – I'm still conversing with an underling.
HERM   It seems you will say nothing that the Father needs.
PROM   I owe him so much, I would gladly pay him back.
HERM   You're using sarcasm on me as if I were a child.
PROM   Aren't you a child, or even stupider,
    if you expect to learn a thing from me?
    There's no humiliation, no device, by which
    Zeus could turn me around to tell him this   990
    until I am released from shameful bonds.
    So let him hurl his blazing fire,
    stir up, confound the world with feathers
    of white snow and thunderclaps.
    None of these things will bend me, so I'll tell
    who's fated to ensure his fall from tyranny.
HERM   Think whether this is any help to you.
PROM   It has all been foreseen and planned.
HERM   You fool – compel yourself, compel yourself at last
    to think correctly in the light of what you're suffering.   1000
PROM   You're troubling me in vain – like talking to the
    sea.
    Don't entertain the thought that I'll be terrified
    of Zeus' will, turn female-spirited
    and beg and plead to that most hated god,

raising my hands in prayer like women do,
to free me from these chains; I never will.

HERM   It seems I'll have to say a lot – and all in vain;
you have neither been softened up or blunted by
my prayers; you're champing at the bit like a young colt
new-yoked, struggling and fighting off the reins.   1010
But all this eagerness is based on weaknesses of strategy;
pure wilfulness, allied with unsound thought,
is in itself quite useless.
Think what a storm and triple wave of troubles
will engulf you, if you're not persuaded by my words –
beyond escape. First, with his thunder and the lightning-fire
the Father will strike at this craggy cliff
and hide your body; you'll be held in an embrace of rock.
After you have endured for an enormous length of time   1020
you will come back into the light. But then Zeus' wingèd
hound, the bloody eagle, greedily
will carve your body into shreds,
creeping unbidden up to feast on you each day,
and he will gorge himself upon your liver, gnawing till it's
    black.
Do not expect this torment to be ended, till
some god appears who's willing to inherit all
your sufferings, and go down to the dark, unlighted gloom
of Hades and the depths around the river Tartaros.
Plan on that basis, since this is no made-up   1030
boast, but all too true. The mouth
of Zeus does not know how to speak
a falsehood; he fulfils his every word. So you
should look around, and think whether you truly would
consider this defiance better than some good advice.

1. DAUGHTER   We think that Hermes' words are very timely;
he has told you to abandon your defiance,
seek the wiser path of good advice.
Obey him; it is shameful for the wise to fail.

PROM   I knew it all, before this god shrieked out   1040
his news; it is no shame in war
to be maltreated by your enemies.
So Zeus can hurl on me his double-pointed
twists of fire; and let the sky be tortured by
the contest of the thunder and convulsive blasts

of angry winds; let the storm shake Earth
from its foundations, roots and all;
let ocean waves with their fierce roar
pile up and bury the stars' paths
across the heavens. Lift my body, hurl it down
into Tartaros' darkness, to the fearful   1050
whirlpools of Necessity;
he will not ever kill me.

HERM   These plans and words
come from a lunatic;
there's nothing in his foolish boast
that isn't discord, mania!
But you, who've sympathized
with his misfortunes, should get out
of here in haste – or else   1060
thunder's inexorable roar
will blast you into madness.

I. D   Say something else; try words which I would listen to,
since what you've tried to bait us with is quite unbearable.
How could you ask me to be such a coward?
I want to suffer with him;
I have learnt to hate all traitors, and
there's no disease I spit away as much.   1070

HERM   Remember what I tell you now,
and when you're hunted down by Ruin,
do not blame your fate, and never say
that Zeus cast you into a torment you
did not foresee. Certainly not; it's you,
yourselves; because of your stupidity, you have been
     caught
in a great net of Ruin you cannot escape –
knowing the consequences, and not
all of a sudden or by stealth.

Exit Hermes, right. Thunder behind the skene.

PROM   Now the earth is shaken   1080
not in words but deeds,
and from the depths the sound of thunder
bellows in response, and fiery coils
of lightning flash, and whirlwinds

twist the dust, the breaths of all
the winds leap on each other
in a civil war;
sky and sea are mingled.
Now the blast from Zeus is visibly
approaching; I am terrified   1090
Oh glory of the Earth, my mother; oh great sky
which turns the sunlight onto everything,
do you see me, and my outrageous sufferings?

Exeunt Prometheus and the Daughters of Okeanos, buried
underground.

FRAGMENTS OF *PROMETHEUS' RELEASE*

Prometheus Bound was part of a connected group of dramas,[1] and was followed immediately by *Prometheus' Release*. There is controversy about whether the author wrote a full trilogy; if so, the other drama was probably *Prometheus the Fire-Bringer*.[2] There is further controversy about whether *Prometheus the Fire-Bringer* preceded *Prometheus Bound* or followed *Prometheus' Release*; in either place[3] there seems too little potential subject-matter for a whole drama (but then, the events of *Prometheus Bound* could be summarized in three sentences!). Like West, I tend to believe that there was a trilogy, with *Prometheus the Fire-Bringer* first, dramatizing the theft of fire;[4] but I would not rule out the possibility that *Prometheus Bound* and *Prometheus' Release* made up a cycle of only two matched and balancing dramas.

Prometheus' Release began with the appearance of a Choros of Titanes (corresponding to the Choros of Okeanides in *Prometheus Bound*). They probably opened the drama with

1. TITAN   We have come ...
    to look upon these sufferings
    of yours, Prometheus, and
    the chains which you endure. ...   (38)

They proceeded to catalogue the lands through which they had travelled to reach him:

[1] I do not accept the theory (e.g. Taplin 1977, 464) that *Prometheus' Release* was a genuine drama written by Aischylos, which inspired another later author to write *Prometheus Bound* as a 'prequel'. Cf. Herington 1979, 424–5.

[2] This was probably a separate work, not simply an alternative title for the genuine *satyr-drama* by Aischylos, *Prometheus the Fire-Kindler* (cf. frag. 36), which does not appear in the ancient catalogue of Aischylean titles.

[3] Cf. the two alternative synopses provided by Griffith 1983, 282–3.

[4] 1979, 132; *contra* Conacher 1980, 103–4.

... and the crimson-floored, the
sacred stream of the Red Sea,
and marsh that flashes brown beside
Okeanos, which nurtures all
the Aithiopians, where the all-seeing Sun
rests his immortal flesh each night
and weary horses, with warm draughts
of gentle water. ....   (39)

Part of Prometheus' response is preserved in a Latin translation
by Cicero. 'It reveals an exhausted and demoralized Prometheus,
much changed from the closing scenes of *Prometheus Bound*;
Oceanus' warning (313–14) has proved true'.[5]

PROMETHEUS   Race of Titanes, kindred to my blood,
   children of Ouranos, you see me bound and chained
   to these sharp rocks, just like a ship in horrid-sounding
   waves which timid sailors bind to shore, fearing the night.
   That's how the son of Kronos, Zeus, has bound me –
   and Hephaistos' hand approved of Zeus' will.
   He drove these wedges in with cruel skill
   and split my limbs apart. Pierced by his craftsmanship
   I suffer wretchedly here, in this outpost of the Furies.
   And now, on every second dreadful day, the servant   10
   of great Zeus flies grimly down, and starts to tear at me
   with hooked talons, ripping my flesh apart in his ferocious
      search for food.
   Then, stuffed and glutted to the full on my rich liver, he
   lets out a mighty shriek, and flies back to the heights,
   brushing his tail-feathers in bloody gore.
   When my half-eaten liver's grown back to full size,
   then he returns in eagerness to his foul meal.
   That's how, tormented, I am fed on by my guard,
   who mangles my live body, in eternal pain.
   For bound, as you see now, in Zeus' chains,   20
   I cannot keep that dreadful bird away from me.
   I have no power to help myself, and I must suffer ghastly
      torments.
   I am in love with death, seeking an end to all my sufferings;

[5] Griffith 1983, 294.

but Zeus' power keeps me far from that fate.
Indeed, this grievous, age-old pain, grown greater over
many horrid years, is now ingrained so deep inside
my body that drips, melted by sunlight, constantly
bespatter these, the rocks of Kaukasos.   (40)

Subsequently Herakles arrived, wandering like Io, and shot the
eagle with his arrows. Like Io, he received advice about his
future journey – the quest for the apples of the Hesperides and
the cattle of Geryon, which will take him to the north and then
west (while she went north, then east).

PR   . . . Go on down this straight path; and first
you'll come to the North Winds; beware
of their great storm and roar; don't let it swirl you up
and carry you away in wintry blasts . . .   (41)

. . . then you will come to the most just
of all mankind, and the most friendly –
Gabioi, where neither plough nor hoe breaks up
the earth, but fields which sow themselves
bear never-ceasing life support for them.   (42)

. . . there you will meet the Lygians, a fearless battle-tribe;
and even you, courageous one, will not find fault
with how they fight. It's fated there
your arrows will not work, and you will not be able to
take stones out of the earth, since all their soil is soft.
But then your Father, seeing you without resource, will pity
     you:
he'll spread a cloud above, and make the whole land dark
with showers of rounded hailstones, which you will throw
and easily drive back the army of the Lygians.   (43)

Did Herakles free Prometheus? If so, with or without Zeus'
consent? The grounds for a settlement between Prometheus and
Zeus are fairly obvious from *Prometheus Bound*; they have little
to do with the profound evolution in the nature of Zeus, from
tyrannical power to wisdom, which has sometimes been alleged
to have been the subject of this cycle of dramas.[6] Prometheus

[6] Cf. e.g. Murray 1940, 87–110 and Reinhardt 1949, 74–5.

almost certainly gained his freedom in return for sharing his secret – the name of Thetis, whose *moira* it was that her son would be more powerful than his father.[7] Perhaps during the action of *Prometheus' Release* Zeus' amorous eye had lighted on her, and the crisis for his régime was imminent; but we simply do not know from the fragments – and therefore should not attempt to conjecture – what happened.

[7] Cf. Conacher 1980, 136–7.

APPENDIX: THE SPURIOUS ENDING TO
SEVEN AGAINST THEBES

In 1848 an ancient synopsis was discovered, which revealed that *Seven against Thebes* was the last drama in the Theban trilogy; since then, the closing scene has been placed under increasing scrutiny. The entry of the Herald at 1005 raises a new issue, dividing the two brothers who earlier in the Finale have been imaged as united in and by their deaths, and returning to the theme of the *polis*, in a way which is inconceivable at the end of a trilogy.[1] It is also clearly implied in *Seven* that the entire house of Labdakos has now been destroyed; this is inconsistent with the survival of the sisters Antigone and Ismene, who appear in this part of the drama, but not elsewhere in Aischylos' version of the story. There are banalities of language in the original Greek; some of these, and repetitive passages, are obvious even in translation. The playwright who wrote 1005–76 also uses some forms of expression which are not found elsewhere before fourth-century texts.

Though there has been much debate,[2] the consensus among modern scholars is overwhelmingly that the lines translated below are not by Aischylos, and that they were written to adapt the drama for a subsequent production, perhaps to form part of a double bill with Sophokles' *Antigone*.

This additional material cannot have been written before around 411–409 BC, since the author depends heavily, both for the language and for the overall conception of his conclusion to the drama, on Euripides' *Phoinikian Women*.[3]

The author of the new ending:

[1] Cf. Hutchinson 1985, 210.
[2] The strongest modern defence of the ending is Lloyd-Jones 1959.
[3] Cf. Hutchinson 1985, 209–11.

1

Inserted after 860

Enter Antigone and Ismene, left.

> But look – here come Antigone   861
> and Ismene, for bitter work;
> I think they will pour out sincere
> laments for their two brothers
> from their lovely chests
> – this grief deserves it.
> First, before they speak, it's right
> for us to make the evil Fury's song
> reach down to Hades, and to sing
> the paian of disaster.   870
> Oh, most unhappy in your sisterhood
> of all who tie a breast-band round their clothes,
> I wail, I weep, there's no deceit to halt
> the true cries from my heart.

2

Attributed some lines between 960 and 1004 to the sisters, and added for them after 995.

> – Above all to me.
> – and especially to me.

3

Added the following scene after 1004.
Enter Herald, left.

HERALD It is my duty to announce decisions reached 1005
 by officers deciding for the citizens of Thebes.

> This Eteokles, because of his goodwill to us,
> it is decided will be buried deep in friendly soil,
> because he died defending us from enemies at our gates;

he reverenced ancestral shrines, and perished without
   blame   1010
– a death such as is fair and beautiful for a young man.

That's what I'm told to say about this man.
As for his brother, this, the corpse of Polyneikes,
must be tossed out unburied, prey to dogs,
because he would have wrecked the land of the Kadmeians,
unless some god had stood against the spear
he wielded; even dead he'll still incur the anger
of his native deities, whom he outraged – this man –
by bringing in a host of foreigners to try to take the city.
That's why it has been ordered he'll be buried   1020
by winged birds, and have dishonourable rites of honour;
   no
libation bearer or grave-digger will escort him,
nor will he have the tribute of shrill mourning-cries;
no friends will honour him by carrying out his corpse.
That's what's been ordered by the men who rule in Thebes.

ANTIGONE   I tell the leaders of the Thebans this;
even if no one else will join in burying him,
I'll bury him, and I will risk the danger
when I've buried my own brother. I am not ashamed
to break faith with the city by this act of anarchy.   1030
Our bond is strange and terrible, forged in the womb –
a mother wretched in her destiny, a father most unfortunate;
that's why, my soul, you must share willingly your sufferings
with him who had no choice, living with one who's dead, a
   kindred heart.

As for his flesh, neither the birds nor dogs,
nor empty-bellied wolves will feed on it; don't anybody think
   they will!
I will myself, although I am a woman,
make a grave and burial with earth for him,
taking the earth folded inside my linen robe,
and I will cover him; let no one think I won't.   1040
A person who has courage finds a way to do her will.
HER   I tell you that the city will not be defied.
ANT   I tell you not to give me orders that can't be obeyed.

HER   The people will be harsh, when they have just escaped
      defeat.

ANT   Let them – but this man won't be left without his burial.

HER   You'll honour with a grave a man the city hates?

ANT   He's not now being greatly honoured by the gods.

HER   They did not punish him until he threw this danger on
      his native land.

ANT   He simply gave wrong back for wrong.

HER   One man wronged him, but he attacked us all.   1050

ANT   Strife is the last of gods – she ends all speech.
   I will bury this man; do not say any more.

HER   You're on your own; I formally forbid you to.

Exit Herald, left.

WOMEN   Oh far-famed, family-destroying
      Furies, you have now destroyed
      all Oidipous' children, utterly.

1. W   *(to the corpse of Polyneikes)*
      What shall I suffer? What shall I do? What
      should I choose? How shall I find the courage
      not to weep for you, and take you to your tomb?
      I fear, I turn away   1060
      in terror of the citizens.

1. W   *(to the corpse of Eteokles)*
      You at least will have a crowd
      of grieving mourners: he, poor man, will not;
      he'll only have one single cry, his sister's funeral
      lament. Who would imagine it?

*The Women divide into two groups, one gathering around each
corpse.*

1/2 W   Let the city do, or not do, what it wants
      to those who mourn for Polyneikes;
      we'll go, we will escort him,
      help to bury him. This grief
      is common to us all, while citizens too often   1070
      change the things they think are right.

1/2 W   We will go with this man, since the city
      and the right go with us.

Helped by the blessed ones and Zeus' strength
he saved Thebes from defeat; our city
was not sacked by waves of foreigners.

*Exeunt Antigone, Attendants carrying the corpse of Polyneikes,
Women right.*
*Exeunt Ismene, Attendants carrying the corpse of Eteokles,
Women left.*

NOTES

Persians

Setting

Concern has been expressed whether the action is located at Sousa (where Dareios' tomb was located in real life), or Agbatana (where the seat of central government was located in Xerxes' time); whether it is located inside a council chamber, or outside the tomb of Dareios; and where this council chamber was located in relationship to the palace of Xerxes.[1] These considerations were of no importance to Aischylos; as Kitto rightly argued, 'the acting area represents Susa – not the Council House or the royal graveyard or the city gates but Susa. The only topographical indication we are given is that the royal palace is somewhere offstage . . . .'[2] *Persians* is set in a single fictive locale, which is not consistent with the real topography of Persia, and does not change at any point in the drama[3] – near an 'ancient building',[4] adjacent to the tomb of Dareios, and not very far from the royal palace.

Persians was created before the introduction of a practicable *skene* building. It is therefore unlikely that the 'ancient building' was represented, since it is only referred to once in the drama, and is never used.[5]

[1] Dale 1969, 119; cf. Wilamowitz cited by Broadhead 1960, xlii.

[2] Kitto 1966, 104.

[3] Against Taplin 1977, 103ff. see Scullion 1990, 98ff.

[4] 141. The setting is not inside it, despite frequent mistranslations of this line; see Broadhead 1960, 66–7. Aischylos imitated the opening words of this tragedy from Phrynichos' *Phoinikian Women*, but clearly did not locate his action inside the council chamber. According to an ancient, introductory note to the text of *Persians*, Phrynichos apparently did; but since there is no certain instance, in all the surviving dramas and fragments, of a tragedy or part of a tragedy in which the *orchêstra* is used to represent an indoor scene, this claim should be treated with caution.

[5] *Pace* Canavan 1972, 61ff. and Hogan 1984, 225. In tragedy the Greek word translated as 'this' at line 141 is often used to refer to buildings or people whom the audience cannot see, but which are near the place represented by the *orchêstra*.

In *Persians*, therefore, as in *Seven* and *Suppliants*, the actors' tent or *skene* was out of sight of the audience – either some distance down a *parodos* or, more probably, on the lower level behind the terrace, tucked close in behind the wall.

The tomb of Dareios is practicable; the drama reaches a spectacular climax with his appearance on top of it at 660, which is not anticipated in any way before the Queen's unexpected return for Scene 2. To avoid interference with the acting and dancing of other scenes, while still giving it a central position, the right place for it is EBC.[6] A mound or tomb erected behind the *orchêstra* circle and against the retaining wall of the terrace would be easily accessible for the actor, who simply ascends a hidden ladder from the lower ground behind the theatre to make a spectacular entrance behind and over the top of the tomb.[7] A mound in this position sets a puzzle to the audience – what is it going to be used for? – but does not pull focus away from the action in the *orchêstra* until it is actually put into use.

Until Dareios' entry draws attention to the mound, the drama is set in a bleak no-man's land. The Elders are placed in the *orchêstra* between the palace down the left *parodos*, which comes as the drama develops to represent security and comfort, and the right *parodos*, which is used only by the Messenger and Xerxes; it represents the outside world, in which the power of Persia has suffered defeat, and from which the news of disaster comes. Dareios' role is then imaged theatrically as mediation; he comes from a tomb which is located between the palace and the disaster, and offers comfort, prophecy and advice from that central position.

The roles are distributed on the assumption that one actor (presumably Aischylos himself) played the 'heavier' roles of the Messenger and Dareios, while a specialist in lighter roles, and in sung lyrics, played the Queen and Xerxes – who indulges in lyric lament.

Persians relies for a great part of its effect on the definition of the Persians as 'other' than Greeks[8] – partly through language,[9] but also

[6] Cf. Hogan 1984, 234.

[7] So too Scullion 1990, 102. I disregard the more extravagant theories – e.g. that the 'steps of Charon' (an underground passageway to the centre of the *orchêstra*, found in the remains of some later theatres elsewhere) were available to Aischylos. There is no trace of them in the physical remains of the Theatre of Dionysos, and (*pace* Taplin 1977, 447–8) no scene in known fifth-century drama where they are needed.

[8] This procedure is so extensive, and so novel, that Hall 1989 argues cogently that *Persians* was the work in which the process studied in her title, 'inventing

through gesture and (perhaps above all) by costuming all the characters in rich, exotic (long-sleeved, ornamented) clothes which mark them out as Asiatic. No Greek characters appear (contrast *Suppliants*); this is natural given the subject-matter, but intensifies the feeling that the Persians are isolated, alien to the codes to which Athenians conform.

Choros 1

Given the small number of surviving dramas, we have no way of knowing whether opening with a choral ode was more characteristic of early tragedy than beginning with a scene spoken by an actor.[10] We are told that Aischylos' opening couplet echoes the first lines of Phrynichos' *Phoinikian Women*, which also dramatized the defeat of Xerxes; but Phrynichos began with an actor scene, since the opening line ('This is about the Persians who are now long gone . . .') was delivered by a eunuch spreading cushions for the Elders' seats. Opening with the entry of the *choros*, as Taplin rightly notes, enables Aischylos 'to build up in a way that could not otherwise be achieved a sense of the communal dread and of the vulnerability of national prosperity which is to be the keynote of much of the play'.[11]

A number of different dramatic techniques are used to achieve this. The first is the steady, almost relentless flow of the opening Choros – especially of the chanted *anapaests*, 1–63, to which the Elders stride in, and take up their positions to begin the *strophic* dance. This is supplemented by thematic use of variations on two recurrent themes – the Persians have gone (1, 12, 29ff.); Elders and wives grieve for their loss, and fear for their future (11–12, etc.); this motif is used to close both the introductory chant (61ff.) and the song as a whole (D and E stanzas, 120ff.). An almost hypnotic power is given to the song by allying this leitmotif effect with the catalogue of names from Persia and its subject states. Whether gleaned from historical record, collected from oral reports at the time of the invasion, or simply invented by Aischylos, these individual names invest the anticipation of disaster with concrete reality. The list also prepares for the equally pointed use

the barbarian', was begun. As far as extant drama is concerned, she is undoubtedly right; however, Aischylos must surely have studied and developed techniques pioneered by Phrynichos in *The Sack of Miletos* and (especially) *Phoinikian Women*.

[9] Hall 1989, 76–9.

[10] Taplin 1977, 61–5.

[11] Ibid. 61. Phrynichos was (apparently) not concerned to create this suspense, since his eunuch announced the defeat of Xerxes in the opening monologue.

of names both in the Messenger's narrative of Salamis, and in the
Elders' angry cross-questioning of Xerxes in the Finale.

The opening chant ends at 64 with the pathos of loss and fear. Then,
as they begin the first strophically responding stanzas (A1–B2), the
Elders sing and dance the expedition's departure. Despite its optimistic
conclusion in B2, this song includes at A1 the yoking of the Hellespont;
this will turn out, in Dareios' account (744ff.), to be the transgression
beyond Persia's *moira* which caused the downfall of Xerxes. Accordingly Aischylos has the Elders suddenly break off their optimistic song,
and insert after the B pair an *epode* (B3, 93ff.) – in which the sudden
danger of defeat by 'a clever god' is prefigured. The intrusion is so
sudden that many editors[12] have attempted to soften its immediacy, by
transposing the stanza to after 112, the last line of C2.

There is no good argument for this transposition, and it destroys the
psychological subtlety of the sequence.[13] The C stanzas are an attempt
by the Elders to regroup themselves, and reassert grounds for optimism
after the terror imposed by the thought expressed in the *epode* B3. But
the attempt rebounds on them; precisely because the Persians have
achieved so much in war by land and sea, they have the potential for
enormous loss; and knowing – as his entire audience knows, but his
characters as yet do not – that such a loss happened to Xerxes,
Aischylos makes the Elders return, in the concluding D stanzas, to the
theme of the introductory chant – their own fear, and the young
women's grief.

Scene 1
Elders and Queen The Queen is introduced at this point to crystallize
in stage terms, around one regal figure, the picture of Persian opulence
and autocracy; to develop the pathos for the fate of Persia's women,
which has already been a theme of Choros 1; and to intensify the
Elders' anxiety for the fate of Xerxes' expedition. This is done through
the Queen's narrative of the portent and the dialogue which reveals the
strength of Athens. The Messenger only brings the news of disaster
when their anxiety has been made specific; and then his opening words

[12] Including the most recent, West 1990b.
[13] *Pace* Winnington-Ingram 1983, 4–5, it would damage the ethical substance
of Aischylos' dramas as well. Throughout *Persians* (esp. 811–12; cf. *Ag* 750ff.),
great military achievements, though hazardous, do not in themselves cause
disaster. In a transposed position as (C3), the B3 *epode* would imply just this.
Further arguments for the original position in Michelini 1982, 78–9.

(252) restore the vast generality of loss, arching right back to the first line of the drama.

The Queen on her re-entry for Scene 2 tells us (607ff.) that she has responded to the disaster by returning without her carriage and fine ornaments; it follows that her first entry here, with the full pomp of oriental royalty, was designed by contrast to introduce a spectacle into the *orchêstra* which can stand for and symbolize the glory that was Persia before Salamis. As when Agamemnon arrives for Scene 4 of *Agamemnon*, the Elders must yield back out of the centre of the playing space towards FR on her arrival; but where Agamemnon's Elders stand their ground to greet their King, the Persians immediately prostrate themselves in reverence before the Queen Mother (152); this establishes at once the totally unhellenic relationship between monarch and subjects in the society portrayed in the drama.[14]

Since the Queen's chariot, and her moment of descent from it, are less pivotal to the scene's meaning than is the case with Agamemnon, and she needs room to move in the *orchêstra* after she has descended from it, a point of rest at BC rather than C is appropriate.[15] The Elders have been rescued by her arrival from a debate which would have proved futile, given that they have as yet no information to discuss about the fate of the army (see 144ff.); falling back to the front half of the *orchêstra*, they now prostrate themselves and address her – in the original, in the more lengthy and elaborate metre of the trochaic tetrameter, which was also used at 215ff. for their response and the dialogue after her narrative.[16]

Aristotle states that the trochaic tetrameter was the original metre of tragedy,[17] and it is conventional wisdom[18] to assume that it is only used in *Persians* because this is the earliest surviving drama, and not to convey a dimension of added excitement and speed – as it is in later tragedy (cf. e.g. *Ag* 1649ff.). However, I suspect that Aischylos used the metre here to convey the tremulousness with which the Elders of Persia respond to their Queen Mother, and the anxiety which has impelled her to leave the palace. It is noteworthy that she only returns

[14] Cf. Herodotos 7.136. In *Ag* Scene 4, Klytaimestra prostrates herself in a grovelling, 'Asiatic' (i.e. Persian) act of king-worship which disgusts Agamemnon.

[15] On the staging of Agamemnon's arrival cf. Ewans 1995, 142ff.

[16] Her account of the dream, like the Messenger's speeches, was written in the normal tragic metre, the iambic trimeter.

[17] *Poetics* 49a21ff.

[18] Cf. e.g. Broadhead 1960, 297–8; Michelini 1982, 42ff.

to the normal iambic trimeter when she has left her chariot, and has been reassured enough by the Elders' declaration of support to begin her narrative of the dream. Modern actors and directors must therefore be aware of the need for a more swift, excitable delivery for 154–75 and 233–48 (also for 697–758 in Scene 3).

The Queen must descend, and interact fully with the Elders, by 170 at latest, if she is to command from the centre of the *orchêstra* as she embarks on her narrative; there is a case in production for bringing her down even earlier, during 162, so she can complement the fluttering anxiety of her tetrameter speech in movement – which will then contrast with the illusory security she achieves by telling them about her dream.

The narrative is lucid, clear and powerful. The allegorical portrait of Asia and Greece precisely prefigures the disaster to come; the end of the dream even anticipates the closing phases of the drama itself, when the figure of Dareios will appear before the arrival of Xerxes in rags. Then the omen symbolizes the passive fall of the noble, imperial eagle before the speed and vicious attack of the hawk; so the speech has figured the loss of Persia to Greece in two different, complementary symbolisms.

This is a superb opportunity for the actor: a well-modulated narrative, precisely structured to grow to two violent climaxes (196, 210), and inviting the player to move around the *orchêstra* to convey the Queen's vision to the Elders and the audience. Then the Queen regains her regal composure – but in words which make it plain, by the sudden pause and appeal to Xerxes' un-Athenian freedom from scrutiny (211–14), that she is all too aware of the dimensions of potential loss.

Again in the original the long-lined metre of the Elders' response evokes the anxiety of the speakers; this almost, perhaps, undermines their optimism (for which the Queen duly reproves them at 520). It is then finally undermined by the last subject which Aischylos raises before having the Messenger return – the remarkable resilience and strength of Athens. The dialogue points the contrast between Athenian swordsmen and Persian archers,[19] then establishes Athens' strengths – the wealth of the Laureion mine (silver, in contrast with their own over-abundance of gold), the lack of a single ruler and the success against Dareios. These words do not simply flatter Aischylos' audience; in context, they are designed to prepare for the Messenger, since they show how the Athenians match and equal every one of Persia's

[19] Each side in historical fact had contingents of men who used the other's preferred weapon – as Aischylos tacitly recognizes at 320 and 460. Hall 1989, 85–6.

strengths. This drives the Queen to retreat away from the interaction – BL, to leave room for the Messenger to run in from the right *parodos* and take the centre.[20]

Salamis and after The Messenger occupies the focus for the remainder of the first half of the drama, with his successive narratives of three chosen parts of the disastrous expedition – Salamis, Psyttaleia and the desperate retreat of the survivors through northern Greece. Since *Persians* has been studied more often from the perspective of history than of drama, this account has been unfavourably compared with the narrative in Herodotos' *Histories*;[21] surprise has even been expressed that an eye-witness could permit himself such latitude. However, Aischylos was not attempting to record the facts in a way which would make him a satisfactory 'source' for the reconstructions beloved of military historians; he uses selection, omission and emphasis to bring out those aspects of the events which will illustrate his theme. The focus throughout is placed on the former greatness of Persia, the vastness of the expedition – and its defeat by a handful of men wielding superior intelligence and acumen, defending their native land with the approval of the gods. The fascination for an Athenian audience will not just have lain in Aischylos' deft emphasis on their own achievement, or on the role of one particular Athenian (352ff.); the peculiar power of these narratives is the playwright's ability to enter entirely into the perspective of the defeated Persians, and make the sequence of events unfold as through their eyes.

As soon as the Messenger has arrived, made for the centre and given his news, he is immediately surrounded by the Elders in a lyric dance of anguish. The initial outbreak of emotion is only quelled after the Queen returns from the perimeter, making the Elders yield towards the front of the *orchêstra*, to give the Messenger a performance space for his speeches. The Messenger is deliberately made to announce the survival of Xerxes first; this enables the Queen to yield back again gracefully towards the perimeter in relief, but it also allows the Messenger to begin his narrative with electrifying force, as he embarks

---

[20] He ignores the Queen on arrival. This is not unusual in the surviving dramas (cf. Taplin 1977, 86–7). It is also good theatre; the Messenger goes single-mindedly direct to the centre, while the Queen's exceptional suffering is marked out by her aloofness, initial silence, and subsequent return at 290 to CL. Her withdrawal clears most of the playing space for the dances of the following *epirrhematic scene*.

[21] Hdt. 8.70ff.

upon the drama's second catalogue of names – now not merely leaders who have gone to Greece, but who have gone for ever.

These speeches are not to be imagined as static performances. They will of course have been delivered from areas near the centre of the *orchêstra*, simply because this is the focal point, commanding the most emphasis, both visually and orally, in the Greek theatre. The narrative is designed to make a particular impact on an Athenian audience; but Aischylos never lets the narrator become detached from his character's perspective. The Messenger's opening words (302ff.) are designed to correct at once the unwarranted optimism of the Queen; and this first catalogue closes with a reiteration that she has, as yet, no idea of the extent of the disaster. The Messenger then challenges his Persian audience to deny the numerical superiority of the Persians (344); and throughout the story of Salamis (352ff.), he illustrates his own view of the events – which will be echoed and legitimated by Dareios; the sheer size of the disaster, and the defeat of an overwhelmingly superior Persian fleet, demonstrate the devastating intervention of the gods, working through the success of the Athenian strategy (353ff., 374). The Queen's response to the narrative of Psyttaleia (472ff.) shows that the Messenger has succeeded in persuading his Persian audience that this viewpoint is true; but he still reiterates the theme in his exit line – again evoking a matching response from the Queen (514–15).

Accordingly, there are several moments where the Messenger's narrative is edged by a persuasive thrust, and these need to be echoed in movement; he must advance towards the Queen and/or the Elders, in their relatively unemphasized positions towards the front perimeter. Elsewhere in the speeches, the whole centre part of the *orchêstra* is at the Messenger's disposal, and all directors will want to explore (as did Aischylos himself) which parts work best as moments of rest, and where the Messenger needs to illustrate and complement the power of his words with gestures and animated movement.[22]

The Queen makes almost the only possible response to such a disaster; she proposes to sacrifice to the gods. The 'false directions' in the last three lines have led to accusations of bad dramatic technique;[23] but Michelini is right to note[24] the parallel and deliberate contrast with

[22] Cf. on a smaller scale the role of the Herald in *Ag* Scene 3; Ewans 1995, 138–41.
[23] Taplin (1977, 92–8) even revived Weil's suggestion that they should be transposed to after 851! *Contra* Broadhead 1960, xxxvii–viii.
[24] 1982, 134ff.

her second exit at 852. Aischylos makes her speak now as if this were
to be her final exit, to heighten the surprise when she reappears after
Choros 2. At 852 the strategy is different; no one in the audience will
expect her to mislead us twice, and so we correctly apprehend then that
she is making her final exit. Aischylos surprises the audience again, this
time because the Queen's intention is not fulfilled; Xerxes enters in
rags, arriving before she has had time to fetch the new robes which
might console him and restore his dignity, and has to face his Elders
alone.

Choros 2

This is the song and dance of lamentation, in which the Elders try – and
fail – to come to terms with the magnitude of the disaster. Aischylos
uses the ode to poise the Elders' response between past and future
events; the chanted introduction (532–47) returns to the theme of
female suffering from Choros 1; with this as a basis, stanza A1 says
what the Messenger could not say, because of his social position and
function, and because he adopts a larger, theological perspective; the
Elders blame Xerxes directly for the disaster, prefiguring their outright
attack on him in the Finale (923ff.).[25] The lyric rapidly reaches its
greatest heights of emotion, as the B stanzas, punctuated by outcries of
despair, evoke the peculiar horror of the deaths at Salamis and Psyttaleia; Aischylos then ends with an evocation of the end of autocracy as a
result of the disaster. In historical fact, the Elders' diagnosis is exagger-
atedly pessimistic; what the Persians did lose after Salamis was Greek
Ionia. Written with hindsight in 472 BC, these stanzas celebrate Ionia's
revolt from subjection, and the increasing power of the Delian League,
which the Athenians had formed after the rout of Xerxes to capitalize
on Persian weakness.[26] The ending is designed to focus on the consequences of Salamis rather than on the event itself; this prepares for the
new direction which the drama now takes.

Scene 2

'In ... the first half of the play, everything hangs together; there is
nothing in the structure that calls for serious criticism. It is a compact

[25] After the two outcries, the responsion between *strophe* and *antistrophe*
places Dareios' undefeated supremacy (552ff.) in direct contrast with Xerxes'
ignominious flight through Thrakia (562ff.).
[26] The Ionian islands are again invoked in Choros 4. The League completed
the liberation of Greek Ionia at the battle of Eurymedon, three years after the
first performance of this drama.

whole, and with suitable alteration of 521–31 could have made a play
in itself that ended with [Choros 2] ... but, though superior in
structure, such a drama would be sadly deficient in moral content, and
to the audience it would appear to celebrate the Greek victory rather
than to present the Persian tragedy. To put both in their true perspective a broader canvas was necessary; hence the ghost scene and
the *kommos*. For neither of these scenes, however, do we find satisfactory preparation.' So Broadhead,[27] attempting to mediate between
his own belief in the value of *Persians* and earlier strong criticism
of this drama as lacking a proper connexion between scenes, a clear
focal point for the action, and a plot 'as this term is commonly
understood'.[28]

These older views are worth citing today, to show how easily an
unacknowledged expectation that Greek tragedy should conform to the
norms of the well-made-play can cause failure to appreciate Aischylos'
dramatic strategy. The Queen's re-entry for this scene is indeed sudden,
and contrary to the false preparation deliberately made on her previous
exit; but Aischylos has aimed for the appearance and prophecy of
Dareios as the climax right from the outset, as clearly as he was to aim
in a later drama towards the murder of Agamemnon.[29] Aischylos never
picks up directly, at the beginning of one scene, on a direction
foreshadowed towards the end of a previous scene. His dramas unfold
organically; each scene, like each phase of growth, is a new and
different contribution to the development of the fully formed whole,
not obviously connected to the previous Scene and Choros. Its true role
is only fully comprehended when the drama is over; but the connexions
are there, in the shifting moods of a drama which unfolds (to use the
Queen's own metaphors as she reappears now, her costume and state
as totally altered after the disaster as her feelings) like the changing
motion of the waves and the winds.

[27] 1960, xxxvi.

[28] Ibid. xxxii, citing Wilamowitz (1914) for 'no connexion' and Kitto (1939
– recanted however at 1966, 103) for 'no focal point'. For 'no plot' cf. e.g.
Vellacott 1961, 18. Broadhead himself (ibid. xl) writes of three main acts
'connected in parallel rather than in series'. With friends like these, who needs
enemies?

[29] Cf. Herington 1985, 145. In *Ag*, the murder is deliberately postponed by
the Kassandra scene, which at first appears to be totally extraneous; yet few
scholars have complained of structural weakness there – presumably because
Agamemnon is not 'early tragedy' but an acknowledged masterpiece. Was
Aischylos infinitely more proficient in dramatic technique at age 67 than at 53?

Like *Agamemnon*, this drama is built upon the homecoming story pattern.[30] The ending is therefore the return of the defeated Xerxes, to show in action in the theatre the full consequences of the defeat at Salamis. However, this spectacle would have no point, until his fall is fully understood, and set in its place in relation to past and future events.[31] Aischylos sets the action during the return of Xerxes, and leaves the final disaster of Plataia to be narrated as a prophecy by Dareios, linked into an overview which places them in the fullest context; this makes the whole sequence of disasters comprehensible, and gives Dareios a basis from which to launch his denunciation of Xerxes' folly. And that moment – the end of the Dareios scene, when it is fully understood both *how* and *why* the power of Persia was crippled by Xerxes' expedition – is necessary preparation for the Finale. It is therefore the focal point towards which the drama aims single-mindedly from the outset, following the pattern of expectation, fulfilment and subsequent apprehension which Aischylos was later to refine still further in *Agamemnon*.[32]

The Queen re-enters almost alone, clothed in black;[33] the contrast between her present mourning and her former chariot, robes of state and many attendants matches and follows on from the despair of the Elders. The dynamics of the stage picture change, as she first addresses the Elders briefly (from BC?), then takes the properties which she and her maidservant are holding up-*orchêstra* towards the mound EBC. This now suddenly becomes the focus of attention, as the two women kneel before it with the offerings of milk, honey, wine and olives,[34] and the drama sets out on what at first sight seems a new direction but is in reality the preparation for its logical climax.[35]

[30] On this pattern cf. Ewans 1982a, 6ff.; on its application to *Persians*, Taplin 1977, 124ff.

[31] In this way the Dareios scene is very similar to the Kassandra scene. Xerxes' return, like Agamemnon's death, is not allowed to take place in the action of the drama until it has been set fully in the context of the past, the hidden present and the future. Cf. Ewans 1995, 149ff.

[32] Ewans 1995, 129ff.

[33] Taplin 1977, 99.

[34] Libation pouring, and invoking a dead king to help, are replicated, with even greater dramatic sophistication, in *L B* Scene 2.

[35] One reason why Aischylos gives no previous preparation, except the presence of the mound, for the appearance of Dareios is that similar scenes of the raising of a dead hero's spirit were (on the evidence of vase-painting) apparently common in early fifth-century tragedy; Green 1994, 17–18.

Choros 3

The spirits of the dead inhabit a shadowy, ill-defined underworld. They are within the power of its ruler, Hades, and the other gods associated with his realm. But they are also in their graves. The dead are present when a dirge is sung for them, and aware of what is done beside their tombs. But the senses are dulled by death, and strenuous effort is needed to ensure that a prayer or offering truly reaches the dead.

These basic conditions of Greek belief lie behind this ode. The Elders must complement the Queen's offerings with a song of sufficient intensity to persuade the gods below to release Dareios (Introduction and A2–B2) and to make the King himself hear them (A1, C1–3). To emphasize the specifically Persian character and extreme emotionalism of this lament, Aischylos once again has the *choros* interject outcries, at the end of both B stanzas. He also used in the original Greek an unsettling variety of metres, including the choriamb characteristic of moods of foreboding or struggle, and the dochmiac, the most excited of all Greek lyric metres. A Persian form of the king's name – 'Darian' – occurs twice;[36] and the Elders refer explicitly in C1 to details of regal costume which presumably were reflected in Dareios' actual costume for the next scene.[37] In these ways the invocation creates a series of exotic effects, in preparation for the sudden appearance of the Shade of Dareios at its climax.

Scene 3

The Shade rises slowly and majestically from behind the tomb, and steps onto it before the first speech.

Dareios' appearance and prophecy form the climax of the drama. Aischylos deliberately disregards historical reality, passing over the expansionist activities of the historical Dareios[38] to create contrasts between father and son. Dareios won an empire by his sound sense, Xerxes lost it by his folly; therefore, Dareios wears his full regal costume, while Xerxes will appear in rags, and Dareios speaks sober

---

[36] 651/672. It directly transcribes the Persian Daryana, as opposed to the hellenized Dareios used elsewhere in the drama.

[37] 661–2 specifically invoke the 'peak' of his tiara, because only kings could wear this ornate head-dress fully upright.

[38] You would not imagine from this scene that the Athenians had repelled Dareios' invasion force at Marathon, much less that the playwright fought there himself, and one of his brothers was killed in the battle.

and eloquent trimeter verse, while Xerxes sings throughout the Finale, sometimes almost incoherently, to express his grief.

Aischylos uses several dramatic devices to highlight Dareios' 'message'. After the powerful invocation in Choros 3, the actual appearance of their dead king's Shade is so awe-inspiring that the Elders are overcome, and unable to communicate with him. Their extreme emotion is (naturally, in Greek tragedy) expressed not by silence but in lyric verse – and so the emotional temperature is brought down only gradually from the intensity reached in the three C stanzas of the preceding Choros. The Shade does not know that Xerxes has led out an expedition and been defeated. This is implausible, given that Dareios is about to show prophetic insight into the future; but it enables the scene to link the events narrated by the Messenger with Dareios' development of the moral truths set out in Choros 1;[39] and it works very well in the theatre, since the *stichomythia* between Dareios and his Queen builds up a tension which demands release. This then occurs in the first of three great speeches, in which Aischylos dramatizes the fundamental beliefs underlying the drama; the way in which Xerxes' voluntary folly has brought down on Persia a *moira*, whose fulfilment could have taken long to achieve (739ff.); the idea of natural limits, and the danger of offending gods (744ff.); the link between sensible restraint and successful rule, in all previous kings of Persia (759ff.); the punishment which awaits the chosen force still in Greece, for desecrating the altars and shrines of the gods (800ff.); and the destructive consequences of excessive greed (822ff.)

Plataia's role in the design of the drama now becomes clear; this final, culminating disaster is not simply reserved for Dareios' speech because to tell it would intolerably overload the Messenger scene, and indeed the whole first half of the drama; nor even for patriotic reasons, since Aischylos underplays the Athenian achievement at Salamis;[40] he also gives the Spartans all the credit for Plataia (817), even though an Athenian contingent played a vital supporting role.[41] In this position, and in Dareios' mouth, 'Plataia becomes a kind of crowning misfortune, exemplifying the whole tragic experience of the Persians'.[42] The appre-

[39] Cf. Michelini 1982, 144.

[40] In particular, he does not refer to the Athenian Aristeides, who planned and executed the deaths of the picked Persian force placed on Psyttaleia (447ff.; Herodotos 8.95).

[41] Herodotos 9.61.

[42] Michelini 1982, 121.

hensions which dominated Choros 1 from B3 to the end have now become reality.

The scene is too long, and too dynamic, for Dareios to remain stranded up on his tomb. He needs to be down in the *orchêstra* by 739 at the latest, since the big speeches cry out for freedom to move, and a commanding central position, to make their delivery effective. Since his opening remarks (to 708) are relatively ghostly and disembodied, and *stichomythia* always implies close engagement, Dareios' best movement cue is the end of the Queen's speech, the news at 714 that Persia is totally defeated. He can then come down, and forward towards her, during the first part of the exchanges that follow, breaking away to take the centre at 739. Note how the Queen responds to his first speech, while Dareios addresses the Elders at the end of this second (784ff.); they have recovered from their awe during his discourse on Persian royal history, and moved closer. The irregular dialogue after the second speech precipitates another 'break-out' by Dareios, for the third and final speech; and at the end he addresses both the Elders and the Queen (829ff.) – implying that before that they are all in front of his dominant position at C/BC. The Elders are to talk sense into Xerxes; his consort is to find good clothes, to take away the humiliation of Xerxes' rags.[43]

After these closing remarks, the Shade retreats again to the tomb: 841ff., like Kassandra's last words in *Agamemnon*,[44] play well if Dareios turns back, on top of it, to deliver the lines just before his final departure.

Choros 4

The shock of Xerxes' appearance, alone and in rags, and the even greater shock that the defeated king expresses himself only in song, have been prepared for by contrast in the decorum maintained both by the Queen and by Dareios. Now that contrast is established still more firmly. Unlike their earlier, more emotional lyric reactions to the defeat, the Elders' song now is a calm, nostalgic summary of the greatness of Dareios' rule. Aischylos once again places focus on the extent to which the Persians had subdued the Ionian islands, because this would mean most to the Athenian audience and their guests from elsewhere in

---

[43] The Queen accepts Dareios' advice (855ff.). Aischylos thus sets up the final surprise of the drama, the entry of Xerxes for the Finale still in rags. Cf. Michelini 1982, 136–7.

[44] Ewans 1995, 151.

Greece; and now the contrasting reminder of defeat at 903ff. is brief, and relatively muted.

Finale

Explicit, open grief was unmanly in ancient Greek ethics. The *threnos*, the ritual lament for death and disaster, was for their community, as in the keening at an Irish wake,[45] normally the work of females. The appearance of Xerxes in rags, and singing throughout the scene,[46] reinforces the presentation of his Persia as decadent and effeminate which has been cultivated throughout the drama.[47] However, the main aim of the scene is to show how the Persians come to terms with the appalling extent of the disaster, and learn to live on.[48]

Xerxes enters alone, but on a tented carriage. This, the scholarly consensus, has been disputed by Taplin,[49] on the grounds primarily that his total isolation in defeat would be best conveyed by entering alone and on foot. However, this requires a very strained interpretation of 1000–1002, which clearly imply that the Elders can see the carriage but not see the troops who would normally accompany it; and the wagon's presence intensifies the pathos, contrasting this last piece of luxury with the abject failure of Xerxes to bring back what really matters to the power of Persia – the men whom he has lost.[50]

The carriage establishes a nice parallel (and contrast) with the entry of the Queen for Scene 1. Like hers, Xerxes' carriage needs to come to rest upstage, between EBC and BC, for the ensuing action to work effectively in the theatre. It gives the king a place to cower as he delivers his opening solo chant, wishing he was dead rather than confronting his Elders; their chanted response (918–21) almost explicitly calls him down and forward to join them in the *kommos* of lamentation. His descent is 'covered' by their chanted prologue at 922ff; during this, he

[45] Macintosh 1994, 33ff.

[46] Played therefore by the same actor as the Queen.

[47] Cf. Hall 1989, 81–5. It is worth noting that two of the kings who notoriously appeared in rags, violating the normal conventions of the Athenian theatre, were barbarians – Xerxes, and the Mysian Telephos in Euripides' drama of that name, which Aristophanes parodied mercilessly in *Acharnians*. (The other ragged king in tragedy was Greek – Menelaos after shipwreck in Euripides' *Helen*.)

[48] Gagarin 1976, 40–42; he traces this element back to 290ff.

[49] 1977, 121–7.

[50] So Broadhead 1960, 223. I understand that Hall will argue the case for the carriage further in her forthcoming edition of *Persians*.

comes forward to C to meet them, so he can begin the sequence of song and dance at 931.

Like the Finale of *Seven against Thebes*, this *kommos* begins relatively coherently, but later becomes more intense and fragmentary in its outpouring of grief. Xerxes was right to fear confronting his Elders, since they place the responsibility squarely on him in 922ff., before the lament proper has even begun; and he begins by accepting all its weight. There is no question now of the Elders educating Xerxes in the wisdom of self-restraint, as Dareios asked them (829ff.); nor of the comfort which the Queen might have given him, to prevent any thought of suicide (837f., cf. 530–1); in this lyric Finale, lamentation is all, and the drama's third and final catalogue of names (954ff.) accuses Xerxes to his face (e.g. 973).

His total inability to reply precipitates the movement at 1002 into the closing pattern, with a closer interchange between the singers. The pathos intensifies further in the E stanzas, with the evocation of Xerxes' empty quiver, his ragged garments and his lack of attendants; and in the F stanzas from 1038 the drama reaches its final pitch of intensity, with both choros and soloist uttering the ancient ritual cry of grief, 'Otototoi' (I leave it untranslated), crying out, beating their chests and tearing their hair and clothes. The tension only eases in the concluding *epode* G3, as Xerxes (since his young guard of honour is now dead) needs his Persian Elders to escort him to his palace, where he will have to live, clothe himself – and continue to rule Persia.[51]

'The long drawn out lament may be boring and monotonous for many modern readers, but it was assuredly not such for the ancient Greek spectator, who was well accustomed to *threnoi* of this kind.'[52] Aischylos did not write this text for readers of any kind, let alone those whose culture educates them to regard public displays of emotion as unseemly. He wrote it for performance before an Athenian audience, who were nurtured on a rich tradition of ritual and cult, and understood instinctively the importance of public expression of grief for pain and humiliation. They heard a script whose texture and shape varies throughout – sometimes subtly, and sometimes violently; and they saw

[51] Being Persian, they will be graceful in their footsteps even in grief; the picture of Xerxes' necessary survival and elegant suffering is deliberately contrasted with the more normal Greek pattern of unmitigated disaster for the king, and the end of his reign in death or exile (e.g. *Seven against Thebes*, Sophokles *Oidipous the King*); Seaford 1994, 355.

[52] Broadhead 1960, 315.

and heard a rich combination of dance and music, by which the actors evoked all the emotions of their characters. The Finale is written with both compassion and power; Aischylos ensures that the spectators are 'not meant to stand outside [the laments] with an attitude of smirking and self-righteous scorn. . . . The audience should feel for and experience the well-deserved but none the less terrible and moving fall of Persia.'[53]

Seven against Thebes

Scene 1

The opening Scene and Choros present a violently contrasted polarity between male and female responses to the state of siege. As the extras playing males file on, old men[1] and boys are mingled with citizens in the small crowd; this opening image brings out, simply and directly, the desperate plight of Thebes.[2]

The men and boys enter slowly and solemnly, and take up position in formation. (Their entry must be as orderly as possible, for contrast with the violent, disorderly entry of the Women for Choros 1.) The best position for passive recipients of an address in the Greek playing space is ELC/EFC/ERC facing the *skene*; this gives the maximum playing area for the actor to present his case to them.

The actor playing Eteokles enters from the changing tent, to signal that he comes, here and in Scene 2, from his home base; the exit after Scene 2, and re-entry from the left *parodos* for Scene 3, indicate that

[53] Taplin 1977, 127.

[1] Eteokles' joke at 12 indicates that some of them sport the paunches which were normally characteristic of old men in comedy; a touch of Aischylean humour, which is often either emended away by editors of the Greek text, or suppressed in translation.

[2] Some expense was involved, since the extras are not used again in this drama; almost certainly therefore they had already appeared in *Laios* and/or *Oidipous*. (Extras are definitely needed to represent the citizens, and effect a proper contrast with the Women played by the *choros*; there is no parallel for the playwright's own Athenian audience being used to represent an imaginary crowd. Cf. Taplin 1977, 129ff.)

Pace Taplin 1977, 134ff., this drama does not begin with a 'cancelled entry' – a tableau taken up, and then imagined to have been there for some time before the action begins. How could the audience have taken the arrival of the extras playing the citizens, in a curtainless, open-air *orchêstra*, as anything but the beginning of the drama?

Eteokles has gone into the city to make the troop dispositions promised at 283ff.

Eteokles enters BC, and the opening part of the speech, in which he tries to 'soften up' his audience by accepting his own responsibility, plays well from BC, advancing gradually to C to begin the direct, forceful address to them at 10ff. This rapidly turns into a plangent appeal to them, and here the actor needs to advance right up to the crowd of extras.

During 21-3 Eteokles is in transition; the actor needs to move back to C, so he may have the fullest command both of his audience of extras and of the audience proper for the news delivered at 24ff. Then 30ff. invite further movement; a second, more vigorous advance towards them – urging them on, perhaps driving some reluctant ones out.[3] As a result, in an unusual effect which vividly conveys the urgency of the scene, the Scout must burst through some of the crowd of departing extras to begin his own speech.

A traditional conception of Aischylean tragedy would have a virtually static Scout deliver his speech to a completely static Eteokles. But the circular *orchêstra* positively invites movement to accompany a speech of this vigour, and in workshopping the scene we rapidly discovered that the speech plays most effectively if the Scout roams around the whole playing space to deliver it, stopping only to emphasize particular points. This disempowers Eteokles, and conveys that initially the terrible power of the Argive Seven overwhelms him. The Scout halts suddenly at a dominant position (e.g. BC) on 64, and delivers the three exit lines almost as an aside – then he is off, as fast as he came.[4]

Eteokles recovers slowly, and with difficulty. There should be a pause after the Scout exits, to demonstrate the power of the attack. Then Eteokles moves gradually away from the subordinate position into which he has been forced (e.g. FR/FL), and makes a firm, careful prayer to all the gods – in designed contrast to the savage rites of sacrifice evoked by the Scout in his description of the Argive champions at 42ff. For this he needs to move gradually up to C or BC, regaining power – and also facing towards the images as the prayer begins, though

---

[3] Taplin (1977, 166-7) is wrong to send the citizens out after 35; either the process of their exit would drown Eteokles' last three lines, or he would have to wait artificially until they have all gone, and then deliver the lines as an address to the air and the sky. *Eu* 232-4 are not a true parallel, since the Furies exeunt immediately after their last line, which is delivered from the perimeter.

[4] Cf. Klytaimestra in *Ag* Scene 3.

perhaps turning round, to face the majority of the audience, for the last few lines. Then he departs.[5]

Choros 1

Aischylos selects special devices to convey the panic of the Women, and mark the contrast between the firm close of the spoken scene and the lyric entry of the *choros*. Their entrance-song is *astrophic* to 108; the lines are obviously divided between all twelve individual singers; and the implied choreography is equally turbulent. Individual choros members enter one by one (as in the notorious first choros of *Eumenides*), and pursue separate, violently emotional patterns of movement to illuminate the text.[6]

The images of the gods are a constant, stable in contrast to the storm of outside noise and inner panic at Thebes. The Women first consider approaching them at 95ff., but are too cowardly to do so (97–8); they do not turn into the upper third of the *orchêstra*, and begin to approach the gods, until the lyrics settle down into matching stanzas at 109ff. However, even here the music remains volatile, and the text still implies subdivision between different singers.[7] Therefore the dance remains free, moving nearer to the images in the A stanzas, but not reaching the periphery of the *orchêstra*.

The violent exclamations at the opening of each of the B stanzas imply that here the Women break away suddenly, circling round the

---

[5] *Pace* Canavan (1972, 91) and Scott (1984, 216), Eteokles should not be present for Choros 1; this would be unnecessary, since there is no need for him to overhear the whole of their invocation to understand the general thrust of what they are doing (the last few lines would be enough to justify his comments at 185–6). It is also unrealistic; 'the reproaches of the man of action in 181ff. lose much of their sense if Eteokles has not been busy offstage' (Taplin 1977, 139–41). The start of Scene 2 is far more theatrically effective if Eteokles enters in haste to begin his attack on the Women.

[6] No offstage sounds are required; the extraordinary imagery (and phrasing – cf. e.g. 103) and the accompanying music and dance fully evoke both the power of the invading army and the Women's terrified response. (Canavan 1972, 76–7 rightly notes that the only 'offstage noise' known to have been used in fifth-century tragedy was the *bronteion* for making thunder; cf. e.g. Sophokles, *Oidipous at Kolonos*, 1455ff.)

[7] Thalmann (1978, 88–9) notes that the gods are approached in a symmetrical sequence after 109, beginning with the city gods and Zeus, then passing via Athena, Ares, Apollo, and Artemis to Hera at 152, before working back through these gods in reverse order. He conjectures that the statues of Zeus and Hera stood at the two ends of the line.

whole *orchêstra*, and only return to a more normal, solemn mood in
the closing C strophic pair, where clearly they face towards the images
and address them directly – probably in a more stable, unified dance by
contrast with what has gone before.

Scene 2

Eteokles re-enters furiously for the confrontation between male and
female which is now almost inevitable, in view of the contrast between
the first Scene and the first Choros.[8] The extent of his anger is conveyed
by the sheer vigour of his response; even these relatively calm supplica-
tions are intolerable to him, under the stress of leading a city under
siege.[9]

Eteokles drives them back towards the front perimeter with the first
five lines, and then circles slowly along the length of their (now subdued
– and therefore, to convey their weakness, scattered) formation during
the second beat to 195, before moving back to a commanding position
at the centre before 200–201. After a pause in which there is no reply,
he turns angrily back towards them with 203.

Then there is a surprise; the Women, far from remaining cowed by
his vigorous rhetoric, as their silence after 202 implies, burst out into a
sung response. Aischylos' decision that they should respond in lyrics
intensifies the emotional level of the action.[10] An *epirrhematic scene*
now unfolds, a subtle and complex confrontation analogous to that
between the Danaides and Pelasgos at *Suppliants* 347ff. Here as there
the power-holding male is forced not (as he had perhaps hoped) to
engage female opponents in logical debate; instead he must oppose
reason and speech to a violently choreographed, emotional presentation

---

[8] This entry is far more effective if he comes back suddenly from a changing-
tent positioned behind the *orchêstra* than if he has to make a long-visible entry
down a *parodos*.

[9] There has been much speculation on the causes of Eteokles' hostility to
women – absent fathers in three generations, alienation from mother earth,
brooding on his mother's incest etc.; for an extreme example cf. Caldwell 1973.
Eteokles' sentiments at 187ff. are unpalatable in the context of modern western
attitudes to gender equality, but do not go much further than normal Athenian
definitions of the demarcation between the male world of politics and warfare,
and the place of females, whose sphere of action was normally confined to the
oikos. The speech is very different in tone and content from the lengthy
ramblings of the two Euripidean males who are overtly misogynistic, and suffer
terribly for it; Iason in *Medeia* (522ff.) and Hippolytos (*Hipp.* 616ff.).

[10] The effect is the direct opposite of the 'stylized formality' diagnosed by
Podlecki (1966, 29).

of the Women's feelings. This is because (despite the vigour with which Eteokles has criticized the Women) both sides are right; male courage is indeed needed in a city under siege – but so too are those invocations to the gods which, with all the men fully occupied, only women can make. Accordingly, Eteokles' task here is not easy; he needs to turn to and move towards the singers of each stanza,[11] delivering an effective response to each one but only gradually calming them until, after his last speech 242ff., there is no counter-attack in song.[12]

Instead – perhaps after a moment's pause, which once again deludes Eteokles and the audience into believing they are all calm – one of the Women expresses panic again. But now the medium is changed; she expresses it in speech, in one line – and so gives Eteokles an opportunity to take up this challenge in a different medium, *stichomythia*. The scene reaches its climax in the exchange which follows, and this works best if the Women's lines are divided between members of the *choros* separated from each other by considerable physical space; Eteokles, after silencing one *choros* member by his response, then has to turn to attack a new outbreak of fear.

The Women have moved up by the images, terrified, at the conclusion of the choreography;[13] accordingly Eteokles has to address members of a group fanned out EBL to EBR, and can only do so effectively from positions somewhere near the centre-line from L via C to R. After one last diatribe against women at 254, he becomes more conciliatory in the closing exchanges, and so silences their outcries; his victory, and the restoration of his power and control, are shown in the theatre when the Women return peacefully to the *orchêstra*. 267–70 were written to cover their move away from the images, and into the front half, to take the emphasis away from them during Eteokles' prayer. That leaves Eteokles with the centre and back centre, from which he can first address the gods in 271ff., and then turn forward on 279 to address the rest of the scene to the Women. He walks to the edge of the playing space during 282ff., and leaves immediately after the last line.

[11] The scene plays much better if an individual *choros* member sings each stanza.
[12] In a fascinating contrast with his own technique in the Kassandra scene in the later *Agamemnon*, Aischylos symbolizes their increasing calm by decreasing the number of lines in each stanza as the subscene unfolds. Eteokles' unyielding position is conveyed by the fact that his spoken responses remain three lines long throughout the exchange.
[13] This is implied by 239ff., and confirmed by Eteokles at 265.

Choros 2

When the Women gave in to him and agreed to be silent, Eteokles
made a concession (268–9, 279–81); they can pray to the gods,
provided they do so with well-omened sounds. Aischylos leads the
audience to expect a second Choros in which the Women gradually
take up a fuller and more confident possession of the *orchêstra* space;
but the ode which they now sing, though much more stable in tone and
content than Choros 1, does not comply with Eteokles' wishes. Moving
away from the images of the gods, they begin by using the whole
performance area to dance both their terror and (in A2, to the same
choreography) a passionate appeal for protection.

Then, in the B stanzas, they evoke the sack of Thebes in a fierce song
of ever-increasing power, wholly viewed from their own position as
women. This leads on to even greater intensity in the C stanzas;[14] the
bloody cries of babies in the first lines of the C1 stanza are to be danced
in parallel with the destruction of life-giving produce in C2, and the
image of plunder and pillage, which closes C1, is set in parallel with
the extraordinarily violent final moments, where the Women picture
newly enslaved girls who are raped, and find release from all their grief
in the moment when orgasm is forced on them.

The background against which Eteokles, in Scene 3, has to defend
Thebes against the onslaught of the seven champions is very different
from the optimistic song which he requested as he left. Choros 2 has
established all too well the reality of what will happen to the city if he
fails to match and overcome all his opponents.

Scene 3

A controversy has developed because Eteokles responds to the Scout's
descriptions of the Argive champions with varying tenses ('I will
place . . .' 407, 'I have set . . .' 447 etc.). Has he already decided who
will defend Thebes at each of the seven gates, or does he choose an
appropriate champion in front of our eyes, to match the character and
boast of the Argive whom the Scout describes?

Most modern scholars feel that 'Eteokles is choosing, of his own
volition and in the light of the opposing champions, defenders for the
city, not simply witnessing in helpless and unspoken amazement the
machinations whereby his previously determined choices are by some

[14] There are also extraordinary poetic devices; for example, the alliteration in
349ff. is an attempt to echo the powerful use of this technique in the original
Greek.

daimonic manipulation perfectly matched'.[15] However, this view is clearly incompatible with 282ff., where Eteokles specifically declares that he is going to choose his champions before the Scout can come back; it is necessary to explain away the past tenses and either ignore those lines, or suspect them of being interpolated.[16]

Wolff[17] argued that Eteokles has already decided which champion will defend Thebes at each of the seven gates: 'the scene shows us recognition, not decision'.[18] This view has had less followers, since the two emphatic future tenses at 407 and 620 would seem to rule it out; but it has been persuasively advocated.[19]

Both theories are too extreme. The text clearly suggests that between Scenes 2 and 3 Eteokles has selected six champions to join him in defence of the seven gates. However, we do not simply watch a recital and matching-up of two separate, pre-prepared lists; in Scene 3 Eteokles chooses which of his seven preselected champions will fight at each of the seven gates, in view of the character of the opponent whom the lot on the Argive side has placed there.

In the words of these speeches two different actions proceed simultaneously; the battle for Thebes is being fought and won in advance, and by correct anticipation of the result when the selected champions fight after Eteokles' exit; and Eteokles' personal *moira* is taking shape, as he assigns six champions other than himself to fight at the first six gates, not knowing that the lot has chosen his brother to attack Thebes at the seventh. With each choice, he comes nearer to the climax of the drama, the moment when he realizes that he must choose to fight against his own brother.[20]

Most of the older critics[21] believed that the six Theban champions came on, played by silent faces, at the start of the scene; each leaves

---

[15] Kirkwood 1969, 13; cf. Taplin 1977, 154 and others.

[16] So Taplin ibid., following Macleod.

[17] 1958.

[18] Burnett 1973, 348.

[19] Burnett 1973, *passim*. Cf. also Cameron 1971, 39ff. and Canavan 1972, 93.

[20] Cf. Ley 1986, 44–48. The principal characters of the *Oresteia* find themselves placed similarly, at the climactic moments, in situations where they must choose between two potentially disastrous alternatives, only one of which can and therefore must be done (Ewans 1995, xxix–xxxiii). I argue in Ewans 1996 that the process by which a *moira* takes shape is fundamental to Greek and Shakespearian tragedy.

[21] Bibliography at Taplin 1977, 150. So too Hogan 1984, 251.

when he has been assigned. Hecht and Bacon revived this idea, supplying each champion with a blazoned shield and an escort of support troops.[22]

This gratuitous spectacle may safely be dismissed, because Aischylos invariably mentions, and uses for dramatic effect, any extras or properties which he introduces into the *orchêstra*; and because the presence of the six other champions would diminish the focus on Eteokles' isolation as the doomed son of Oidipous.[23] The battle between Thebans and Argives is fought by proxy, through description, imagery, movement and dance. Just as the attackers are unseen, so too are the defenders.

However, this does not mean that nothing happened in the playing space during the scene. On the contrary, the vigour of the movements needed in Scene 1, when the Scout communicated to Eteokles, and to the audience, the power and savagery of the Argive Seven, prefigures an equally strong use of movement in this scene as well. The contrast between the first and third scenes lies in the fact that now Eteokles has retrieved the inner strength, and so the ability, which he needs to counter-attack against the boasts and shield-devices of the attacking champions. This must be shown by assertive, firm counter-movements during each of his first six speeches, in deliberate contrast both with his temporary defeat in Scene 1 and with the outburst at the climax of this scene.

Six pairs of speeches are followed by a seventh for the Scout, whose personal impact on Eteokles is so great that it breaks the pattern. The symmetry between these successive pairs is denoted by a sequence of short, strophically responding choral stanzas which mark the first six pairs off from each other; the violence of Eteokles' response to Polyneikes' challenge then deprives the Women of the chance to sing a seventh stanza. These stanzas are usually regarded as an almost trivial background commentary, musical interludes between serious speech and therefore sung (and danced, if at all) from a muted and passive position towards the front of the *orchêstra*.

This is unlikely. It is obvious as soon as the scene is put into rehearsal that the choral stanzas are a major component in the structure. Aischylos has by this point devoted two choral odes and one scene to making his audience take the viewpoint of the unmarried women seriously; their successive responses to the pairs of champions oscillate between hope, confidence, fear and expectation, inflect our view of Eteokles' success in each of his responses, and so prepare the audience for the end of the scene, where the pattern is broken, as the Scout announces Polyneikes and then leaves abruptly. Then, in a remarkable inversion of roles, the Women address the curse-driven Eteokles from a position of authority (676ff.) and their unsuccessful attempt to dissuade him forms the climax of the drama.[24]

Accordingly these choral interventions should be performed, to make an adequate impact, as sudden repossessions of the *orchêstra*.[25] The *choros* members should yield, after their two symmetrical speeches of announcement at the start of the scene,[26] into the position of minimum emphasis in the Greek theatre space – EFR–EFC–EFL; and then suddenly surge forward, temporarily occupying as much as possible of the playing area, during each of the brief lyrics, before retreating again out of an emphatic position so they can hear (and respond to) the next phase of the combat.

This is a metaphorical duel between the Argives, who are represented in the vigorous speeches and movements of the Scout, and Eteokles.[27] Each attacking champion wields a shield, whose device symbolizes the magic with which he seeks to overwhelm his opponent, and makes clear the nature of his boast. Because the scene has often been thought to be primarily verbal and theatrically static, much interpretative zeal has been devoted to the imagery of the shields and their emblems;[28] but the subtleties of literary interpretation have sometimes obscured the through-line of the scene. Aischylos develops here the contrast which was established in Scene 1, between Eteokles' steady and just appeals for civic defence and the violence of the Argive oath and lot-drawing. This contest has two basic axes: the contrast between random chance

[24] For a contrasting view cf. Burnett 1973, 348; for her, the description of each defender increasingly proves the foolishness of the Women's terror. In my judgement Aischylos evokes the Women's terror of the Argives so powerfully in the earlier scenes and odes not to demonstrate their folly but to dramatize the extent of the danger from outside which Eteokles must successfully oppose by his dispositions in this scene.

[25] Cf. the brief choral odes in the second half of *Libation Bearers*; Ewans 1995a, 163–4.

[26] These, of course, are designed to prefigure the symmetry of the speeches between the two men whose arrival is being announced.

[27] Perhaps the general area of the playing space which the Scout occupies draws closer to that of Eteokles, and becomes more invasive, as the scene proceeds.

[28] Cf. especially Bacon 1964, Zeitlin 1982 and Thalmann 1978.

on the Argive side and careful, rational selection by Eteokles; and the contrast between values – a self-destructive impiety in all but one of the attackers and a love of native city, and respect for true excellence, in Eteokles and all of his six Theban champions. The power of the scene lies in the irony with which – after the example of Amphiaraos outside the sixth gate warns that the threshold of the city is not a simple dividing line between excellence inside and excess outside – the respecter and champion of a patriotic and true modesty becomes overwhelmed, in his choice for the seventh gate, by those very qualities of passion and excess against which he has so far fought successfully, on behalf of the city.[29]

1 **Proitos' gate; Tydeus, Astakos** Tydeus' maddened rage and over-boastful shield are opposed by a man who honours Modesty, and fights for the Justice of his parents and his motherland; this is the keynote, the fundamental difference between the Argives and the Thebans. Accordingly it is stressed in the sung response of the Women, and developed in the contrast between the next three pairs. There is also another theme; the internal dissension inside the Argive camp,[30] and the inability of the just and truly noble prophet Amphiaraos to coexist with the excesses of the other champions, are established here, in preparation for the sixth gate.

2 **Elektran gate; Kapaneus, Polyphontes** The theme of great strength allied with arrogance is developed in Kapaneus; physically a giant, he comes with an even more excessive boast, defying Zeus himself. Eteokles duly chooses against him a man of firm strength, who has the goodwill of the gods. Again the Women's dance stresses the arrogance, reminding the audience also, as they express their fear of rape, of the realities of a city's sack which they evoked so vividly in Choros 3.

[29] Although Aischylos departs from the actual topographical order of Thebes' gates (see Glossary), there seems to be no particular significance to the gate assigned to each pair of champions, with the exception of the fourth.

[30] Thalmann (1978, 34) sees a correspondence between this dissension and the tension inside Thebes between Eteokles and the Women. This should not be pressed too far; for the ancient Greeks, internal strife between the males of a fighting force was a far more serious problem than a conflict between a unified male fighting force (as Thebes, under Eteokles' command, clearly is in this drama) and the panic of unmarried women.

3 **Neis gate; Eteoklos, Megareus** Eteokles' near-namesake is a similar opponent. The Scout's narrative evokes the champion's power through a vivid description of his armoured horses, and of his shield – where once again the boast is that the bearer is more powerful than a god. Eteokles, and the Women, both stress the contrast between Megareus, fighting for his home, and the haughty words of the Argive attacker.

4 **Gate of Athena Ogka; Hippomedon, Hyperbios** Like the attacker at the second gate, Hippomedon is described in terms of sheer size and terrifying aspect; his shield-device, the fire-breathing monster Typhon, and his war-cry both emphasize his rage and excess of frenzy. By contrast this gate lies beside the temple of the goddess of wisdom herself, and the defender exhibits all the qualities which made up human excellence in Greek eyes; perfection of physical form and of spirit, and military excellence.

Zeus was challenged overtly at the second gate; here again the Argive shield-device challenges the supreme god, with its image of one of his ancient enemies. Eteokles in reply describes a Theban shield-device for the only time; Hyperbios bears Zeus himself upon the shield, making the Theban response precisely appropriate. The Women's stanza, like Eteokles' speech, therefore stresses their (justified) confidence that Zeus will prevail.

5 **Northern gate; Parthenopaios, Aktor** The ground-pattern of the scene has been established at the first four gates; now the issues become more complex. Parthenopaios is overboastful not through excessive arrogance, but because he is young and untried – on the threshold between boy and man. And his shield-device contains the first direct, specific reference to Thebes, and to the past history of its royal family. Against him Eteokles places Aktor, a man of deeds rather than words, and images a Sphinx beaten down outside the city walls.

This response is less deft than those before. The Scout did not suggest that Parthenopaios brags on at length, as Eteokles implies at 557–8; and Eteokles does not refer to the defeat of the Sphinx by his father Oidipous, even though this would have had great point in the context.[31] The Women's lyric response to this pairing and the next is correspondingly less hard-edged than before; an emotional reaction, a prayer

[31] It was the subject of the *satyr-drama* which followed *Seven against Thebes* in the original performance.

which contrasts with the moral conviction expressed in their responses to the first four pairs.

6 Homolian Gate; Amphiaraos, Lasthenes After his less than perfect response to Parthenopaios, Eteokles is set a far greater challenge. Amphiaraos reciprocates Tydeus' contempt for him; he criticizes Tydeus for insane excesses, characterizes the whole expedition as madness, and goes on to mount a trenchant critique of Polyneikes' attack upon his native land. In this way the two main themes of Eteokles' ripostes to the first four attackers are echoed – but now from the other side of the walls.

Amphiaraos is a man of complete excellence – symbolized by the absence of any sign from his shield, and expressed in the famous line (592) 'he/does not just want to seem, but actually to be the best'.[32] Eteokles finds, and carefully develops, the only possible counter-attack; conceding Amphiaraos' personal excellence, he argues that it is neutralized by the impious, overboastful company into which he has entered. Lasthenes' wisdom, strength and determination to preserve his native land will hardly be needed. The Women sum up, dancing a prayer for victory (like stanza C1, without moral comment) as if this were the end. The Scout's next move, and his final speech, completely disrupt this pattern.

7 The seventh gate; Polyneikes, Eteokles Amphiaraos' words looked back, to the attacker at the first gate – and forward, to the seventh. They established in advance the wrongness of Polyneikes' cause, even before we hear from the Scout Polyneikes' ferocious determination for victory, and his claim to be led by Justice. Eteokles' riposte, once he has recovered from the shock, is a simple denial of the opposing claim, in contrast with the clever reinterpretations which he offered for the first five opponents. Morally, Polyneikes is in the wrong – rash, unjust, and attacking his native land.[33]

---

[32] According to Plutarch (*Life of Aristeides* ch. 3) at this moment all eyes in the audience turned to a prominent citizen of Athens, Aristeides (nicknamed 'the just'). Podlecki (1966, 36–40) shows it is unlikely that Aischylos intended an allusion to him.

[33] Gagarin (1970, 122) notes the one-sidedness of Eteokles' claim, and speculates that some of the events in *Oidipous* might have presented Polyneikes' claim to justice in a more favourable light. There has been a tendency to accept Eteokles' claims uncritically, partly for the good reason that Polyneikes is attacking his native land, accompanied by five impious foreigners – and partly

Most modern scholars insist that Eteokles' decision, and his inflexi-
bility when the Women attempt to dissuade him, show the influence of
madness; a Fury, sent by the gods, imposes on him that self-destructive
blindness which the Greeks called *Ate*.[34] This reading diminishes the
power and subtlety of Aischylos' psychological insight. Eteokles first
has a moment of agony, as he recognizes the fulfilment of the Curse of
Oidipous; he is then shown, under extreme external pressure, thinking
rationally through to a decision to act.[35] But the decision is monstrous,
since it involves the shedding of kindred blood; the Women's response
to Eteokles is so passionate simply because he is intent on causing near-
indelible *miasma* by fighting his own brother.

However, Eteokles is not irrational or insane. His lines remain
spoken right to the end of the scene, and therefore never rise to the
passionate level of emotional expression which in Greek tragedy is the
domain of the lyric. In this scene, the power of his father's Curse is not
shown through a sudden outburst of madness in the central figure. The
Fury or Curse manifests itself not by affecting character or psychology
but in the situation revealed at the seventh gate. On the Argive side, the
lot has assigned Polyneikes to the seventh gate, and in Thebes Eteokles
has chosen to deploy the other Theban champions at the first six gates,
leaving the seventh to himself. Hermes the god of luck has created one
side of this situation (508); Apollo the enforcer of oracles has created
the other (798ff.).

Eteokles could choose someone else to fight Polyneikes; this is implicit
in the phrasing of 672ff. The popular view of Greek tragedy as doom-
laden is not supported by the text, here or anywhere else in Aischylos'
surviving tragedies. Eteokles chooses to fight his brother himself

for the bad reason that the city authorities roundly condemn Polyneikes in the
spurious ending, and this judgment is echoed by Kreon in Sophokles' *Antigone*.
In Aischylos' Finale, the Women view the two brothers even-handedly; a shift
from presenting Eteokles in a bad light towards the end of *Oidipous* to the
hostile view of Polyneikes in this scene would be totally compatible with the
methods of the *Oresteia* and with what we can guess about the Danaid trilogy;
and the equivalence now between the two brothers – Justice fighting against
Justice, as at *L B* 461 – would be fully established if Eteokles also claimed
Justice by having her as the motif on his shield (Winnington-Ingram 1983, 32;
cf. Zeitlin 1982, 144).

[34] Powerfully argued by Solmsen 1937, and often echoed since.
[35] Cf. Lattimore 1964, 7–8; 'The curse, the fate, the action and the choice all
coincide'. The emotional sequence in his response is very similar to that of
Agamemnon at Aulis (*Ag* 193ff.). Note also the parallel between the Women's
response here and the violent emotional reaction of the Elders at *Ag* 218ff.

because it would be *aischron*, shameful, for him not to; and the avoidance of shame was the most powerful motivation for the adult male *agathos* in Greek society.[36] Argive lot and Theban choice have placed both brothers at the final gate, and it would be shameful to back down from that placement; Polyneikes has himself challenged Eteokles to fight him, 635ff., and it would be shameful to decline the challenge. Eteokles accepts the symmetry – king against king, brother against brother; his decision is made. With an abrupt call for the last piece of full *hoplite* armour to complete his preparations, he strides towards the right *parodos*, which leads out to the city walls.

One of the Women prevents his exit;[37] in six stark lines she puts into the scales against him the threat of indelible *miasma*. The issue at the climax is absolute – *aischron* against *miasma*; and this is brought out into the open by Eteokles' response. To oppose him, the Women use the only weapon they can; they burst into lyrics, surrounding him with entreaties in song and dance, pitting the full force of their emotions against his intransigence in an *epirrhematic scene*, in deliberate echo of Scene 2; but the appearance of Polyneikes against the seventh gate reveals to Eteokles that the Curse of Oidipous is present, a hostile daimonic force which can only be released in death.

Eteokles, in his responses to all four of their stanzas, regards himself as doomed; but the Women correctly show that this is not so. The Curse is like a storm, now seething with its rage; and like a storm, it too will blow itself out. All he has to do, to survive, is stay in shelter till then (698ff.).

In the last moments of the scene, Aischylos selects the medium of a rapid-fire *stichomythia* to show why Eteokles cannot accept this sound advice. The Women's crucial plea is 716; 'the god rewards even ignoble victory'; but they cannot persuade a Greek *agathos* to avoid *miasma*, when they have to concede that the invisible 'victory' won by doing so is ignoble, because it involves a cowardly avoidance of an enemy's

---

[36] Adkins 1960, 30ff.; cf. Winnington-Ingram 1983, 38ff. Hutchinson (1985, 149) recognizes the power of *aischron* in this situation, but argues that 'such feelings of shame in themselves are honourable, but morally it is better to defy them than to shed the blood of one's own family. That act violates the moral laws of the Aischylean world ... and Eteokles' utterances are so written as to betray that his desire is wrong.' In performance, however, such a detached moral judgement misses the point; for the spectator, issues of right and wrong are entirely overset by Aischylos' illumination of how and why a man could be brought to a point where he feels he must choose to fight his own brother.

[37] See below.

NOTES

challenge. In Eteokles' reply, Aischylos used the technical term *hoplite*, identifying his character with the largest and most socio-politically important single group in his audience. Fifth-century Greeks defined male excellence by a man's ability to stand with his fellow-citizens in defence of the city. Therefore, no man could give in to this plea.

And so he goes; both choosing, rationally, to avoid *aischron* and recognizing that he is impelled by the daimôn of the royal house. Having subdued the Women who earlier stood in his way by his intransigence, he leaves by the right *parodos*. It has by now been totally established as leading to the battlefield; and so, for Eteokles, it leads to death.

Eteokles must look like a hoplite when he leaves, to give this scene full visual meaning. The call for greaves at 675–6 has led to a flurry of imaginative modern stage directions, ranging from a servant entering hastily to put on his greaves[38] through to a full arming sequence during the rest of the scene.[39]

The movements needed to illuminate this intense verbal combat absolutely rule out having the actor playing Eteokles encumbered and upstaged by the business of being armed by extras.[40] It would be a disastrous production error to inhibit Eteokles from movement, or to obscure our clear sight of him and interaction with the actor during the climax of the whole drama.

Were even the greaves brought on? This is more plausible; if a slave emerged instantly after 676 to fulfil the order, this stage business would give time for one of the Women to address 677ff. to Eteokles before he leaves. There is however far more dramatic meaning if the obstacle which makes him stop for the speech at 677ff. is the speaker herself, moving swiftly to intercept Eteokles as he strides towards the *parodos*.[41] Lines 675–6 play best as an address to an unseen offstage servant by an Eteokles actively moving towards departure: and the problem of arming disappears if Eteokles comes in for Scene 3 fully armed, apart from his greaves; this costume change from Scenes 1 and 2 establishes

[38] E.g. Vellacott 1961, 108.

[39] E.g. Hecht & Bacon 1973, 30–3, where the weapons are brought on by a bevy of slave girls (!).

[40] The issue here is theatrical practicality; Hogan (1984, 261–3) rightly criticizes Taplin's characteristic attempt (1977, 158ff.) to rule out an arming scene by an argument from theory.

[41] There is then also more pathos created by the contrast at the end, when the Women's appeals have all failed, and they do not try to prevent his exit after 719.

at 375 his awareness that the moment for action is now, and his own readiness to join the battle.

Choros 3

The exit of Eteokles shows in concrete theatrical terms that the Curse, the Fury of Oidipous, has re-emerged. In the first three stanzas the Women recognize this; then from B2 onwards the action of this drama is set in the context of the past events of the trilogy, which now surface – for the first time, apart from line 70.[42]

The power of this Choros lies in the directness and simplicity of the treatment, the way in which the Women – retaining the authority which they gained, for the first time, at the end of the previous scene – plumb the depths of these appalling events from the first crime right down to the fratricide. Aischylos deliberately keeps the emotional tone low-key, preparing by contrast for the heights of grief to which the Women will rise in the funeral lament which dominates the Finale.

The choreography must match this mood; the opening is muted and subdued,[43] and the dance must rise only gradually to a peak of intensity in the C stanzas. Then Aischylos pursues the same strategy again (but now over the span of two rather than three strophic pairs), returning to relative peace in the D stanzas and then pressing rapidly forward, to achieve the fullest intensity in the final pair.

Scene 4

Because of the extent of the lamentation to follow, Aischylos makes the announcement of the brothers' deaths as brief and sparse as possible; and because of the emotional intensity to be unleashed in the Finale, he keeps the exchanges between the Scout[44] and the Women as stylized as possible. The stylization of the *stichomythia*, the compression and formality with which the moment at which the Women apprehend is

---

[42] This is the principal difference between the *Oresteia* and what we can guess from *Seven* about the way Aischylos dramatized the Oidipous legend. *Eumenides* takes up at once, in Scene 1, the issues which were raised by *Libation Bearers*, and even the scene of action – Apollo's shrine at Delphi – had been foreshadowed in the last scene of the previous drama.

[43] *Pace* Thalmann 1978, 104. The ionic metre of the A stanzas is not 'wild', and the terror which they express is not 'the high point of the choros' fear'. That came earlier, in Choros 1.

[44] This Messenger is played by the actor who played the Scout in Scenes 1 and 3, and there is no reason why he should have changed his costume. He would therefore have been perceived by the audience as being the same character.

dramatized, add to the power of the sequence; their emotion only becomes overt in the lyrics of the Finale.

This is the first low-key scene since the opening tableau. Apart from a few moments in the *stichomythia*, where members of the *choros* move towards the Scout, crowding in nearer to him, it profits from a relatively small amount of movement by either of the characters. Again, Aischylos is preparing by contrast for the Finale.

Finale

The closing sequence is an extended *threnos* for the two dead kings. Once more, as in *Persians*, an Aischylean drama adopts at its close a tone and feeling far removed from the stoic, austere reception of grief with which Anglo-Saxon criticism is more comfortable.[45] Aischylos' use of a female *choros* is now given its final justification, for the role of women in a Greek funeral was to lament.

The Finale begins slowly and gently; in the introduction and the A strophic pair the Women state simply what has happened and what they must do. Then Aischylos introduces the two bodies into the *orchêstra*, making the objects of their grief visible. They are placed at the centre, symbolically positioned LC and RC, and become the focus for the songs and dances of grief in the remainder.[46]

Both tempo and intensity vary, as the *threnos* becomes more and more miserable and introverted through the B to E strophic pairs; then the form and tempo both change violently. Aischylos has established from B1 onwards a pattern, in which one soloist sings the first lines of each stanza, and it is then completed either by the whole *choros* in unison,[47] or – in the E stanzas, preparing for the change of form in F – by other soloists. Suddenly this pattern is broken; the E pair turns out to have an *epode* also, and in this and the final F group of stanzas the lament is tossed rapidly between individuals, almost out of control of their syntax in the intensity of their grief. The only point of restraint and solidity here lies in the three-line utterances which conclude F1 and

[45] Macintosh 1994, *passim*, has however demonstrated the affinities between Greek and Celtic perceptions of death as a process, and consequently between Greek and Celtic mourning rites both in life and in drama. Hutchinson 1985, 180 rightly notes the more sober and restrained tone of this lamentation, when compared e.g. with the Finale of *Persians*.

[46] Aischylos composed an *epode* (A3), a special stanza isolated from the flowing pattern of responsion, to cover the time the extras take to bring the corpses to the centre.

[47] This is a conjecture – but a very plausible one.

F3. Then in the final stanza form dissolves completely; F3 responds to nothing, and has no calm of any kind. The tempo should relax slightly from 998, as a precarious stability is provided for the last seven lines (they are slightly longer and more coherent, and each begins with the cry 'Oh . . .').[48]

Aischylos as playwright provided himself as director with a Finale which centres totally around the music and dance of lamentation; a scene which, if performed with adequate intensity of expression, can generate great emotional power. By ending the trilogy in this way, Aischylos ensured that the audience's closing focus is entirely concentrated upon the sufferings of the last two descendants of Labdakos, the horror of fratricide and the power of Oidipous' Fury.

After all the actors have filed out of the *orchêstra*, the images of the gods remain – the gods who have saved Thebes, as the Women begged them in Choroses 1 and 2, but have calmly watched the final destruction of the royal family.

The spurious ending to this drama, which follows 1004 in our manuscripts (see Appendix) is alien to Aischylos' drama not only because of its banal and sometimes inept poetic style, but also because it heads off in a new direction, pulling focus abruptly back to the city, which has receded from view since Eteokles' departure. It also introduces two characters – Antigone and Ismene – who (for all their subsequent importance in Sophokles) are superfluous to Aischylos' version of the story. In *Seven against Thebes*, the entire royal house is eliminated when the brothers' deaths fulfil the curses of Oidipous.[49]

Suppliants

Roles

Physical appearance is vital to the production of this drama. Strong gender and Greek/barbarian polarities underlie and contrast with the

[48] The emotional balance of the final stanza is so finely achieved, grows so naturally out of the intensity of E3–F2, that I am tolerably certain we have the end of Aischylos's drama intact.

[49] Cf. Hutchinson 1985, 210. The case against rejection is made most strongly by Lloyd-Jones 1959; cf. also Hecht and Bacon 1973, 7–8. Their arguments have not won acceptance. Seaford (1994, 139) conjectures that the spurious ending displaced a real one in which a cult was founded; as he notes, many tragic endings show the inauguration of ritual. But this is not universal even among the small amount of tragedies that have survived; his speculation is therefore unprovable.

discovery of a kinship between the Aigyptians and the Argives.[1] The
Argives represent the Greek norm; against it are set the dusky features
and exotic costume of Danaos and his daughters. The Herald and his
men are even darker, their black limbs contrasting with white linen
clothes. The doubling of Danaos and the Herald allows one actor to
retain blackened limbs and a dark mask throughout, while the other
plays Pelasgos.

The only hand props are weapons, and the suppliant wands and
female waistbands which themselves become the 'weapons' of the
otherwise helpless suppliants. The set is dominated by the altar, and
statues of the twelve Olympians, which stand round the rear perimeter;
like all other properties in Aischylos, these will play a crucial role in the
drama.

Choros 1

The Danaides arrive in Argos, take refuge as suppliants from their
pursuers, and establish a relationship with the place to which they have
come.

Aischylos dramatizes this action in an extended choral ode (180
lines, including the final repeat of the refrain, after H2);[2] almost as long
as Choros 1 in *Agamemnon*, and no less important. Before placing the
Suppliants in interaction with the Argives, he establishes the seriousness
of their predicament and the range of moods in which they react to it,
while also beginning to alert the audience to the moral complexities of
the situation which will unfold.

The entry chant (1–49) divides naturally into two sections, perhaps
chanted by the leaders of two subgroups of six. It establishes the main
elements of the situation: that their flight was voluntary, that they have
a claim on Argos and its gods because they are descendants of Io, and
that they hate the sons of Aigyptos. The opening mood is confidence
and passionate, but self-controlled emotion.[3]

Ironies begin at once. The Danaides will commit a 'blood-crime' (6);
the olive branches are indeed, in their hands, 'the weapons of a

[1] Compare the development of an understanding between Athena and the
Furies in *Eumenides*, despite her initial astonishment (and muted distaste) at
their appearance.

[2] This repeat, regarded as essential by most modern scholars, is omitted in
the manuscript, and therefore is not included in the sequence of line numbers.

[3] The metric pulse is firm and vigorous; contrast, for an example of the
metrical and syntactic devices which Aischylos could use to express fear, the
opening of Choros 1 in *Seven against Thebes*.

suppliant' (21; Pelasgos rightly notes their war-like demeanour by his comparison with Amazones at 287–9); and as the lyrics begin they compare their cries to those of the nightingale who had killed her own son. Throughout the drama Aischylos sets up a complex oscillation between images of their helplessness, which establish their absolute right to protection from forced marriage, and images of their power which look forward to the murder of the sons of Aigyptos.

The introduction is declaimed almost as an address to the audience: but when the ode first opens out into fully sung lyrics, they turn inward (A1–C1); they address the stanzas to each other, and the mood is meditative, almost self-indulgent. But the strategy changes at 78; the Suppliants turn for the first time fully towards the images, and address the appeal in C2 and D1 outward, to the gods.

Traditional interpretations used to stress Aischylos' 'theology', reading such stanzas as 86ff., and the whole of Choros 3, as an 'advanced' statement by the author, setting the Greeks on the road towards monotheism. This forgets that the Danaides are dramatic characters – in a specific situation, and with their own particular needs. A Greek prayer had to establish that the suppliant's claim is valid, and that it would be *aischron* for the god or goddess if they did not respond.[4] The Danaides address Zeus because he is the only god who cares for suppliants; also because he is their ancestor, and they have a claim of *philia* upon him.

Far from expressing confidence, the Suppliants are seeking reassurance as they sing and dance this section. Aischylos shows this by 'syncopation', pairing stanzas by sense across the symmetrical patterns of metre and choreography which link *strophe* with *antistrophe*. C2 is here paired in content with D1, D2 with E1: this establishes a remarkable effect which culminates when the picture of Zeus' invisible power (101ff.) is set by the metre and choreography in parallel with the self-destructive desire of the sons of Aigyptos (109ff.)

The mood turns more emotional at 112ff. Aischylos changes the metre,[5] interjects inarticulate cries after the second lines of the F stanzas, and adds to each stanza from here to the end a refrain,

---

[4] This can be in view of past and/or promised future service (as with the first prayer in surviving Greek literature, by Chryses to Apollo in the opening narrative of the *Iliad*); it is better, if possible, to urge a claim of blood-kinship – as the Danaides do (168ff.; cf. 524ff.). The Greek word *euche*, normally translated 'prayer', really denotes a legitimate claim to a god's assistance.

[5] In the Greek original, iambo-choriambics were succeeded by pure iambics.

breaking out from and building on the dilemmas in the two F stanzas and the hope in the two G stanzas. The build-up is steady to 154ff.; in the final H stanzas the Suppliants assert just how far they will go if their appeals are not granted. Aischylos is not interested in creating the shock of surprise when they threaten to hang themselves at 455ff. Instead, he establishes in advance the limits within which the confrontation with the Argives must work. Will the Suppliants be as intensely committed as this dance suggests? If so, then they will truly have power over their hosts.

Scene 1

By the end of Choros 1 the Suppliants are in full possession of the *orchêstra*. They have established a provisional relationship with the soil of Argos and its gods. However, their survival will depend on establishing a relationship with the inhabitants. The approach of the Argives therefore drives them back to huddle near the altar, relying on the images of the gods for protection. Later, however, they will move back into possession of the *orchêstra*, at times surrounding Pelasgos to put pressure on him: and when they return to near the images it will not be in a huddle, but spread out in power; when they unleash their ultimate threat, one *choros* member stands beside each of the twelve Olympians.

This very substantial scene, taking the action to the half-way point, shows the Suppliants' first encounter with the Argives and the way in which they gain the King's protection. Pelasgos' attitude, strength and tone change constantly,[6] under the force of the social and moral pressures which the Suppliants impose on him as the scene unfolds. These are shown both by the sequence of their movements and through the use of different formal means; Aischylos incorporates speeches, an extended *stichomythia*, an *epirrhematic* subscene, and a short lyric (Choros 2), to mark out various degrees of intensity, and different patterns of interaction, as the scene unfolds.

The Argives Approach (176–233) Danaos frames this scene; his advice to his daughters opens the scene, and his departure for Argos to lay the groundwork for Pelasgos' address to the *demos* concludes it. When,

---

[6] 'Apprehension, open-heartedness, decisiveness and caution flicker through [his] every speech'; Raphael and McLeish 1991, xxix. They draw an important distinction between the continual unfolding of characters in flux in Aischylos, and the detailed elaboration of fixed, 'given' characters in Sophokles and Euripides.

and from which direction, did he enter – at line 1, with the Suppliants, remaining up-*orchêstra* until they have finished their dance, or now? Entry at line 1 would pull focus from Choros 1; and this ode is much longer than the first Choros in *Libation Bearers*, which is the only Aischylean parallel for an entry with the *choros* by a character who remains silent until it has been sung.[7] Danaos has motivation to enter just before 176; prefiguring his role when he re-enters twice later, this entry is motivated directly by the need to bring his daughters news.

Which way does he come? If from the right, from the shore. He would then appear to arrive in the sacred grove later than his daughters, but still apprehend the approach of the Argive army before they do. If from the left, he has been scouting out the land ahead of them; but how did he get there from the boats, without being seen by the audience? Both are strange; but the left is the better alternative.[8]

It is a standard tragic technique for one solo actor or *choros* member to prepare the *choros* character for the appearance of a new character;[9] but the use of Danaos to narrate the approach of the Argive army serves two further purposes. Firstly, it opens the dialogue between father and daughters, which is continued in Scenes 3 and 5. Danaos reveals almost at once his fear that the Suppliants have a temperament which may well take them beyond the submission and deference which the Greeks expected from young women (197ff.; they do obey him now – at least until 506ff.!). It is probable that the relationship between Danaos' view of his paternal role, and Danaides who go beyond a normal Greek daughter's role and are prepared to be independent, even disobedient, was an ongoing theme in the trilogy; Scene 5 might be

[7] Furthermore, Elektra is strongly motivated to come in with – indeed, leading – the *choros*, while Danaos has no such motivation. Taplin (1977, 193–4) believes that his 'very close relationship' with his daughters, and the reference to him at 11f., justify entry at line 1, and simply assumes that 'had we more of Aeschylus there would doubtless be others [parallels to the silent entry of Danaos and Elektra]'. The argument is circular. Why should there be?

[8] There might be a parallel with Elektra's *second* entry in *Libation Bearers* (Ewans 1995, 175); she enters right before 585, crosses silently to the *skene* doors and enters the palace before the *choros* re-enter. This could establish the case for Danaos to pass in silence through the *orchêstra* before the Suppliants enter; but I find it very hard to believe that the first action the audience saw in this drama was Danaos entering, miming a silent exploration of the area and then departing in the direction of the city to explore further, before the *choros* enter for line 1.

[9] Cf. e.g. the speech by an Elder before the entry of Agamemnon's Herald in *Ag* Scene 3.

laying the groundwork for subsequent development of their interaction in the second and third dramas.

Secondly, the sequence containing Danaos' description and advice vividly illustrates in theatrical terms the vulnerability of the Suppliants and the precariousness of their position. The opening narrative whips up their anxiety, and breaks down their confident possession of the whole *orchêstra*; they should retreat by 186 away from where the Argives will enter, i.e. to EFR. Danaos by contrast, after delivering the beginning of the narrative from C, presumably approaches the Suppliants to cajole them, on and after 184; but by 200 he must have reached BC, standing by the altar and encouraging them to join him there.

One of the Suppliants agrees to this at 208; however, it is clear from 222ff. that they do not immediately move back to the images. This is because the invocations to the gods in 213ff. are only effective if played from a distance, i.e. with the *choros* across the middle of the *orchêstra* CR–CL; they actually retreat, to huddle by the images of the gods, only at 226ff.

Danaos addresses 222–5 to his daughters; but the rhetoric at 226ff. is plainly designed to cover their retreat. He therefore needs to advance to the centre for these lines, delivered to the air and sky. The opening position is thus reversed by the time Pelasgos enters; Danaos is now at the centre, the Suppliants up by the altars – with the suppliant wands in their left hands (193–4), leaving them free to extend their right hands in the ritual gesture of supplication.[10] Only then does Danaos leave the centre, to take up an appropriately de-emphasized position (e.g. EBR/RC).

Pelasgos speaks, and interrogates the Suppliants (233–346) Pelasgos enters L, and his soldiers take up position EFL, to give him room to move, and also to place them in a position which counterbalances the Suppliants.[11] Meanwhile the King, during his opening lines, inspects

[10] Belfiore n.d., 7–8.

[11] *Pace* e.g. Taplin (1977, 201), Pelasgos must enter on foot. There is simply no room in a 20m *orchêstra* for one or more chariots, together with the complex movement and choreography needed to realize the rest of this scene in performance. Pelasgos needs to be able to move, almost immediately; and there is no particular point to be made by having him descend from a chariot (contrast *Ag* Scene 4).

Pelasgos is to be imagined as having advanced ahead of his full forces, accompanied only by his bodyguard. There must be enough soldiers to split into two groups at the end of this scene – one to attend Danaos, the other Pelasgos. I

the newcomers and then proceeds to the centre – establishing at once that this is his own territory, and nearing the Suppliants again only at 243 ff., when he wishes to elicit a reply from them.[12]

250 ff. demand extensive movement around the *orchêstra*, as Pelasgos circles to display his power and the extent of his realm.[13] He must be back at the centre for 260 ff., in which the *orchêstra* is totally identified with the Apian land; and the story which he chooses to tell about it is rich in resonance for the future. 'Ancient murders' caused a particularly virulent *miasma* to break out in this land once – and the threat of another such *miasma* is present in the subsequent action, both in the pollution which would be caused if the Suppliants hang themselves on the gods' images, and in the pollution which the Danaides will themselves inflict on Argos when they murder their husbands.

Under close questioning, the Suppliants use their detailed knowledge of Argive mythology to establish their claim to a bond with Pelasgos' kingdom not merely as suppliants but as *philoi*, blood-relations. Aischylos dramatizes this sequence as an extended *stichomythia*, with the King as interrogator and therefore 'leader' after 298. This is natural, since Argos is his territory, and the Danaides should be passive, both as females and as suppliants; but this passivity is only superficial, since by the ways in which they answer him, the Suppliants are effectively leading the action.[14] The movement must bring this dynamic out; the sequence plays best if individual Suppliants move forward, away from

suggest a company of eight or ten, matched in Scene 4 by an equal number of Aigyptians. The total at 914 would then be 30 or 34, which allows around 10 square metres per person – enough space for a vigorous blocking of the confrontation, while also bringing sufficient men into the playing area to give physical reality to the threat of violence.

[12] The translation tries to bring out the guarded understatement of 245; the Danaid deflects the focus at once from the Suppliants' own appearance to the vital question of the power and authority of the Argive who has come to meet them.

[13] In Aischylos' vision of prehistory Pelasgos' kingdom embraces virtually the whole of classical Greece; his northern boundary extends from the Thrakian border in the east right across to Thessaly and Dodona (i.e. from Bulgaria to southern Albania and north-west Greece). The trilogy, in dramatizing the union of Io's Aigyptian descendants with the original 'Pelasgian' inhabitants, shows how the people we call Greeks (Latin 'Graeci') gained one of their own names for themselves, 'Danaoi'.

[14] Weir Smyth (1922, 28 ff.), Lembke (1975, 34 ff.) and some others attribute the dialogue so that the Suppliants lead the *stichomythia*. This destroys the subtlety of the scene.

the altars, as they deliver 290ff.,[15] gradually surrounding him and including him in their formation by the time they have reached their objective, and state it clearly, at 324.

Pelasgos breaks out in 325ff., retreating from immediate assent to this direct demand. They pursue him with vigour – first with a short but moving speech (328ff.), and then in an adversative, highly confrontational *stichomythia* (335ff.).[16] If the full effect is to be gained here, seven different Suppliants should advance directly towards him, one on each line. This drives the King forward until he acknowledges for the first time his fear of the situation; the Suppliants then change tactics and dramatic form.

Epirrhematic scene and coda (348–438) They now appeal to him in song and dance. This makes their demand more passionate; but it also relaxes the tension, since these media are more stylized, the content more elaborated and less pithy than dialogue. Accordingly, his responses can now also become more meditative. Pelasgos is trapped in the middle of a circle of dancing *choros* members, who simply ignore each of his (virtually static) five-line responses by continuing the sequence of dances. By the end (407ff.), though his simile is fine and his rhetoric is powerful, Pelasgos' dilemma has not changed in any way since 342ff. He must either choose war with the Aigyptians, or incur the anger of Zeus.

One new element has been introduced. Pelasgos surprises the Suppliants when he reveals (366ff.) that he is a constitutional monarch, accountable to the *demos*. Although Athenian tragic dramatists had little knowledge of early Greek social structures, and no obligation to reproduce them,[17] there are parallels for this organization in the society

[15] When they come away from the images, the Suppliants leave their wands behind standing erect, as emblems that they are suppliants to the gods of Argos; Pelasgos sees the branches overshadowing the gods' seats at 345–6, when the young women have left the images, and are pointing back towards them.

[16] I have supplied two lines of dialogue to fill the loss of sense after 337.

[17] The surviving dramas make it plain that playwrights were free to reconstruct prehistoric conditions as they wished, to reflect the contemporary concerns and issues which they sought to dramatize for the Athenian audience. Early Spartan kings act tyrannically in (e.g.) Euripides' *Andromache* to reflect the loathing for that city and its way of life felt by many Athenians during the Peloponnesian War; by contrast Theseus is portrayed as a democratically accountable monarch in Euripides' *Suppliants* and Sophokles' *Oidipous at Kolonos*.

depicted in Homer; Garvie is also right to note[18] that the role played by the *demos* may have become more important after Pelasgos' death, especially if the Danaides murdered the sons of Aigyptos while staying in accommodation provided by the citizens of Argos.[19] However, Pelasgian Argos follows all the principles which Athenian democrats would approve; and it is likely[20] that democracy had been restored at Argos itself by 464. Athens was moving towards the alliance with Argos which she made in 461 (and which Aischylos explicitly praised in 458 in *Eumenides*)[21] – a fundamental realignment of Greek power relationships, in which the pro-Spartan, right-wing policies of Kimon and others were defeated. Aischylos' portrait of Pelasgos not only welcomes this but signals the nature of the enlightenment which, in his vision, Athenians and Argives share; a commitment to democratic process, and a determination to sustain Greek ideals against barbarism at all costs.[22]

Since Pelasgos (reasonably) remains undecided, the Suppliants launch an even more passionate lyric appeal; a short and intense ode is interpolated into the fabric of the scene. As the performance unfolded, Choros 2 must at first have seemed like a continuation of the *epirrhematic scene* – until the song proceeds beyond its first stanza without a response from the King. The effect is to highlight the extent of Pelasgos' dilemma, through the increased pressure which the Suppliants place upon him.[23]

Pelasgos decides to stand aloof; the Suppliants force him to commit himself (438–524) Once again, Aischylos opens Pelasgos' speech with rich imagery, to denote the extent of his dilemma. In *Eumenides*, the goddess of wisdom herself manages to transcend the dilemma which she so clearly articulates at *Eu* 470ff. Pelasgos is not so fortunate. He decides that the price of kindred bloodshed (with the implication of 'indelible' *miasma*) is too high; and resolves to take no part in the

[18] 1969, 153.
[19] Cf. Winnington-Ingram 1983, 63–4.
[20] Forrest 1966, 221ff.
[21] *Eu* 762ff.; cf. Ewans 1995, 213 and 215.
[22] Forrest ibid.; cf. Podlecki 1966, 50ff., Garvie 1969, 144–6. *Contra* Lloyd-Jones 1974, 359–60 and Garvie 1969, 150ff.
[23] The short ode, interpolated into the course of a scene, has parallels in Aischylos in two even shorter, single-stanza odes, Choros 2 in both *Libation Bearers* and *Eumenides*. In all three cases a solo actor remains present, absorbed in reflection.

dispute (452ff.). Presumably with these lines he turns away from interaction with the Suppliants, ready to take his men and return to the city.

His intention is undermined by a *coup de théâtre*. It is clear from the closing phase of the scene, in which he persuades the Suppliants to come out into the sacred grove, that they have returned long before then to a position at the rear perimeter of the *orchêstra*, under the protection of the images of the gods. When did they move there?

They cannot be out of the *orchêstra* while they are still dancing Choros 2 but a fierce point is given to the climax of the scene if by 460ff. each Suppliant is standing – for the first time – beside the image of an Olympian,[24] ready to give immediate effect to 466 if Pelasgos does not reverse his decision. Accordingly they must have moved earlier – before 455, since movement during the *stichomythia* would pull focus.

There are two options. The Suppliants can counter-move in a 'dramatic' silence while Pelasgos begins to move towards his intended exit after 454: but it is more effective in Greek tragedy to move during rather than between speeches, and a break in flow is unwanted at this point in the drama. It is therefore better for them to start moving around 450, signalling by the movement that they intend to undermine Pelasgos' decision. The silent repositioning, if completed in time for 456 to follow on directly from – and fulfil the meaning of – 455, places appropriate emphasis on the opening of the *stichomythia*.

In this dialogue Pelasgos is drawn up-*orchêstra*, nearer and nearer to them, to increase the impact of the shock at 466. This then leaves the bulk of the *orchêstra* before him, available for the movement which is then needed, as he turns away from them after 457 and regains control. In his third and last speech of introspection he finally leaves dilemma aside, and moves forward into a decision, represented by the acknowledgement of Zeus' power in 478-9.

Once his decision has been (almost passively) made, Pelasgos regains a more dignified tone for his address to Danaos, matched by Danaos' reply. Danaos then leaves with some of the suppliant wands, and half Pelasgos' bodyguard – and Pelasgos is alone with the Suppliants. Their tone now demonstrates once again the flexibility which is a principal feature of their character throughout the drama; now they have

[24] This effect must not be spoiled by anticipation; their huddle by the altar earlier in the drama should therefore be far more passive than the position which they take up now.

achieved their aim, they revert to obedience and timorousness (perhaps there is even a small subgroup which hesitates to quit the images at all?). By contrast Pelasgos regains full regal authority, taking the centre as soon as Danaos has left, removing their fears, and dominating to the end of the scene through the confident structure and tone which Aischylos has provided for his exit speech.

Choros 3

Now the Suppliants all come forward, repossessing the whole *orchêstra* with confidence. They have secured protection by Argos; and the first half of the drama is over. There is a period of relative security (lasting until the end of Choros 4) before the arrival of the Aigyptians forces the action to its climax.

Their dance is in three parts. They begin (A stanzas) with a *euche* addressed to the (near-central) image of Zeus; in the B and C stanzas they dance out the story of Io's wanderings; then they return to the theme of the power of Zeus (D, E stanzas).

The Suppliants sing about Io, and dance out her sufferings, because Zeus showed his power when he healed Io (535, returned to and elaborated in the D1 stanza at 574f.); and he healed her from a punishment which was unjustly inflicted (562). If he could cure their ancestress, and transform her back from the monstrous shape which Hera had inflicted upon her, then he can surely deliver them from an equally unjust persecution, when it is only inflicted by human beings; and as their relative, he *should* do this, or he will have failed to help his *philoi*.[25]

---

[25] Cf. Finley 1955, 200: 'her suffering was inseparable from her destiny as bride of Zeus, but though they know her final rest, they cannot conceive a like mood for themselves, understanding as yet only flight and rejection'.

Accordingly, Lembke's reading of Io (1975, 12–13) as symbolically 'a monstrously egocentric child' should be rejected. Io did not transform herself, and Hera did not transform her because Io resisted her own sexuality, since in the *Suppliants* version she became Zeus' lover willingly. *Pace* Lembke, and Murray 1958, myths cannot be made to mean anything whatever, disregarding their inner structure. (There is more psychoanalytical speculation – Hera as the oidipal/pre-oidipal mother, forbidding and punishing infantile desires; the gadfly as phallic symbol, etc. – in Caldwell 1974.) Hera is angry partly because she has been personally wounded by Zeus' infidelity, and partly because as the goddess who defends marriage she disapproves in principle of sexuality outside marriage.

For further discussion of Io, Zeus and Hera cf. Belfiore n.d., 11ff. As she notes, Io is not in this drama a virgin subjected by Zeus to sexual harassment (as she is in *Prometheus Bound*). There is therefore no parallel between Zeus'

This view is one-sided. Zeus' sexual desire for Io angered Hera and caused Io's sufferings in the first place; Io attained peace not by staying a virgin, but by accepting Zeus as her lover and becoming pregnant; and the loathed sons of Aigyptos are descendants of Io – and of Zeus – as well. It must be suspected that Aischylos developed these perspectives in *Aigyptians*. If so, the choreography here needs to express not confidence but over-confidence.

Scene 2

The return of Danaos brings the Suppliants' attention back from their ancestor on Olympos to their human father. He rapidly takes up a position BC, where he can draw their attention from the focus on Zeus at the end of Choros 3, to narrate the success of Pelasgos' persuasion with the assembly. And this short scene is the start of the increase in Danaos' power, which is demonstrated in his triumphal return with bodyguard in Scene 5, preparing for him to become King of Argos in *Aigyptians*.

The joy and power of the narrative are such that the actor will need to move substantially after 611 (or at least 615); it is then most effective if Danaos does not, when he ends, remain in the *orchêstra* EBC; this would pull focus from Choros 4. It makes better theatre sense if Danaos now leaves right, to scout out the ground back towards the sea, and re-enter for Scene 3 from there – in symmetry with his earlier entry from the left, with the news that the Argives were coming from that direction.

Choros 4

The *choros* turn once more to the images to begin a dance of benediction and thanksgiving. Only the evocative magic of lyrics can bridge the gulf between the human and divine.

The tone of this Choros is often compared with the last section of the finale of *Eumenides*. The ideas are similar; but the Danaides are not goddesses, and their position now is far less certain than that which had been guaranteed to the Furies by Athena. For this reason the metre of Choros 3, in the Greek original, is predominantly dochmiac – always

union with a willing Io (whom he rescues as god of suppliants when she reaches Egypt) and the pursuit of the Danaides by the sons of Aigyptos. Cf. Belfiore n.d. 12ff. against (among many) e.g. Murray 1958, 35, Garvie 1969, 224 and Friis Johansen/Whittle 1980, 39. If there is any parallel between Io's situation and that of her descendants, it might lie in Hera's persecution of Io, like the Aigyptian pursuit of the Danaides. Belfiore explores this possibility ibid.

in tragedy the metre of anxiety. Choreographers and directors need to bring out the Suppliants' unease; only if Argos continues to live up to the 'Athenian' virtues of awe for the gods, holding by their commitments and democratic process will the Suppliants themselves be safe.

The Suppliants also – understandably – continue to see the situation only from one point of view. If this *is* their native land, then is it not also the native land of the sons of Aigyptos as well? Their own refuge in Argos will create exactly that evil which they now repeatedly pray the gods to avert; civil war and consequent *miasma* (A1, B1, C1). It may even be that D1 is ironically prophetic, since after the initial battle in which Pelasgos died the Argives probably did give the sons of Aigyptos 'fair settlement of claim' rather than provoke more warfare. If the settlement included their marrying the Danaides, that led directly to the murders which inflicted indelible *miasma* on Argos.

Accordingly, this dance is full of irony at the expense of the singers. The parallel in *Eumenides* is not the Finale but Choros 4, in which the Furies celebrate the justice of Athena and her city without its occurring to them for a moment that the Athenians could do anything so foolish as freeing Orestes from their pursuit.

Scene 3

After the calm, the storm. Aischylos now builds tension steadily from here to the climax, the re-entry of Pelasgos at the two-thirds point. This scene is symmetrical with the opening of Scene 1.[26] Once again Danaos enters – this time from the opposite direction – to bring the news of approaching, potentially hostile forces; and once again the vulnerability of the Suppliants is conveyed in the *orchêstra* by their almost immediate retreat from command of the full playing space. They gather fearfully around him as soon as the import of his narrative is plain (they could even do this on 714, with 'the ship' as trigger words): they completely disregard his pleas for calm, and his insistence (731) that they should have faith in the religious power of this place.

Aischylos emphasizes their desperation. Danaos ends his speech with a typical two-line gnomic close, showing that the speaker is about to leave. His daughters prevent him, once again surrounding the solo actor (from 735) with a full *choros* dancing and singing: this becomes an *epirrhematic scene*. Unlike 347ff., this is of brief duration (only four stanzas); and the solo actor prevails. Pelasgos was forced to silence by

---

[26] Cf. Taplin 1977, 209ff.

their onslaught: Danaos' confidence in the Argives is firm, and justified, but he can only leave when he has silenced their terror (764ff.).

Some writers have criticized Aischylos, alleging that Danaos leaves the playing space only so that the two actors are available to play the Herald and Pelasgos in Scene 4.[27] There are however four good reasons for his departure:

1 Danaos has a good motivation to leave his daughters – to fetch help. They have to stay by the images of the gods, which guarantee – or should guarantee – safety; he must go, or the Argives will not know of the Aigyptian landing in time.

2 Even if a third actor had been permitted when this drama was staged,[28] a physically helpless old father would be redundant in Scene 4. *Pace* Aristophanes' 'Euripides',[29] Aischylos never, in the surviving dramas, leaves a silent character in the *orchêstra*, pulling focus from the action for no purpose.

3 It is an effective, well-tried dramatic device in rescue-story fiction, both ancient (cf. e.g. Euripides *Iphigeneia among the Taurians*) and modern, for the forces of evil almost to achieve their goal before salvation arrives.

4 The main subject of this tragedy is the ebb and flow of the Suppliants' emotions, as their bid for freedom seems at one moment to be secure, at others vulnerable. Scene 3 is the first stage in the graphic decline of their confidence; it is highly effective in performance because, during this scene, the Danaides try to cling to their father, and his departure at the end allows all their fears to emerge, in the next Choros.

Choros 5

The Danaides disregard their father's closing assurances; they cannot feel safe; and they dance a turbulent song of anxiety.[30] In this ode the Suppliants are so terrified that they cease to recognize, and so temporarily break down, the boundary between the 'safer' area directly under

[27] E.g. Taplin (1977, 21): 'It is ... awkward that Danaos should not be there for his daughters' greatest ordeal.'

[28] Different sources ascribe the introduction of a third actor to Sophokles and Aischylos. The innovation was in use before the *Oresteia*, which was performed five years after the probable date of *Suppliants*.

[29] *Frogs* 911ff.

[30] Despite its textual violence, the ode is, in the original Greek, in the relatively calm iambic metre, with few syncopations. Aischylos sets the turbulence of their desires in counterpoint with their impressive ability to express them.

the gods' protection and the remainder of the *orchêstra*, representing
the outer parts of the sacred grove. They now trust neither in the gods
nor in the Argives, and the dance uses the whole *orchêstra* to represent
the world from which they need to escape, because no part of it now
gives them any prospect of salvation. Hence the desperation, ever
increasing until in the final strophic pair they turn to the one god in
whom they have any hope at all – their ancestor, the god of suppliants,
lord Zeus.[31]

Scene 4

The drama reaches its climax, one of the most powerful in the surviving
Greek tragedies.

Who attacks the Danaides? Although Gilbert Murray's spectacular
Aischylos is no longer in favour, two recent editions[32] assign the
Herald's lyrics to a *choros* of Aigyptian sailors. There are however
several reasons to reject this:

1 Heralds normally came to present demands, both in tragedy and
in real life, as solo speakers accompanied by a silent escort.[33]

2 The entry of the Herald singing, and the gradual transition back
to speech, make a normal and coherent sequence, while the sudden
emergence of a solo Herald as spokesperson, after a *choros* of Aigyptians has sung, and then suddenly falls silent, would make a very odd
effect.

3 The appearance of a singing *choros* of anonymous Aigyptian
sailors would be confusing and strange, if – as is probable – the sons of
Aigyptos themselves formed the *choros* in the next drama.

Aischylos achieves a high level of intensity not by massing large
numbers of actors – though the *orchêstra* is now relatively full by his
normally modest standards – but by a combination of visual, musical
and verbal effects with action, expressed in the choreography. The
choros are in long robes, exotic to Greek eyes (234ff.); their masks and
hands present dark skins. The Aigyptian men have black limbs showing

[31] There are repeated overtones which point to just how far this desperation
will drive them in the subsequent action of the trilogy – in the phrasing at 799
and 807. After all, Zeus may have heard their prayers now (624); but he did
not, in the sequel, save them from violation by the sons of Aigyptos; they had to
do that themselves, by committing murder. Cf. 1048ff., whose truth is more
than half accepted by the Suppliants in the last words of this drama.

[32] Friis Johansen/Whittle 1980, 173ff., West 1990a, 152ff. *Contra* Taplin
1977, 216–17; cf. Garvie 1969, 193–4.

[33] Cf. Lloyd-Jones 1974, 367–8.

under short white tunics (719–20); their leader, as he moves towards them, looks to the Suppliants like a spider in a black dream (887–8). They are confronted by Pelasgos with Argive soldiers in full Greek military equipment.

The lyrics are of exteme tension, with violent language, interruptions, and exclamations;[34] the discipline of strophic responsion is not achieved until 843; and, although the Herald calms down to the level of speech at 872, the Suppliants remain in highly excitable lyrics.

The action clearly begins with the Suppliants in a terrified huddle near the images; in the opening moves the Herald and his men first enter and gain mastery of the *orchêstra* (he should most naturally deliver his first few lyrics from C), and then circle round, with the Herald advancing as he dances like a spider to drive the Suppliants back towards the right *parodos*.

This implies that the main action at first takes place towards the rear of the *orchêstra*; but the Suppliants meet his commands with defiance, as the strophic lyrics begin at 843. This passage works best with individual *choros* members breaking out from the group of Suppliants, dancing against him with gazelle-like leaps on each of their individual stanzas, while the other Suppliants stand firm, holding faith in the grove and gradually counter-advancing against the Herald and his men, getting away from BR and forcing the Herald back into the L segment.[35]

At 880 the dynamics of the scene change. The key to understanding the remainder is to note that the actual moment of physical violence, when an Aigyptian lays hands on a Suppliant, is delayed right down to at least after 904, perhaps even after 908. Aischylos prefers to escalate the scene of seizure by the ebb and flow of words, dance and song, only allowing physical contact in the last moments before the rescuers arrive.

The tide turns in the Herald's favour after 882–3; the Suppliants' reaction is no longer defiant. Perhaps he should here draw a sword or a long knife, to emphasize visually his power, and the violence which

[34] The Greek text is highly corrupt, and much of this translation is based on speculative restorations by modern scholars. The distribution of some lines is also uncertain; in particular the opening, which could read (cf. West 1990b): HERALD Aaah!/I'm here to seize you/from the ship, now on the land./ SUPPLIANTS You'll die before you do it. Ptah!/Go straight back down/into the ship.

[35] More conservative critics might insist that the lyrics must have been sung and danced by the whole *choros* – in which case the space needed to play this sequence means that the *choros* will retrieve even more of the playing area by 880.

they see in the C stanza refrains; during this passage he comes closer and closer to them, driving them towards the exit like sheep in a pen. The literal repetition of the last four lines of C1 in C2 conveys that they are trapped,[36] and it is best if his men move against them for the first time during the two matched pairs of trimeters which he speaks after C1 and C2.

The D stanzas (one line each!) are the shortest responding lyrics in surviving Greek tragedy. I conjecture that Aischylos wrote this because after 903 the women are totally hemmed in; almost motionless, about to be physically overpowered – some perhaps already forced out of the playing area into the mouth of the right *parodos*. Then they see Pelasgos in the distance, and call to him. And so the 'last-minute rescue' takes place in front of us; it is not narrated, as so often in the later dramas of 'catastrophe survived'.[37]

Pelasgos' sober and arresting words immediately create a re-formation in the *orchêstra*, and the movements now take a more solid and restful form to match the return to spoken verse. The Argive troops enter behind their general, and advance into the L segment; the Suppliants take refuge behind them ECL/EFL; and the two leaders confront each other in the centre, each with his soldiers behind him. Visually, it is now the Herald who is being pushed towards the R *parodos*; he is forced to give ground by 930 at the latest, so leaving BC/ C as a commanding position for Pelasgos' closing address to him at 938f. (The advance to C is of course needed to help build the rhetoric at 942f.)

The Herald attempts a two-line riposte at 950–1 – spoken from the mouth of the *parodos* as 'last words', but answered by Pelasgos, who needs to go briefly towards BR to deliver his reply to the Herald's departing back; this gives him an easy position from which to address the Suppliants, if they are still FL, and coax them back towards the centre of the *orchêstra*.

Choros 6

What happened next? The choral chant starts with the content we would expect – thanks to Pelasgos, and a request for Danaos to return to them. Then there are serious problems with the text; the sudden, silent exit of the King and his men, and the almost immediate re-entry

[36] Cf. the repetition of the first two stanzas of the *Eumenides* Finale, to express the Furies' anger and frustration after their defeat.
[37] This is the title of Burnett's study of Euripides' 'tragedies of mixed reversal'.

of Danaos, also attended, are unparalleled in the surviving Greek tragedies, feel alien to all the conventions of Athenian tragedy, and play badly even in the more fluid and eclectic modern theatre. Taplin is right to argue[38] that something has been lost here – probably two or three pairs of lyric stanzas, designed to create a sufficient feeling of time passing for Danaos' entry to be reasonably separated from Pelasgos' exit; and that the lines about maidservants[39] which stand in the MS as the 'conclusion' to this ode have been interpolated, probably from elsewhere in the trilogy.

Scene 5

Aischylos now begins to foreshadow what was probably the main development in the plot between the close of *Suppliants* and the beginning of *Aigyptians*; the death of Pelasgos in battle, and the selection of Danaos by the Argives to be their king. Danaos returns with a large escort – probably twelve in number to equal the Suppliants themselves, since they turn in the Finale into a matching supplementary choros which answers them and warns them about the future.[40] A costume change, to near-regal magnificence, would also be appropriate, as a literal demonstration of the generosity which the Argives will show to the Suppliants themselves, when they go into the city. Danaos must also dominate his daughters physically; in the opening section he addresses from C or BC a choros standing passively in the front segment of the *orchêstra*.

The Suppliants have gained what they wanted; but in a characteristic Aischylean move (seen also at the end of *Agamemnon* and *Libation Bearers*), their position begins to be undermined in advance, in preparation for the action of the next drama in the trilogy. It may well be appropriate to play Danaos from 991 as an old man musing, with Polonian lechery, on the erotic power of his daughters (and therefore circling closely among them as he delivers the lines): what he says remains absolutely true, despite the sardonic echo of his chosen word

---

[38] 1977, 222.

[39] 'Line up/in your places, dear attendants, just/as Danaos appointed each of you/to one of us to be her maidservant.'

[40] See below. This increase in numbers would effectively show Danaos' increase in *time*, in contrast with the small group of perhaps four men whom Pelasgos gave him at the end of Scene 1. Hall (1989, 156) notes that personal bodyguards were a mark of the tyrant, and this grant may prefigure Danaos ascending to the throne, in the next drama, in a manner reminiscent of a despotic coup.

'ripeness' in the pert reply at 1014; Aphrodite herself, when she appeared in *Danaides*, developed the main idea of 1000ff. in cosmic terms.

Perhaps Danaos' control over his daughters, re-established now by sheer rhetorical power, was one of the main strands in the plot of the next drama. Did he command them to kill the sons of Aigyptos on the marriage night, and did Hypermestra therefore defy her father as well as her sisters? Danaos here presents a combination of near-regal authority with sexual prurience, which presages a fascinating treatment of his role, if he advised or persuaded the Danaides to murder their cousins.

Finale

The Suppliants have suffered greatly to preserve their integrity and their father's honour; but they are also attempting to resist an inexorable natural process, presided over by one of the most powerful goddesses. To bring this out further, Aischylos chooses not to let the Suppliants simply sing and dance themselves out in procession to Argos. That would be an effective ending to this drama; the Danaides have won this space, and won in this space; the contrast is total between their fearful entry alone, from the right *parodos* at the start and their escorted exit left, to Argos, now. But it would not look forward to the next drama. He therefore composes contrasting dances of love and abstention; a supplementary *choros* break into song and dissent, when the Suppliants once again express their resistance to a forced marriage,[41] to bring out this point even more firmly than Danaos has.

Who is that *choros*? Traditionally the lines were assigned to some Maidservants of the Suppliants, on the basis of the lines addressed to them, which stand in the MS at the end of Choros 6; but the text here is too forthright for maidservants; and there is no place for maidservants in *Suppliants*, since their silent presence throughout would totally undermine the fundamental image of a sudden, helpless flight from the Aigyptians. Indeed, the idea that Aischylos could tolerate a group of twelve maidservants either pulling focus, unmentioned, for the duration

---

[41] However, the supplementary *choros* misses the overtone in the phrasing of 1031–3; the Danaides may seem to be contemplating suicide when they speak of death as a consequence of forced marriage; but their language is deliberately ambiguous, so Aischylos encourages his audience – not for the first time in this drama – to think rather of murder.

of the drama or entering unmotivated after 979 shows little regard for his dramatic skill. It is therefore rightly dismissed by Taplin.[42]

Three candidates remain; the escort of Argive men, a new supplementary *choros* of Argive women, and Danaos himself.[43] Taplin's personal preference for Danaos seems eccentric; these lines in the Finale convey a vision of sexuality which is distinct from Danaos' combination of authority and prurience; the lyrics seem designed to offer a supplementary admonition to the Suppliants, the more powerful because it comes not from their father but from a more objective, more moderate source.

Argive Women are favoured by two translations, that of Lembke and of Raphael/McLeish. However, I cannot accept Lembke's view that 1034ff. are 'women's words'.[44] All of these lines could be sung by men; and there is added point if males admonish the Danaides, since they will ultimately have to come to terms in some way with male power and male sexuality. There are also no lines to introduce a new supplementary *choros* of women.[45]

I therefore agree with Friis Johansen and Whittle that Aischylos experimented here with the technique which he used again with Pylades in *Libation Bearers*; having repeatedly seen Argive Soldiers enter and leave the *orchêstra* as silent faces, the audience has been lulled into assuming that they are simply extras and will never play a speaking or singing part. Suddenly, and surprisingly, that expectation is reversed; and Aischylos makes the reversal most effective by swinging the Suppliants, in the A stanzas, into lyrics typical of the beginning of an exit song of praise for their new location. This is then suddenly interrupted, as the Argive soldiers burst into a counter-song and temporarily prevent their exit, interposing their own dance between the Danaides and the left *parodos*.

---

[42] 1977, 230–80.

[43] McCall (1976, 124) argues valiantly that there is no supplementary *choros*, and the A to C stanzas were divided between two groups of Danaides. It seems to me that the lines assigned in this translation to the Argives are impossible for any of the Danaides to sing, at this stage in their psychological development.

[44] 1975, 100. (Raphael & McLeish offer no argument for their preference.) The women's movement could do without the assumption – itself both sexist, and harking back to Romantic mystiques – that anything to do with sexuality is in some way more the domain of females than males. Seaford (1987, 114–15), reinforces the case for a male/female division by bringing out parallels between this Finale and wedding songs, which were normally sung antiphonally by *choroses* of young men and young women.

[45] Contrast *Eumenides* 1005, 1026.

The conflict is escalated in the C stanzas, where subdivision conveys the tension created by the Argive intervention; it is only resolved (for the moment) in D2, when the Suppliants accept the unarguable message of 1061, and attempt in the exit stanzas to create a prayer which will achieve what they want, while accepting realistically that they cannot expect to have a perfect life. As they leave, the images of the gods remain – inscrutable. They will not necessarily give the Danaides what they desire.

Fragments

33 Fishermen

The second of the two fragments includes a marginal line marker for line 800. *Satyr-dramas* were shorter than tragedies; *Kyklops* has 709 lines, and *Trackers* is unlikely to have been much longer; this scene therefore probably comes from late in *Fishermen*. It is impossible to know what happened earlier, since the two fragments present a self-sufficient unit of the action. Danaë is landed, rescued, and appropriated by the Satyrs and Silenos.

It is easier to conjecture what happened afterwards. Lines 18–20 foreshadow the return of Diktys, to claim possession of the chest and its contents from Silenos; presumably their dispute was interrupted by a god or hero, who rescued Danaë and made amends to her on behalf of Zeus.[1]

The *choros* appear not to be present for 1–20; it is probable therefore that there has been a change of scene, from another location to the lonely shore on which the action is now set. This change of scene, like others in Greek drama, would have been indicated by the exit of the *choros* together with the placement of a new property – in this case the chest containing Danaë and Perseus.[2] Silenos and Diktys mime search-

[1] By convention Zeus, as the supreme god, never appeared in tragedy (Aischylos, characteristically, broke this convention in his lost drama *The Weighing of Souls*). A god who had impregnated a virgin had another reason not to appear in person – embarrassment; cf. Athena's appearance on behalf of her brother Apollo at the end of Euripides' *Ion*.

[2] There are only two actors, and no scene changes, in the first three surviving tragedies. The use of three actors, and the change of scene, might suggest that *Fishermen* belongs to the last years of Aischylos' life, after the introduction of the *skene*. The scene changes in *Libation Bearers*, *Eumenides* and Sophokles' *Aias* involve a shift between a focus around the *skene* doors and a focus around a new prop set in the centre of the *orchêstra*. This would also appear to be the case in *Fishermen*. Since *Ambassadors to the Isthmian Games* definitely requires

ing around the *orchêstra*, much like the Furies at the start of *Eumenides* Scene 3, or the Sailors and Tekmessa at Sophokles *Aias* 866ff.

The chest became the main focus of attention for the remainder of the scene, and the Satyrs and Silenos dance around Danaë and Perseus; so the logical place to preset the chest (and some rocks; cf. line 6) is the centre of the *orchêstra*.[3] Silenos and Diktys, soon after they enter (or re-enter) from a *parodos* to begin this scene, must have established by mime that the extreme front part of the *orchêstra*, and/or the front rows of the spectators in the *theatron*, now represent the sea.[4]

When the text resumes at 765, Danaë has plainly left the chest – presumably miming terrified but futile attempts to escape from the satyrs who surround her. By 782 she needs to be back at C, just in front of the chest, for the invocation to Zeus; this position is needed both so she can deliver the speech effectively, and so the Satyrs can begin the dance from positions surrounding her and Perseus.[5] They will then yield back to the perimeter, making room for Silenos' extended solo,[6] and returning to dominate the *orchêstra* only at 811ff. This marks the start of a hymeneal exit song, which was presumably first delayed by Danaë's resistance, and then interrupted either by the return of Diktys or by the intervention of a god. In either case, if *Fishermen* followed the pattern normal in other *satyr-dramas*, Silenos and the

three actors and the *skene* (see below), both our surviving substantial fragments of Aischylean *satyr-drama* probably date from the period when he was at the height of his dramatic powers, between the Danaid trilogy and his death.

[3] Agamemnon's grave in *L B*, Athena's image in *Eu* and Aias' body in Sophokles' drama (concealed, like Danaë's chest, behind a natural feature, some bushes), were all placed by stagehands at the centre of the *orchêstra* before the action began in the new location. Cf. Ewans 1995, 174–5 and 201.

[4] The front of the *orchêstra* and the first rows of seats are the most effective parts of the Greek theatre to use for an imaginary world into which the characters look, since the maximum number of spectators can see and interact with the actors' masks. Cf. the use of the same parts of the theatre to represent the dark and muddy world of Hades at Aristophanes, *Frogs* 270ff.

[5] Clear visibility between the castaways and the Satyrs is necessary so the child actor playing Perseus can react to the dance in a way which makes theatre sense of 795. While this could also be done if Danaë and the chest are preset at EBC, such a position makes 765ff. very hard to play, and forces Silenos and Diktys to act the discovery scene at 7ff. in a weak position, remote from most of the spectators.

[6] Long solo songs are unparalleled in tragic drama until the late fifth century, and in Aristophanes' *Frogs* (1329ff.) 'Aischylos' mocks 'Euripides' for using them. This fragment shows that Aischylos himself was happy to include monodies in a *satyr-drama* over sixty years earlier.

satyrs will have achieved liberation from their servitude to Diktys'
brother Polydektes (the King of Seriphos), and Danaë will have found
a more appropriate husband.

35 Ambassadors to the Isthmian Games

This fragment must date from Aischylos' last years, since it requires a
practicable *skene* representing the temple of Poseidon, and three actors
to play Silenos, Hephaistos and Dionysos. The dramatic line is well
defined and clear, even though the subject-matter is obscure. The satyrs
have, for unknown reasons, been given images of themselves – probably
masks – by a very gifted craftsman, who is almost certainly Hephaistos;[7]
they hang these up as votive offerings to Poseidon, but are then rebuked
by Dionysos – who perhaps, given the title of the drama, had sent them
as ambassadors to the Isthmian Games at Corinth, expecting then that
they would rehearse for a display of dances or for the choral contest,
but now finds that they have been training to compete as athletes in the
Games. However, they side with their new friend – who has already
given them some dangerous tools[8] (69ff.), and now brings them further
'toys', whose identity cannot be conjectured. Presumably however they
returned to their old master, Dionysos, before the end of the drama.

During the opening section the Satyrs, as they chant, first show the
images to each other, then gather by line 18 in front of the *skene*; they
fasten the images to its façade. They are all close to the *skene*, and
facing it, during the following lines, so Dionysos surprises them by
entering behind their backs at 23. The action after that clearly involves
a free performance by Dionysos, ranging all around the *orchêstra*, and
driving them before him, fairly continuously up to 77. However, his
strategy does not succeed; they are clearly unfazed by his anger, and
they re-form in 79ff., ready to make an entrance into the temple. This
is however interrupted by Hephaistos' entry with new properties, just
before the fragment ends.

[7] Lloyd-Jones 1963, 546–9.
[8] Perhaps javelins; Lloyd-Jones ibid., following Snell.

GLOSSARY OF PROPER NAMES

Where other narratives conflict with Aischylos, the information provided relates only to the version used in these dramas.

The names of Persian commanders in *Persians* are glossed only when we know something about them from other sources.

Places in Prometheus' account of Io's wanderings (*P B* 700ff.) are grouped together in a single entry under IO.

ACHAIANS Aischylos normally follows Homer in using Achaians as a synonym for Greeks, reflecting the Achaian pre-eminence, especially throughout the Peloponnese, in the time at which the dramas are set. At *Persians* 488, however, he refers specifically to the Achaians of Phthia in southern Thessaly.

ACHERON A river in the underworld.

ACHILLEUS Son of Peleus and the nymph Thetis; king of Phthia in Thessaly. His quarrel with Agamemnon, leader of the expedition against Troy, is the central strand in the plot of Homer's *Iliad*.

ADRASTEIA 'The Inescapable'; a goddess who punishes rash speech.

ADRASTOS King of Argos in *Seven*; father-in-law of Polyneikes, and leader of the expedition against Thebes.

AGBATANA The capital of the kingdom of Media, afterwards the summer residence of the kings of Persia.

AIAS Son of Telamon and lord of Salamis; when the Greek chieftains awarded the arms of Achilleus to Odysseus rather than to him, he attempted to kill them all. However, Athena inflicted madness upon him, and he killed sheep and cattle instead. When he returned to sanity, he committed suicide in shame.

AIGYPTIOI Inhabitants of Aigyptos' kingdom.

AIGYPTOS Eponymous king of Aigyptos, modern Egypt; son of Belos, twin brother of Danaos.

AITHIOPIA Territory to the south of Egypt.

AITNA Modern Etna; town and volcano in north-east Sicily.

AKTAION A Theban prince, who offended Artemis by boasting he could hunt better than she. She turned him into a stag, and his own hounds tore him apart on Mt Kithairon near Delphi.

AKTOR   A defender of Thebes, brother of Hippomedon.

AMAZONES   Warrior women who lived in the Black Sea region.

AMPHIAROS   Son of Oikleus, one of the Seven against Thebes; a prophet as well as a warrior.

AMPHION   King of Thebes, husband of Niobe. He killed himself after the deaths of his children.

ANDROS   An island in the Aigeian Sea, south-east of Euboia.

ANTIGONE   Daughter of Oidipous, sister of Eteokles and Polyneikes.

APHRODITE   Goddess of love. Her 'fertile corn-land' at *Suppliants* 554–5 is Phoinikia.

APIS   A son of Apollo, a healer, who gave his name to the land around Argos.

APOLLO   Son of Zeus and Leto, and brother of Artemis; a major Greek god, worshipped especially at Delos and Delphi. God of archery (and so particularly able to protect his friends and send sudden death on his enemies); music and painting; purification from *miasma*; healing from disease; and prophecy.

ARES   The god of war, son of Zeus and Hera.

ARGOS   (1) With Sparta, one of the two most important cities in the Peloponnese. It is located in a level, fertile plain in the north-east Peloponnese, just west of the river Inachos. (2) The hundred-eyed, son of the Earth, appointed by Hera to guard Io. Hermes killed him at the command of Zeus.

ARIOMARDOS   Governor of Thebes in Egypt in Aischylos; two men of this name appear in Herodotos (7.67 and 78).

ARSAMES   A son of Dareios, commander of the Arabian and Aithiopian forces in Herodotos; in Aischylos, ruler of Memphis.

ARTAPHRENES   (1) *Persians* 21: a general at Marathon, who in Xerxes' invasion commanded Mysian and Lydian forces. (2) *Pers.* 776ff.: probably the 'Intaphrenes' of Herodotos' account (3.70 and 78) of the conspiracy which resulted in Dareios' ascent to the throne.

ARTEMIS   Sister of Apollo; a virgin goddess, imaged as a huntress, who is naturally called on by unmarried women in *Suppliants* and *Seven*. As a female counterpart to Apollo, she both inflicted and could cure diseases in women. She was also protectress of the young, and the goddess who presided over childbirth.

ASOPOS   A river in Boiotia.

ASTAKOS   The father of Melanippos.

ATHENA   Goddess of wisdom, and patron deity of Athens.

ATLAS   A Titan, brother of Prometheus, condemned by Zeus, in punishment for the war of the Titanes against the Olympians, to bear the weight of the heavens upon his shoulders.

AXIOS   A river in Makedonia, flowing into the Aigeian Sea.

BABYLON   Formerly the capital of the independent empire of Nebuchadnezzar (604–562), the chief city of Mesopotamia became the third capital of the Persian empire after Kyros conquered it in 538.

BAKTRIA   The most distant territory of the Persian empire, east of the Caspian Sea.

BELOS   Son of Libye, father of Aigyptos and Danaos.

BEREKYNTHIA   The part of Phrygia, in the north-west of Asia Minor, ruled by Tantalos.

BOIOTIA   Plain in central Greece, north-west of Attika; the principal city was Thebes.

BOLBE   A lake in Makedonia.

BOREAS   The North Wind, who abducted Oreithyia.

BOSPOROS   The 'cow-crossing', name given both to the narrowest part of the Hellespont, and to the strait between the Sea of Azov and the Black Sea.

CHALKIS   The principal city of the island of Euboia.

CHIOS   Large island in the Aigeian Sea, off the coast of Lydia.

CHRYSA   City on the coast near Troy.

DANAE   Daughter of Akrisios king of Argos. He imprisoned her in a tower of bronze, because an oracle foretold that her son would kill his grandfather. Zeus visited her in a shower of gold, and made her pregnant. Akrisios shut up both mother and child in a chest, which he cast into the sea. *Fishermen* dramatizes what happened when they came ashore on the island of Seriphos.

DANAIDES   The daughters of Danaos.

DANAOS   Son of Belos, twin brother of Aigyptos. He was granted the kingdom of Libye by Belos, but fled with the Danaides to Greece. After the death of Pelasgos he became ruler of Argos.

DAREIOS   King of Persia 521–485. He suppressed rebellion in Babylonia, invaded Skythia, subdued Thrakia and Makedonia, and sent an expeditionary force against Athens in revenge for Athenian assistance during the revolt of the Ionian Greeks. Aischylos was among the Athenians who defeated this force at Marathon in 490.

DELPHI   A town in Phokis, on the slopes of Mt Parnassos, site of Apollo's principal oracle.

DEMETER   Sister of Zeus, goddess of agriculture and of all the fruits of the Earth.

DIKTYS   A fisherman, brother of Polydektes, the king of the island of Seriphos.

DIONYSOS   Son of Zeus and Semele; god of ecstatic possession, fertility, and the life-force, both creative and destructive – especially as manifested through liquids; the sap of young trees, the blood of young animals and humans, and wine. His followers are called Bakchantes, after his alternate cult-name Bakchos.

DIRKE   One of the two rivers of Thebes.

DODONA   A small city in southern Epiros, in north-west Greece, the site of a famous oracle of Zeus.

DORIS   A small and mountainous district of north-west Greece.

EDONIANS   Inhabitants of the part of Thrakia between the river Strymon, the frontier with Makedonia, and the river Nestos.

ENYO   A goddess of war, companion of Ares.

EPAPHOS   Son of Io and Zeus, founder of the royal line of Egypt. His name literally means 'touch', in memory of the healing touch of Zeus by which he was conceived.

ERASINOS   A river of the plain of Argos.

ETEOKLES   Son of Oidipous and brother of Polyneikes.

ETEOKLOS   An Argive, one of the Seven against Thebes.

EUBOIA   A long island in the Aigeian, lying off the coasts of Attika, Boiotia and southern Thessaly.

EUROPA   Daughter of Agenor, king of Phoinikia. Disguised as a bull, Zeus made off with her and swam to Krete, where she became the mother of Minos, Rhadamanthos and Sarpedon.

EURYMEDON   One of the most conspicuously arrogant suitors of Penelopeia, during Odysseus' absence from Ithaka.

GABIOI   A Thrakian tribe.

GATES   Aischylos orders the seven gates of Thebes in a different sequence from that of topographical reality. This table presents his arrangement, with their physical position, working clockwise from the northern gate, shown by the number in brackets:

1 Gate of Proitos (2). Proitos was an obscure Theban hero.

2 Gate of Elektra (4). The southern gate. The 'Elektra' is unknown,

but is not to be identified with Orestes' sister in the legends of the house of Atreus at Argos.

3 Gate of Neïs (7).

4 Gate of Athena Ongka (5). 'Ongka' was a cult-title of Athena at Thebes; its meaning is unknown.

5 Northern Gate (1).

6 Homolian Gate (3).

7 Not named in *Seven*; in real life Hypsistai/Kreneai (6).

GERYON A three-bodied monster, who lived in Erythia – 'the red island', so called because it lay far in the west, under the rays of the setting sun.

GLAUKOS A fisherman from Anthedon in Boiotia; he ate a magic, 'ever-living grass' which transformed him into a sea-god who could foretell the future.

GULF OF MELIA A deep inlet at the border between Greece and Thessaly, behind the north-west point of Euboia.

HADES Brother of Zeus and Poseidon, husband of Persephone. Zeus' counterpart below the Earth, the ruler of the underworld to which human souls pass after death. His kingdom is often called 'Hades', abbreviated from 'Hades' halls'.

HALYS The chief river of Asia Minor, falling into the Black Sea; it was the boundary between the original empire of the Medes and Persians, and the Lydian and Phrygian lands which Kyros conquered.

HEKTOR Eldest son of Priam of Troy. His death at the hands of Achilleus, and the ransoming of the body by Priam, form the narrative climax of Homer's *Iliad*.

HELEN Daughter of Zeus and Leda, half-sister of Klytaimestra; wife of Menelaos, later mistress of Paris.

HELLAS The Greeks' own name for their country, which is elsewhere called Greece from Roman *Graecia*.

HELLESPONT The narrow strait which connects the Sea of Marmora with the Aigeian Sea; the boundary between Europe and Asia.

HEPHAISTOS Son of Hera; the god of fire, and craftsman of the gods.

HERA Wife of Zeus, and goddess of marriage. She had a large temple at Argos and was the principal goddess worshipped there.

HERAKLES Son of Zeus by Alkmene, wife of Amphitryon; the greatest Greek hero, and the only one to receive the same worship as a god after his death. He was driven mad by Hera, and killed his children. To expiate this crime, Apollo's oracle ordered him to serve Eurystheus, king of Tiryns, for twelve years. The Labours of Herakles are the superhuman feats which Eurystheus demanded of him.

After the end of his labours, his wife Deianeira gave him a cloak spread with a poison which she wrongly thought to be a love-potion. Dying in agony, he had a funeral pyre built for him on the slopes of Mt Oita, and commanded his son to set it on fire. He was then raised to the heavens by Zeus, and reconciled with Hera.

HERMES   Son of Zeus and Maia, herald and messenger of the gods. He was the god who escorts travellers, and conducts souls between the worlds of the living and the dead; also the guardian of paternal rights, and the god of deception and trickery.

HIPPOMEDON   One of the Seven against Thebes.

HISMENOS   One of the two rivers of Thebes.

HYPERBIOS   Brother of Aktor; one of the seven defenders of Thebes.

IDA   The chief mountain of Phrygia, in the region surrounding Troy.

IKARIA   An island in the Aigeian Sea.

INACHOS   An Argive, father of Io. He gives his name to the main river of Argos territory.

IO   Daughter of Inachos, founder of the first royal line of Argos. The story of Zeus' desire for her, her transformation into a cow by Hera, and her long journey to Egypt, are told – in significantly different versions – in *Suppliants* and *Prometheus Bound*.

In *PB* she is depicted as having travelled north-west from Argos to Dodona in north-west Greece, on the border between Molossia and Thesprotia; then to the Gulf of Rhea at the north end of the Adriatic. Storms drove her north until she reached Prometheus' rock, which is imagined as lying in an uninhabited part of Skythia, far to the north of Greece.

The author appears to place the Chalybes, a Skythian race of iron-workers, on or upcountry from the north-west coast of the Black Sea. From their territory Io goes north along the west bank of an imaginary river Hybristes ('violent'), which flows into the Black Sea roughly where the Dnieper does; this river has its source towards the far north of the continent, in a mountain called Kaukasos (not to be identified with the range to the east of the Black Sea, known to most Greeks and in the modern world by that name). Returning down the Hybristes' east bank, she reaches the Amazones just west of Lake Maiotis – the Sea of Azov. However, the author is aware that normal mythology placed the Amazones south of the Black Sea; Prometheus therefore prophesies their relocation to Themiskyra in the north of Asia Minor – but wrongly identifies this area with Salmydessos, which was actually in Thrakia, on the south-west coast of the Black Sea.

Io then crosses the Isthmos of Crimea; her wanderings in Asia take her into fantastic territory – based however, as Bolton (1962) has shown, on central Asian folk-tales which Aristeas heard among the Issedonians, and recorded in his poem *Arimaspeia*. She encounters the three Graiai ('old women') and their winged sisters the Gorgones (normally located in Libya). The mention of the Arimaspians near the river Plouton ('wealth') reflects the fact that the Urals were rich in gold. Finally she circles round to the Far East, where the author locates the Aithiopians. She then follows the river Aithiops – presumably south-west – to the sources of the Nile. Heading north along the banks of the Nile, she reaches real geography again at the First Cataract, and travels north to Kanobos.

IONIA The west coast of Asia Minor and the neighbouring islands, colonized in early times by the Greeks.

ISMENE Daughter of Oidipous, sister of Eteokles and Polyneikes.

ISTHMIAN GAMES One of the four great panhellenic festivals, held at Korinth in the second and fourth years of each Olympic cycle.

KADMOS Son of Agenor the king of Phoinikia, and brother of Europa; the founder of Thebes.

KANOBOS City on the coast of Egypt, just east of Alexandria; Io's final resting place in *Prometheus*. In *Suppliants* she goes on to Memphis.

KAPANEUS One of the Seven against Thebes. In vase-paintings, and in Sophokles' *Antigone* (134ff.) Zeus did indeed hurl a thunderbolt against him as he assaulted the city, as Eteokles prophesies at *Seven* 444ff.

KARIA A district in the south-west of Asia Minor.

KENEA The north-west promontory of Euboia, opposite Thermopylae; site of a temple of Zeus.

KERCHNE A village near Argos.

KILIKIA A district in the south-west of Asia Minor.

KISSIA In real life the district of central Persia in which the winter capital, Sousa, was located; Aischylos writes as if it were a separate fortified city.

KNIDOS An island-port, linked to the mainland of Karia by a causeway.

KOKYTOS A river in the underworld; its name means 'wailing' (lamentation).

KOLCHIS   Region to the north of the Black Sea, inhabited by the Amazones in *PB*.

KOTYTO   An indigenous Thrakian goddess, whose orgiastic rites were taken over by Dionysos.

KRONOS   The youngest of the Titanes; son of Ouranos and Ge (Heaven and Earth); he deprived Ouranos of the government of the world, and was himself dethroned by his own son, Zeus.

KYPRIS   'The Kyprian goddess' – i.e. Aphrodite, who was born from the foam of waves on the shore of Kypros.

KYPROS   Large island off the south coast of Asia Minor.

KYROS   Founder of the Persian empire; he conquered the Medes, Lydia, the Greek cities of Asia Minor and the Babylonian empire. He was killed in 529 during an expedition against the Massagetai of Skythia.

LAIOS   King of Thebes. His failure to keep the terms of an oracle that he should die childless led to the sufferings of the royal house, and its destruction in the third generation by the mortal combat of Eteokles and Polyneikes.

LASTHENES   One of the seven defenders of Thebes.

LEMNOS   Large island in the north Aigeian Sea.

LERNE   A district near Argos, with a lake and a small river.

LESBOS   A large island in the Aigeian, off the coast of Mysia in Asia Minor.

LETO   Mother of Apollo and Artemis.

LIBYE   Eponymous ruler of Libya.

LICHAS   Herald and servant of Herakles, who brought him Deianeira's poisoned robe; Herakles hurled him into the sea.

LOXIAS   Probably 'the crooked one'; a cult title of Apollo, referring to the obscurity of many of his oracles.

LYDIA   Central western district of the peninsula of Asia Minor; an early seat of Asian civilization.

LYGIANS   Inhabitants of the region of southern France around Marseilles.

MAGNETIKE   A coastal region of Thessaly.

MAIOTIS   Lake north of the Black Sea; the modern Sea of Azov.

MAKEDONIA   The region to the north of Greece, where the rivers Lydias, Axios and Strymon flow into the Aigeian Sea.

MARATHON   Village and plain on the east coast of Attika, site of the defeat of Dareios' invasion force in 490.

MARDOS   The usurper, known in Herodotos (3.61ff.) as Smerdis, who pretended to be a son of Kyros, and ruled the Persian empire after the death of Kyros' heir Kambyses.

MARIANDYNOI   A tribe on the north coast of Asia Minor, near the Black Sea; noted for their funeral dirges.

MEDES   Strictly, inhabitants of the kingdom north of Persis; after its incorporation into the Persian empire 'Medes' became a frequent synonym for Persians.

MEGABATES   Cousin of Dareios, and father of one of Xerxes' four admirals.

MEGAREUS   Son of Kreon, and a descendant of the Sown Men; one of the seven defenders of Thebes.

MELANIPPOS   A defender of Thebes in *Seven*; descended from one of the Sown Men.

MEMPHIS   A major city of ancient Egypt, on the west bank of the Nile, just south of the Pyramids.

MENELAOS   Son of Atreus, husband of Helen; joint leader of the expedition to Troy with his brother Agamemnon.

MESSAPION   A mountain on the coast of Boiotia, opposite Euboia.

METIS   The name given uniquely in *Suppliants* to Prokne, who killed her son Itys to take revenge on her husband Tereus for raping her sister Philomela. Prokne became a nightingale when she prayed to be changed into a bird to escape from Tereus' pursuit; the sad song of the nightingale is her lament for Itys' death.

MINOS   Son of Zeus and Europa; king of Krete, and after his death one of the judges in Hades.

MYKONOS   An island in the centre of the Aigeian Sea.

MYRMIDONES   Inhabitants of Phthia, the kingdom ruled by Achilleus.

MYSIA   The north-west corner of Asia Minor.

NAIADES   The nymphs of fresh water – rivers, lakes, streams and springs.

NAUPAKTOS   A small town in Lokris, with a good harbour on the north side of the Korinthian Gulf.

NAXOS   An island in the centre of the Aigeian Sea.

NEMESIS   The goddess who personifies anger and divine retribution.

NIOBE   Daughter of Tanatalos, and wife of Amphion, king of Thebes. She boasted that she was a better mother than Leto, because she had more children; Apollo and Artemis killed her children in revenge.

ODYSSEUS   King of Ithaka, husband of Penelopeia. He returned from the Trojan War, after ten years at war and a further ten of wanderings;

his wife was under intense pressure to remarry from over one hundred suitors. Using his great bow, and with the help of his son Telemachos and two of his retainers, he killed them all.

OIDIPOUS   Son of Laios, and ruler of Thebes after he rid the city of the Sphinx, until he discovered that his wife was his own mother.

OIKLEUS   Father of Amphiaraos.

OINOPS   Father of Hippomedon and Aktor.

OITA   A mountain in southern Thessaly, scene of Herakles' self-immolation.

OKEANIDES   The daughters of Okeanos.

OKEANOS   A Titan, lord of the river which surrounds the continents.

OLYMPOS   Mountain in the north-east of mainland Greece, the dwelling-place of the gods.

OREITHYIA   A daughter of Erechtheus, king of Athens; she was abducted and married by Boreas.

OURANOS   The first supreme god; his name means 'heaven'.

PAIONIA   Territory of the Paionians, around the river Axios in Makedonia.

PALAICTHON   Literally 'ancient land'; the name of Pelasgos' father in *Suppliants*, sprung from the soil; the first human to live in Argos.

PALLAS   A cult-title of Athena, of unknown origin and meaning.

PAMPHYLIANS   Migrants from Troy, who settled in and around Kilikia.

PAN   The god of flocks and shepherds. The island which Aischylos refers to as 'a haunt of Pan' was called Psyttaleia; modern historians dispute whether it is Lipsokoutáli or St George.

PANGAIOS   A mountain range in Edonian territory, on the borders between Makedonia and Thrakia.

PAPHOS   Old and New Paphos were two towns on the west coast of Kypros.

PARIS   Son of Priam and Hekabe, often called Alexander. His abduction of Helen caused the Trojan War.

PAROS   An island in the Aigeian Sea.

PARTHENOPAIOS   'The maiden-faced'; son of Atalanta from Arkadia.

PATROKLOS   Son of Menoitios, intimate friend since childhood of Achilleus. His death at the hands of Hektor precipitated Achilleus' return to combat in the Trojan War.

PELASGIANS   Inhabitants of Pelasgian Argos.

PELASGOS   Son of Palaichthon, and king of Argos in *Suppliants*. His kingdom, as Aischylos imagines it, extends over most of later Greece.

PERRHAIBOI   Inhabitants of the regions west of Mt Pindos, and around Dodona.

PERSEUS   Son of Danaë by Zeus; thought by some Greeks to be the eponymous ancestor of the Persians.

PHILOKTETES   Son of Poias, the most celebrated archer in the Trojan War. On the way to Troy a snake bit his foot; this produced such an intolerable stench that the Greeks, on the advice of Odysseus, abandoned him on the coast of Lemnos. However, an oracle told the Greeks that Troy could not be taken without the arrows which Herakles had bequeathed to Philoktetes, and in the tenth year of the war Odysseus had to go to Lemnos and persuade him to come and fight.

PHOIBOS   Cult title of Apollo, meaning 'bright'.

PHOINIKIA   Mountainous strip of land on the Syrian coast; its chief port, Tyre, was the centre of Persian naval power.

PHOKIS   Region of northern Greece, north-west from Boiotia.

PHRYGIA   The region of north-west Asia Minor in which Troy is sited.

PINDOS   A mountain range in north-west Greece.

PLOUTON   'The giver of wealth'; a name for Hades, since crops and minerals come from below the earth.

POLYNEIKES   Son of Oidipous, and brother of Eteokles; he persuaded the Argives, under his father-in-law Adrastos, to march against Thebes so he could reclaim it as his inheritance.

POLYPHONTES   One of the seven defenders of Thebes.

PONTOS   The Black Sea.

POSEIDON   Brother of Zeus, god of the sea.

PRIAM   King of Troy.

PROMETHEUS   A Titan, the benefactor of mankind who stole fire from the gods. His name means 'forethought'.

PROPONTIS   The Sea of Marmora.

RHADAMANTHOS   Son of Zeus and Europa. He fled from Krete in fear of his brother, king Minos, and married Alkmene in Boiotia. He was conspicuous for his justice, and became after his death one of the judges in Hades.

RHODOS   Large island in the south-east Aigeian, off the coast of Karia.

SALAMIS   (1) An island separated by a narrow channel from the west coast of Attika; legendary home of the hero Aias, and part of Athenian territory since Solon. (2) Colony of Salamis 1, in the island of Kypros.

SAMOS   An island off the coast of Ionia, of great importance in the late sixth century under its ruler Polykrates, before its conquest by Persia.

SARDIS   Capital city of Lydia, a rich independent kingdom in Asia Minor until it was conquered by Kyros.

SARPEDON   A son of Zeus by Europa, king of Lykia, a small district on the south side of Asia Minor. He and his brother Glaukos play a major part as warriors on the Trojan side in the *Iliad*. His 'sandy headland' is on the coast opposite the east end of Kypros.

SEMELE   Daughter of Kadmos and Harmonia; sister of Agauë, the mother of Pentheus. She was loved by Zeus, who promised to give her anything she wanted. Hera was jealous of Semele; she appeared before her in disguise, and persuaded her to ask Zeus to show himself before her in all his majesty as the god of thunder. She did this, and was consumed by lightning; but Zeus saved her son Dionysos.

SILENIAI   Part of the coast of Salamis.

SILENOS   The father of the satyrs; a selfish, alcoholic and lecherous old man who was also the tutor of Dionysos, and an inspired prophet.

SOLOI   Small town on the island of Kypros.

SOUSA   The winter capital of the Persian kings.

SOWN MEN   On arriving at the site which later became Thebes, Kadmos killed a snake or dragon which guarded a well sacred to Ares. Athena commanded him to sow the monster's teeth; a host of armed men sprung up from them. He flung stones among the men so they fought each other, until only five were left; they were called the Spartoi or Sown Men, and their descendants became the nobility of Thebes.

SPARTA   Principal city and most powerful military force in the Peloponnese.

SPERCHEIOS   A river in southern Thessaly, flowing into the Gulf of Melia.

SPHINX   A monster, with a woman's head, a lioness' body and the wings of an eagle; she persecuted Thebes until Oidipous solved her riddle and was rewarded with the throne and the widow of the previous king, Laios.

STRYMON   A river in far north-east Greece, on the border between Makedonia and Thrakia.

STYX   The principal river of the underworld; its name means 'hateful'.

TANTALOS   Son of Zeus by a nymph; father of Pelops and of Niobe.

TARTAROS   River and region in the deepest part of the underworld, where the Titanes were imprisoned by Zeus.

TEIRESIAS The former prophet of Thebes, whom Odysseus summoned up from the underworld during his wanderings.

TELAMON King of Salamis, father of Aias.

TENOS An island in the Aigeian Sea, directly south-east of Andros.

TEREUS See METIS.

TETHYS A female Titan, wife of Okeanos and mother of the nymphs of the sea – the Okeanides or Daughters of Okeanos – and the nymphs of rivers.

TEUTHRAS An early king of Mysia, father of Telephos.

THEBES The principal city of Boiotia.

THEMIS The goddess of the order established by law and custom; her name means 'right'.

THESSALY The plain surrounding Larissa in north-west Greece.

THETIS A sea-nymph, daughter of Nereus, wife of Peleus, and mother of Achilleus.

TITANES The sons and daughters of Ouranos and Earth. They ruled the world under Kronos, the second supreme god, until he and they were overthrown by Zeus in the battle of the Titanes.

THRAKIA The relatively uncivilized tribal lands north of the part of the Aigeian coastline between the river Strymon and the Hellespont.

TMOLOS A mountain in Lydia.

TYDEUS Son of Oineus, father of Diomedes; he fled from his native Kalydon to Argos after murdering a kinsman, married one of Adrastos' daughters and became one of the Seven against Thebes.

TYPHON/TYPHOS A hundred-headed, fire-breathing monster; he challenged Zeus after the fall of the Titanes, was blasted by a thunderbolt, and was buried under Mt Aitna.

XERXES Son of Dareios, king of Persia from Dareios' death in 485 until he was assassinated in 465.

ZEUS The most powerful god; son of Kronos and Rhea. Originally a sky and weather god, his weapon was the thunderbolt. He punished oath-breaking, and some other kinds of wrongdoing; in particular, the table of hospitality was sacred to him as the protector of the rights of guests – strangers, beggars and suppliants – and hosts. However, Zeus did not make the world, and he was not omnipotent or omniscient. Despite his great and wide-ranging powers, other gods as well as human beings could defy him (at their own risk).

GLOSSARY OF GREEK WORDS

agathos   A good or noble man – head of an *oikos* by virtue of a combination of birth, wealth and military ability.

agora   The market-place or city square; the centre of political, legal and social life in the city-states of ancient Greece.

aischron   'Shameful'. The avoidance of shame, and the pursuit of actions which will increase *time*, are the fundamental motivations of the *agathos* throughout the classical period.

anapaests   The metre of the chanted sections of a Greek tragedy, midway in intensity between speech and lyric song. Often used as accompaniment for the entrance-march of the *choros*.

astrophic   Greek lyric verse is *astrophic* when it lacks the formal patterning of *strophe* matched with responding *antistrophe*. *Astrophic* verse is equivalent to a free, blank verse in English.

ate   'Blindness' or 'destruction', a *daimôn* which can be inflicted on a human being by the gods.

bronteion   The machine for producing the special effect of the sound of thunder. Later tradition says that stagehands rattled a barrel of small stones; but shaking a large sheet of thin copper would also have been feasible in fifth-century technology.

choros   Literally song (and dance) – denotes either the group of twelve *choros* members or the odes (songs) that they perform.

daimôn   A god or god-like power; *daimones* are often what we, like the later Greeks, would call personifications of abstract forces – e.g. Madness, Fear, Persuasion.

demos   The citizen body of a democratic *polis*.

dithyramb   A song and dance in the form of a choral hymn, usually including a narrative. These *choroses* were originally connected with the worship of Dionysos; at the Festival each of Athens' ten tribes presented two 'circular *choroses*', one of fifty men and one of fifty boys, to compete with *dithyrambs* in two different competitions.

drama Lit. 'thing done/enacted'; the normal term at Athens for the combination of speech and song, movement and dance which comprises a tragedy or comedy.

echthros Enemy; in Greek the polar opposite of *philos*, referring therefore to all who are not either members of the family or *xenoi*, unless they can prove themselves to be well disposed.

ekkuklêma The rolling-out machine, used in tragedy when the pressure of events inside the building represented by the *skene* has such implication for the public forum outside that they must be seen (as they could not if simply displayed in the entrance, because of shadows).

epirrhematic scene An exchange (*amoibaion*) between solo actor and *choros*, in which one or both sing.

epode A third stanza, sometimes added as a tailpiece after a pair of *strophe* and *antistrophe*; in the same metres but not responding exactly in its structure to those stanzas.

euche The normal Greek word for 'prayer', its fundamental meaning is 'boast'. This reflects the extent to which a Greek prayer is an assertion that the person praying has done (or has undertaken to do) a specific service to the god or goddess if the prayer is answered.

hoplite A heavily armed footsoldier, clad in bronze armour with sword and round shield. Hoplite 'phalanxes' (formations with rows of hoplites each guarding with his shield the sword-arm of the man to his left) were by Aischylos' time the main feature of Greek land warfare. Hoplites ranked midway between the aristocracy, who could afford to be cavalrymen, and the lower ranks, who on land could only be light-armed slingshot throwers, but during the fifth century increasingly came into their own as the men at the oars in sea battles.

kommos A lyric lamentation, sung by the *choros* and one or more solo actors.

kômos The festivities or revelry which gave its name to *komoidia* (comedy), the 'song of revelry'.

mainades Followers of the god Dionysos, possessed by the bakchic frenzy – a trance-like state in which superhuman feats of strength are possible.

mechane The crane used in and after the late fifth century to swing into view gods and other characters who are to be imagined as flying into the playing area.

miasma   Pollution; the word embraces both literal dirt and what we would call psychic pollution automatically incurred by breaches of taboo, e.g. bloodshed.

moira   A person's share or lot in life; the 'destiny' which is not a predetermined fate, but gradually takes shape as a human life unfolds, under the guidance of three ancient goddesses, the Moirai.

nomos   The single Greek word which includes both orally transmitted 'custom' and written 'law'.

oikos   The great household, consisting of an *agathos*' family and the dependants who work for him, which was the basic unit of Greek society.

orchêstra   The dance-floor, almost certainly circular, on which tragedies were performed.

parodos   One of the two entrance-ways, one on each side of the *orchêstra*. By a convention reflecting the reality of the theatre's location, the *skene* left *parodos* was imagined as leading to 'downtown' from the place where the action was set, and the *skene* right *parodos* to the countryside and to other *poleis*. Some scholars, following the spurious ch. 13 of Aristotle's *Poetics*, use this term to indicate the entry-song, the first choral ode of a tragedy or comedy. They favour the synonym *eisodos* for the side entrance-ways.

philia   A friendship or alliance, bound by loyalty or blood-relationship; it especially included relatives and other members of your own household. A person so bound to you was your *philos*; plural *philoi*.

poiêtes   Lit. 'maker', 'creator' – the man who was writer, composer, choreographer and director of a *drama* (also, until Sophokles, the leading actor).

polis   A city which, with its surrounding territory, was also an independent state; the largest social unit in ancient Greece after their formation in the eighth to sixth centuries.

polites   A citizen member of a *polis*; i.e. an adult male related by blood to an *oikos* and/or to a tribe recognized as belonging to the families which had originally constituted that *polis*.

satyr-drama   The farcical and ribald afterpiece to each competitor's offering of three tragedies. The *choros* played the role of the half-animal, half-human satyrs, and their father Silenos was normally one of the characters.

skene   Lit. and until *c.* 460 a tent in which the actors changed masks and costumes. By the time of the *Oresteia* it was a wooden building behind the *orchêstra*, with a pair of double doors and a practicable roof; it could be used to represent e.g. a palace, house, temple or tent.

stichomythia   Lit. 'step-speech'; a dialogue sequence of rapid cut and thrust, in which normally the speaker changes every line.

strophe, antistrophe   Lit. 'turn' and 'counter-turn'; the metrically responding stanzas (A1, A2; B1, B2 etc.) in solo and choral lyrics.

theatron   The 'seeing-place' – the part of the theatre in which the audience sat.

theios   Divine; marvellous.

thiasos   A company of worshippers, singing and dancing in praise of Dionysos.

threnos   A song of lamentation, with a ritualistic character.

timê   Honour or status; always in terms of concrete possessions and/ or privileges.

tragoidia   The Greek term for the genre, of wider application than modern 'tragedy', since it includes dramas (e.g. *Eumenides* and Sophokles' *Oidipous at Kolonos*) in which catastrophe is avoided or survived, and dramas which modern critics would regard as nearer to melodrama (e.g. Euripides' *Orestes* and *Helen*). The reasons for the name, which means 'goat-song', are obscure. In late antiquity it was believed that a goat was the prize at the first tragic competitions. Some modern scholars have argued that the name was derived originally from the goat-like dance of satyrs; others that *tragoidoi* are goat-singers because the *choroses* of tragedy were of young men on the verge of manhood, and therefore shared the uninhibited behaviour of the goat; others again that tragedy might be named after the lamentations which followed the ritual slaughter of the he-goat in spring.

xenos   A person who has contracted or inherited a relationship with the head of an *oikos*, or has arrived and is about to contract a relationship by exchange of gifts, which binds them and their descendants whenever they visit each other's territory. The relationship is reciprocal, regardless of who is acting as 'guest' or as 'host' at any one time, and it transcends any regional grievances or enmities.

SUGGESTIONS FOR FURTHER READING

Arnott, P. (1989) *Public and Performance in the Greek Theatre*, London. The best book on this subject, covering a wide range of features of the Greek Theatre.

Ewans, M. (tr.) (1995) *Aeschylus: The Oresteia*, London. The companion to this book, containing Aischylos' only surviving trilogy. The introduction deals in more detail with the theatre space and performance style of Aischylean tragedy.

Hall, E. (1989) *Inventing the Barbarian: Greek Self-definition through Tragedy*, Oxford. Chapter 2 is the most important recent study of *Persians*.

Herington, J. (1986) *Aeschylus*, New Haven. A rhetorical book, excellent in its insistence on the animate nature of Aischylos' universe; flawed by the conviction that *Prometheus Bound* is authentic.

Jones, J. (1962) *On Aristotle and Greek Tragedy*, London and New York. A fine book – though its prose style is sometimes opaque. It opens with an effective polemic against scholarly refusal to accept the re-dating of *Suppliants*.

Kitto, H. D. F. (1966) *Poiesis: Structure and Thought*, Berkeley. His chapter on *Persians*, though polemical and overwritten, remains the best introduction to this drama.

Ley, G. (1991) *A Short Introduction to the Ancient Greek Theater*, Chicago. The best introduction for students and readers new to the subject.

Rehm, R. (1992) *The Greek Tragic Theatre*, London. The most recent introduction to the nature and context of Greek tragic performance.

Seaford, R. (1994) *Reciprocity and Ritual; Homer and Tragedy in the Developing City State*, Oxford. A complex, sometimes difficult book which provides the best account of the development of tragedy and its role in the *polis*.

Taplin, O. (1977) *The Stagecraft of Aeschylus*, Oxford. Primarily concerned to establish the exact moments at which the named characters enter and exit, this large book also provides insights on many other staging matters. It blends lucid, sometimes excellent discussion of important issues with pedantic scholarly disputation. A knowledge of Greek is required for full understanding.

Thalmann, W. G. (1978) *Dramatic Art in Aeschylus' 'Seven against Thebes'*, New Haven. This detailed monograph is more literary than its title suggests, and is hard to follow without a knowledge of Greek; it is still rewarding.

Walcot, P. (1976) *Greek Drama in its Theatrical and Social Context*, Cardiff. A short and excellent book.

Winnington-Ingram, R. P. (1983) *Studies in Aeschylus*, Cambridge. Essays which offer stimulating literary interpretations of the dramas.

Other References Cited in the Introduction and Notes

Adkins, A. W. H. (1960) *Merit and Responsibility; a study in Greek Values*, Oxford.

Bacon, H. H. (1964) 'The Shield of Eteokles', *Arion* 3, 27–38.

Baldry, H. C. (1956) 'The Dramatization of the Theban Legend', *Greece & Rome* 25, 24–37.

Belfiore, E., n.d. 'Aeschylus: *Suppliants*' chapter in *Murder among Friends: Violation of Philia in Greek Tragedy* (unpublished).

Bolton, J. D. P. (1962) *Aristeas of Proconnesus*, Oxford.

Broadhead, H. D. (ed.) (1960) *The Persae of Aeschylus*, Cambridge.

Burian, P. (tr.) (1991) *Aeschylus; The Suppliants*, Princeton.

Burnett, A. P. (1971a) Review of Garvie *Aeschylus' Supplices; Play and Trilogy*, *Classical Philology* 66, 54–61.

Burnett, A. P. (1971b) *Catastrophe Survived: Euripides' Tragedies of Mixed Reversal*, Oxford.

Burnett, A. P. (1973) 'Curse and Dream in Aeschylus' *Septem*.' *Greek, Roman and Byzantine Studies* 14, 343–368.

Cairns, D. L. (1993) *Aidôs; the Psychology and Ethics of Honour and Shame in Ancient Greek Literature*, Oxford.

Caldwell, R. S. (1973) 'The Misogyny of Eteocles', *Arethusa* 6, 197–231.

Caldwell, R. S. (1974) 'The psychology of Aeschylus' *Supplices*', *Arethusa* 7, 45–70.

Cameron, H. D. (1971) *Studies on the Seven against Thebes of Aeschylus*, The Hague.

Canavan, J. P. (1972) *Studies in the Staging of Aeschylean Tragedy*, (Columbia University PhD thesis) Ann Arbor.

Conacher, D. J. (1974) 'Aeschylus' *Persae*; a Literary Commentary' in *Serta Turyniana* (ed. J. H. Heller), Urbana.

Conacher, D. J. (1980) *Aeschylus' Prometheus Bound: A Literary Commentary*, Toronto.

Connor, W. R. (1989) 'City Dionysia and Athenian Democracy', *Classica et Mediaevalia* 40, 7–32.

Cunningham, M. (1953) 'A Fragment of Aeschylus' *Aigyptioi*?', *Rheinishes Museum* 96, 223–31.

Dale, A. M. (1969) *Collected Papers of A. M. Dale* (eds. Turner and Webster), Cambridge.

Dyson, M. (1994) 'Prometheus and the wedge: text and staging at Aeschylus *PV* 54–81', *Journal of Hellenic Studies* 144, 154–6.

Else, G. F. (1965) *The Origin and Early Form of Greek Tragedy*, Harvard.

Ewans, M. (1977) *Janáček's Tragic Operas*, London.

Ewans, M. (1980) 'Aeschylus and Wagner: Stagecraft and Meaning in the *Oresteia* and the *Ring*', *Proceedings of the Australasian Languages and Literature Association*, 20, 357–67.

Ewans, M. (1982a) 'The Dramatic Structure of *Agamemnon*', *Ramus* 11.1, 1–15.

Ewans, M. (1982b) *Wagner and Aeschylus: the 'Ring' and the 'Oresteia'*, London.

Ewans, M. (1993) 'Racine's *Phèdre* and Greek Tragedy', *Prudentia* suppl. vol., 89–102.

Ewans, M. (1996) 'Patterns of Tragedy in Sophokles and Shakespeare' in *Tragedy and the Tragic* (Silk, M., ed.), Oxford.

Finley, J. (1955) *Pindar and Aeschylus*, Harvard.

Forrest, W. G. (1966) *The Emergence of Greek Democracy*, London.

Friis Johansen, H. and Whittle, E. W. (eds.) (1980) *Aeschylus; The Suppliants*, Copenhagen.

Gagarin, M. (1976) *Aeschylean Drama*, Berkeley.

Garvie, A. F. (1969) *Aeschylus' Supplices; Play and Trilogy*, Cambridge.

Garvie, A. F. (ed.) (1986) *Aeschylus, Choephoroi*, Oxford.

Goldhill, S. (1987/1990) 'The Great Dionysia and Civic Ideology', *Journal of Hellenic Studies* 107, 58–76; revised version 1990 in Winkler and Zeitlin.

Gould, J. (1973) 'Hiketeia', *Journal of Hellenic Studies* 93, 74–103.

Green, J. R. (1994) *Theatre in Ancient Greek Society*, London.

Green, J. R. and Handley, E. (1995) *Images of the Greek Theatre*, London.

Griffith, M. (1977) *The Authenticity of 'Prometheus Bound'*, Cambridge.

Griffith, M. (1978) 'Aeschylus, Sicily and Prometheus' in *Dionysiaca* (ed. Dawe, R. D. and others), 105–139.

Griffith, M. (ed.) (1983) *Aeschylus: Prometheus Bound*, Cambridge.

Hammond, N. G. L. (1972) 'The Conditions of Dramatic Production to the Death of Aeschylus', *Greek, Roman and Byzantine Studies* 13, 387–450.

Harrison, J. E. (1912) *Themis; a Study of the Social Origins of Greek Religion* (includes an Excursus by Gilbert Murray on 'The Ritual Forms preserved in Greek Tragedy), Cambridge.

Harrison, T. (1991) *The Trackers of Oxyrynchus*, 2nd edn, London.

Hecht, A. and Bacon, H. (trs.) (1973) *Aeschylus: Seven against Thebes*, New York.

Herington, C. J. (1970) *The Author of the Prometheus Bound*, Austin.

Herington, C. J. (1985) *Poetry into Drama: Early Tragedy and the Greek Poetic Tradition*, Berkeley.

Hogan, J. C. (1984) *A Commentary on the Complete Greek Tragedies; Aeschylus*, Chicago.

Hutchinson, G. O. (ed.) (1985) *Aeschylus: Septem Contra Thebas*, Oxford.

Kirkwood, G. M. (1969) 'Eteokles *Oiakostrophos*', *Phoenix* 23, 9–25.

Kitto, H. D. F. (1939) *Greek Tragedy*, London.

Kitto, H. D. F. (1966) *Poiesis; Structure and Thought*, Berkeley.

Lattimore, R. (1958) *The Poetry of Greek Tragedy*, Baltimore.

Lattimore, R. (1964) *Story-Patterns in Greek Tragedy*, Ann Arbor.

Lembke, J. (tr.) (1975) *Aeschylus: Suppliants* (intro. by W. Arrowsmith), New York.

Ley, G. (1986) 'On the Pressure of Circumstance in Greek Tragedy', *Ramus* 15, 43–51.

Ley, G. (1993) 'Monody, Choral Song, and Athenian Festival Performance', *Maia*, n.s. 2, 105–24.

Lloyd-Jones, H. (ed.) (1963) 'Appendix containing the more considerable fragments published since 1930' added to Weir Smyth, H. (ed. and tr.), *Aeschylus Vol. II* Cambridge, Mass.

Lloyd-Jones, H. (1959) 'The End of the *Seven against Thebes*', *Classical Quarterly* n. s. 9, 80–115.

Lloyd-Jones, H. (1974) 'The Supplices of Aeschylus; the New Date and Old Problems', *L'Antiquité Classique* 3, 356–74.

Long, A. A. (1970) 'Morals and Values in Homer', *Journal of Hellenic Studies* 90, 121–39.

Macintosh, F. (1994) *Dying Acts: Death in Ancient Greek and Modern Irish Tragic Drama*, Cork.

McCall, M. (1976) 'Secondary Choruses in Aeschylus' *Supplices*', California Studies in Classical Antiquity 9, 117–31.

Melchinger, S. (1974) *Das Theater der Tragödie*, München.

Melchinger, S. (1979) *Die Welt als Tragödie, vol. 1*, München.

Michelini, A. M. (1982) *Tradition and Dramatic Form in the Persians of Aeschylus*, Leiden.

Murray, G. (1940) *Aeschylus: the Creator of Tragedy*, Oxford.

Murray, R. D. (1958) *The Motif of Io in Aeschylus' Suppliants*, Princeton.

Page, D. (ed.) (1957) *Aeschylus, Agamemnon* (with J. D. Denniston), Oxford.

Pattoni, M. P. (1987) *L'Autenticità del 'Prometeo Incatenato' di Eschilo*, Pisa.

Pickard, J. (1893) 'The Relative Positions of Actors and Chorus in the Greek Theatre of the V Century BC', *American Journal of Philology* 14, 68–89, 199–215 & 273–304.

Pickard-Cambridge, Sir A. (1946) *The Theatre of Dionysos in Athens*, Oxford.

Pickard-Cambridge, Sir A. (1962) *Dithyramb, Tragedy and Comedy* (2nd edn rev. by T. B. L. Webster), Oxford.

Podlecki, A. (1966) *The political background of Aeschylean tragedy*, Michigan.

Radt, S. (ed.) (1981) *Tragicorum Graecorum Fragmenta Vol. 3; Aischylos*, Göttingen.

Raphael, F. and McLeish, K. (trs.) (1991) *Aeschylus; Plays: One*, London.

Read, L. (1993) 'Social Space in Ancient Theatres', *New Theatre Quarterly* 36, 316–328.

Rehm, R. (1988) 'The Staging of Suppliant Plays', *Greek, Roman and Byzantine Studies* 29, 263–307.

Reinhardt, K. (1949) *Aischylos als Regisseur und Theologe*, Bern.

Robertson, D. S. (1924) 'The end of the *Supplices* trilogy of Aeschylus', *Classical Review* 38, 51–3.

Scott, W. C. (1984) *Musical Design in Aeschylean Theater*, Hanover.

Scullion, J. C. (1990) *The Athenian Stage and Scene-Setting in Early Tragedy*, (Harvard PhD thesis) Ann Arbor.

Scully, S. and Warren, R. (trs.) (1995) *Euripides; Suppliant Women*, New York.

Seaford, R. (ed.) (1984) *Euripides: Cyclops*, Oxford.

Seaford, R. (1987) 'The Tragic Wedding', *Journal of Hellenic Studies* 107, 106–130.

Sidgwick, A. G. (ed.) (1903) *Aeschylus: Persae*, Oxford.

Sikes, E. E. and Wilson, St. J. B. V. (eds.) (1906) *The 'Prometheus Vinctus' of Aeschylus*, London.

Sissa, G. (1990) *Greek Virginity*, Cambridge, Mass.

Solmsen, F. (1937) 'The Erinys in Aischylos' *Septem*', *Transactions of the American Philological Association*, 68, 197–211.

Spatz, L. (1982) *Aeschylus*, Boston.

Tanner, R. G. (1975) 'Goats, Pity and Fear', *Hetairos* 2, 3–6 & 21.

Tucker, T. G. (1889) *The Supplices of Aeschylus*, London.

Vellacott, P. (tr.) (1961) *Aeschylus: Prometheus Bound and other Plays*, Harmondsworth.

Vernant, J.-P. (1980) *Myth and Society in Ancient Greece*, Brighton.

Vickers, B. (1973) *Towards Greek Tragedy*, London.

Weir Smyth, H. (ed./tr.) (1922) *Aeschylus Vol. I*, Cambridge, Mass.

West, M. L. (1979) 'The Prometheus Trilogy', *Journal of Hellenic Studies* 99, 130–48.

West. M. L. (1990a) *Studies in Aeschylus*, Stuttgart.

West, M. L. (ed.) (1990b) *Aeschylus: Tragoediae*, Stuttgart.

Wilamowitz-Moellendorf, U. von (1914) *Aischylos: Interpretationen*, Berlin.

Winkler, J. and Zeitlin, F. (eds.) (1990) *Nothing to do with Dionysus? Athenian Drama in its Social Context*, Princeton.

Winnington-Ingram, R. P. (1985) 'The Origins of Tragedy' in Easterling, P. and Knox, B. (eds.) *The Cambridge History of Classical Literature Vol 1*, 256–63, Cambridge.

Wolff, E. (1958) 'Die Entscheidung des Eteokles in den *Sieben gegen Theben*', *Harvard Studies in Classical Philology* 63, 89–95.

Zeitlin, F. (1982) *Under the Sign of the Shield*, Rome.

SOURCES FOR THE FRAGMENTS

Everyman	Loeb	Radt	Source
30	284	451q	*Oxyrynchus Papyri* 20.2256.
31	285	73b	Papyrus first published by Lefebre in 1920.
32	189	350	Plato *Republic* 383A.
33	274	46–7	Papyrus first published by Vitelli-Norsa in 1933 and *Oxyrynchus Papyri* 18.21 61 (1941).
34	273	25e	*Oxyrynchus Papyri* 18.2159.
35	276	78	*Oxyrynchus Papyri* 18.2162.
36	278	204b	*Oxyrynchus Papyri* 20.2245.
37	285	281a	*Oxyrynchus Papyri* 20.2256.

Fragments of Prometheus' Release

Everyman	Griffith	Source
38	5	Arrian *Peripl. Pont. Eux.* 19.1–2.
39	6	Strabo *Geogr.* 1.2.27.
40	8	Cicero *Tusc. Disp.* 2.23–5.
41	11	Galen *Comm. on Hippocr. Epidem.* 6.1.29.
42	12	Steph. Byz. *Lex.* 7.5.5. s.v. 'Abioi'.
43	14a	Strabo *Geogr.* 4.1.7.

TEXT SUMMARIES

Persians

The action is set in Sousa, the capital city of Persia; it dramatizes the events leading up to the return of Xerxes from his naval and military expedition to subdue Greece.

Xerxes' Elders brood on the scale of the expedition, the fact that there has been no news, and the grief of the women who have been left behind. The Queen joins them, troubled by an ominous dream.

A Messenger arrives, to tell them that the army has been utterly destroyed. He gives an eye-witness account of the Battle of Salamis, in which a Greek fleet defeated a vastly superior Persian force; the loss of a special force of Persian commanders placed on a small island; and the sufferings and further losses endured by the Persian army, as they made their way back through northern Greece and Thrakia.

The Queen resolves to sacrifice to the gods, and the Elders lament the disaster which Xerxes has caused. Then the Queen returns, resolved to summon up the Shade of the previous King, her husband Dareios. The Elders sing and dance an exotic ode and Dareios appears on top of his tomb. The Queen tells him what has happened, and Dareios recognizes that his son has brought down on Persia a catastrophe which could have been deferred. He prophesies the defeat at Plataia of the chosen force which Xerxes has left behind in Greece, because they have damaged the altars of the gods. The Shade returns to Hades, and the Queen returns to her palace.

Xerxes enters, alone and in rags. He sings an extended lament with the Elders, in which they angrily accuse him and he accepts responsibility for the disaster.

Seven against Thebes

The drama is set in Thebes, under siege by an army led by Adrastos, King of Argos. Eteokles the son of Oidipous delivers a call to arms to a group including all the able-bodied men of Thebes, and hears from a Scout that the enemy have selected seven of their fiercest captains to fight to the death against Thebes; one will lead his troops against each of the city's seven gates.

The Unmarried Women of Thebes enter suddenly, terrified by the enemy onslaught. Eteokles with great difficulty subdues their panic, and persuades them to pray to the gods for Thebes to survive. However, their prayers end in vivid evocations of plunder and rape in a conquered city.

The Scout returns, and describes to Eteokles each of the seven Argive champions and his boast against the city. For each one Eteokles devises an appropriate response, and assigns one of seven chosen Thebans to defend the city at that gate. Before the seventh gate stands his own brother, Polyneikes; he is resolved to fight Eteokles, and either die, or kill him and return to rule the city. Despite the Women's anguished attempts to dissuade him, Eteokles departs to fight him.

The Women brood upon the history of the royal house – the crime of Laios, and the incest and parricide of his son Oidipous. Then the Scout returns for the last time, with the news that the city is saved – but the royal brothers have killed each other in hand to hand combat.

Attendants bring in the corpses of Eteokles and Polyneikes, and the drama closes with an extended lament for them.

Suppliants

The drama is set in a sacred grove outside Argos, in the earliest period of Greek history. The daughters of Danaos enter, fleeing from their cousins the sons of Aigyptos, who want to marry them against their will. Their father appears, bringing the news that an Argive force is arriving; he advises them to take refuge at the images of the gods.

King Pelasgos arrives with an escort of Soldiers. The Danaides claim kinship with the Argives, proving to him that they are descendants of Io, once a priestess in Argos; she fled, transformed by Hera into a cow because Zeus had made love to her. When she reached Egypt, Zeus transformed her back into human form, and made her pregnant with the first of a line of kings. They call on Pelasgos to save them from their pursuers, both as suppliants and as kin; when he hesitates, they threaten to pollute the land irrevocably by hanging themselves upon the images of the gods. He finally commits himself, sends Danaos into the city to place tokens of supplication on the other altars there, and leaves to persuade the citizen assembly to protect the Danaides.

They sing the legend of their ancestress, Io. Danaos returns, to tell them the citizens have voted with full authority to support them; the Danaides respond with a song of thanksgiving. Then Danaos brings the news that he can see a fleet coming to land, manned by troops with dark skins; he tells them to stay by the sacred altar, while he leaves to fetch help.

A Herald enters, with Aigyptian forces. As he and his men are about to seize the Danaides, Pelasgos returns with Argive soldiers and orders him to stop. The Herald backs down, but as he leaves tells Pelasgos that war is inevitable.

Pelasgos departs. Danaos returns, richly clothed and with a body-guard. He advises his daughters to preserve their chastity, after all they have suffered so far. They begin an exit-song – but are warned by the Argives that the goddess of love cannot be resisted, and perhaps they may even marry the sons of Aigyptos after all. They pray to Zeus, their ancestor, that this will not happen.

Prometheus Bound

The drama is set in front of a rock, overlooking a chasm, far to the north of Greece. Power and Violence, male and female executioners of Zeus' will, lead in Prometheus, and make Hephaistos, the craftsman of the gods, bind him and pinion him to the rock. After they have left, Prometheus laments his fate.

He is joined by the daughters of Okeanos, who have been roused by the noise of the hammering. He tells them that Zeus has punished him because he took pity on mankind, stole fire from the gods and gave it to them.

Okeanos appears, on a winged bird. He offers to help Prometheus by entreating Zeus to release him. Prometheus tells him he would be wasting his time, and Okeanos departs.

Prometheus describes to the Okeanides the wretched state of man-kind before he gave them the knowledge which allowed civilization to develop.

Io suddenly enters, a young woman with the horns of a cow. Prometheus coaxes her into telling her story. She was continually harassed by dreams that Zeus wanted to sleep with her, until Zeus' oracle commanded her father to throw her into exile. Then horns grew on her head, and gadfly bites forced her to wander from land to land. Prometheus prophesies her lengthy future wanderings in the east, and her eventual release when she arrives in Egypt. He also tells her the story of the Danaides, and claims that Zeus will be forced to release him because he knows that Zeus' eye will fall on a woman, who is fated to bear a son mightier than his father.

Gadfly bites afflict Io again, and she departs in agony. Prometheus reiterates his defiance of Zeus, and Hermes appears, demanding to know which sexual union will bring Zeus down. Prometheus defies him, and Hermes tells him that if he does not tell, Zeus will bury him underground for thousands of years, then bring him back into the light and send the additional torment of an eagle which will devour his liver every day. After initially begging Prometheus to yield, the Okeanides suddenly defy Hermes, and resolve to share his sufferings. Hermes departs, and the drama ends as thunder and lightning announce the impending cataclysm.

ANCIENT CLASSICS
IN EVERYMAN

Legends of Alexander the Great
edited by Richard Stoneman
*The fascinating adventures of
a dominant figure in European,
Jewish and Arabic folklore until
the fifteenth century*
£5.99

**Juvenal's Satires with the
Satires of Persius**
JUVENAL AND PERSIUS
*Unique and acute observations
of contemporary Roman society*
£5.99

The Epicurean Philosophers
edited by John Gaskin
*The surviving works and wise say-
ings of Epicurus, with the account
of his natural science in Lucretius'*
On the Nature of the Universe
£5.99

**History of the
Peloponnesian War**
THUCYDIDES
*The war that brought to an
end a golden age of democracy*
£5.99

The Discourses
EPICTETUS
*The teachings of one of the
greatest Stoic philosophers*
£6.99

The Education of Cyrus
XENOPHON
*An absorbing insight into the
culture and politics of Ancient
Greece*
£6.99

The Oresteia
AESCHYLUS
*New translation and edition
which analyses the plays in
performance*
£5.99

Suppliants and Other Dramas
AESCHYLUS
*New translation of Aeschylus'
first three surviving plays and
the earliest dramas of western
civilisation*
£5.99

The Odyssey
HOMER
*A classic translation of one of
the greatest adventures ever told*
£5.99

The Republic
PLATO
*The most important and
enduring of Plato's works*
£5.99

All books are available from your local bookshop or direct from:
Littlehampton Book Services Cash Sales, 14 Eldon Way, Lineside Estate,
Littlehampton, West Sussex BN17 7HE (*prices are subject to change*)

To order any of the books, please enclose a cheque (in sterling) made payable to
Littlehampton Book Services, or phone your order through with credit card details (Access,
Visa or Mastercard) on 01903 721596 (24 hour answering service) stating card number
and expiry date. (*Please add £1.25 for package and postage to the total of your order.*)

In the USA, for further information and a complete catalogue call 1-800-526-2778

DRAMA
IN EVERYMAN

The Oresteia
AESCHYLUS
*New translation of one of the
greatest Greek dramatic trilogies
which analyses the plays in
performance*
£5.99

**Everyman and Medieval
Miracle Plays**
edited by A. C. Cawley
*A selection of the most popular
medieval plays*
£4.99

Complete Plays and Poems
CHRISTOPHER MARLOWE
*The complete works of this great
Elizabethan in one volume*
£5.99

Restoration Plays
edited by Robert Lawrence
*Five comedies and two tragedies
representing the best of the
Restoration stage*
£7.99

**Female Playwrights of the
Restoration: Five Comedies**
edited by Paddy Lyons
*Rediscovered literary treasures
in a unique selection*
£5.99

**Plays, Prose Writings
and Poems**
OSCAR WILDE
*The full force of Wilde's wit
in one volume*
£4.99

**A Dolls House/The Lady from
the Sea/The Wild Duck**
HENRIK IBSEN
introduced by Fay Weldon
*A popular selection of Ibsen's
major plays*
£4.99

**The Beggar's Opera and
Other Eighteenth-Century Plays**
JOHN GAY et. al.
Including Goldsmith's She Stoops
To Conquer *and Sheridan's* The
School for Scandal, *this is a volume
which reflects the full scope of the
period's theatre*
£6.99

**Female Playwrights of the
Nineteenth Century**
edited by Adrienne Scullion
*The full range of female nineteenth-
century dramatic development*
£6.99

All books are available from your local bookshop or direct from:
Littlehampton Book Services Cash Sales, 14 Eldon Way, Lineside Estate,
Littlehampton, West Sussex BN17 7HE (*prices are subject to change*)

To order any of the books, please enclose a cheque (in sterling) made payable to
Littlehampton Book Services, or phone your order through with credit card details (Access,
Visa or Mastercard) on 01903 721596 (24 hour answering service) stating card number
and expiry date. (*Please add £1.25 for package and postage to the total of your order.*)

In the USA, for further information and a complete catalogue call 1-800-526-2778